Macmillan Topics

Teacher's Book

Susan Holden

MACMILLAN

Macmillan Education
Between Towns Road, Oxford OX4 3PP
A division of Macmillan Publishers Limited
Companies and representatives throughout the world

ISBN–13: 978-0-230-00974-5

First published 2006

Note to Teachers

Permission to copy
The material in this book is copyright. However, the publisher grants permission for copies to be made without fee on those pages marked with the photocopiable symbol. Private purchasers may make copies for their own use or for use by classes of which they are in charge; school purchasers may make copies for use within and by the staff and students of the school only. This permission does not extend to additional branches of an institution, who should purchase a separate master copy of the book for their own use. For copying in any other circumstances, prior permission in writing must be obtained from Macmillan Publishers Limited.

Illustrated by Oxford Illustrators Ltd
Original cover design by Topics –The Creative Partnership
Additional cover design by Laila Meachin
Original Design by Topics – The Creative Partnership
Additional Design by Lenn Darroux, ParaGrafic

The authors and publishers would like to thank the following for permission to reproduce their relevant material:
Happy Birthday Words and Music by Patty S Hill and Mildred Hill copyright © Summy Birch-Birchard Music A Division of Summy-Birchard Inc., USA/EMI Music Publishing, London, WC2H 0QY 1935 renewed 1962, reprinted by permission of WarnerChappell Music Ltd.
Yellow Submarine Words and Music by John Lennon and Paul McCartney copyright © Sony/ATV Music Publishing (UK) Limited 1966, reprinted by permission of the publisher. All Rights Reserved.
Michelle Words and Music by John Lennon and Paul McCartney copyright © Sony/ATV Music Publishing (UK) Limited 1965, reprinted by permission of the publisher. All Rights Reserved.
Text about Franz Ferdinand and 8 lines from You See Her by Franz Ferdinand, reprinted by permission of Supervision Management.

Authors Acknowledgements

The author is very grateful to the whole Macmillan Education editorial, production and marketing team who have worked on this project at great speed and with such enthusiasm.

She would especially like to thank:
- Julie Brett, for managing the project throughout with such understanding, flexibility and good humour;
- Clarissa Horwood and Katherine Anderson for much needed and sympathetic content editing at a late stage;
- Sue Bale for her initial enthusiasm;
- Kate Melliss for her ongoing support and advice;
- Cristina Roberts,Wilma Moura and the editorial team in Brazil for their work on the initial concept;
- Chris West and Jeremy Dieguez for providing the logistical framework.

She would also like to thank Don Byrne for his critical and constructive suggestions while this material was being written.

Printed and bound by Martins the Printers Ltd

2010 2009
10 9 8 7 6 5 4 3

Topics

Contents

Introduction

D. **Worksheets and Tests Answer Keys**

E. **Audio Magazine Audio Scripts**

Introduction

A. Macmillan Topics: **The Series**

This teacher's book covers all the titles in the macmillan topics series. It contains:

- An introduction to the series.
- Generic ideas to use with any title.
- Specific ideas to use with each title.
- Eight photocopiable worksheets and a test for each title.
- Answer keys for the worksheets and tests.
- Tapescripts for the two audio cds.

1. Language levels and titles

Each title in the series focuses on a specific factual topic. It explores different aspects of this through a series of articles presented in magazine format. These articles are written in a variety of text styles and registers and are presented in a highly visual way.

The series is organised into five language levels, with a choice of titles at each level. The criterion for these levels is 'language for recognition', not 'language for production'. However, if the students are interested in a topic, or attracted by the look of a specific article, they will also often be able to read above the apparent language level.

Beginner ***People*** ***Places***
Simple sentence structure
Verbs *'to be'* and *'to have'*
Present simple (common verbs used in clear contexts)
Adjective + noun

Beginner plus ***Animals*** ***Sports***
Simple sentence structure
Present simple
'Can' for ability
Adjective + noun
Frequency adverbs

Elementary ***Festivals*** ***Environment***
Simple sentences with clauses linked by *'and'* and *'but'*
Present simple (wider range of verbs)
Present continuous tense
'Can' for ability
Adjective + noun
Frequency adverbs

Pre-intermediate ***Communication*** ***Entertainment***
More complex sentence structures
Present simple
Comparatives and superlatives

Intermediate ***Consumers*** ***Travel and Tourism***
Complex sentence structures
Present perfect tense
Conditional clauses with *'if'* and *'when'*
Present and past passive voice

2. The vocabulary range

The series is rich in vocabulary, with the conscious aim of developing the students' ability to cope with unfamiliar language appropriate to each specific topic. Key lexical items in each article are highlighted and glossed in the word file on that page, in order to provide immediate support with british and american english variants noted.

Articles about 'real' topics use a certain amount of specialist language which is not normally contained in a textbook. The 'check it out' section on page 2 of each title contains relevant examples of this language. This page gives specific reference material for the students which they can extend with their own examples. In addition, in areas such as science, technology, entertainment, communications and sport, many english words are already used in the l1, either as direct imports or in a recognisable form. As a result, identifying cognates and easily-recognised words provides useful clues for overall understanding.

3. Projects and mini-projects

The topics series is ideal for using reading as a basis for project work. Each article has an accompanying 'mini-project'. These provide an opportunity for the individual student to use his or her personal knowledge or to explore the topic further. These mini-projects suggest specific activities to do before reading an article, or as a follow-up to it. They can be done individually, in pairs or groups. The aim is to encourage the development of personal skills.

These mini-projects are indicated by different icons at each level:

The projects page at the end of each title presents more extensive projects linked to the overall topic. These, as well as the projects on some of the worksheets, can also be easily linked to other school subjects.

4. Using the content: crosscurricular teaching and the CLIL classroom

The topic-centred nature of the series makes it easy to connect english language learning with other school subjects. Many of the articles at all levels relate to subjects such as art and design, science, history, geography and l1 (mother tongue) language and literature. These content links are highlighted in the teacher's notes for each title.

In CLIL classrooms, where some of the content teaching is carried out through the medium of english, the topics material can be used by both the english language and the subject teacher, working either together or separately.

5. Developing intercultural awareness

Many of the texts and projects invite the students to contrast the information about an aspect of another culture with what they know – or can discover – about it in their own cultures. Through reading and discussing the articles, they have the opportunity to find out more about both other cultures and unexpected aspects of their own.

6. The users

The macmillan topics series is very flexible and can be used in a number of different teaching contexts:

- In full-time education for both english language and clil classes;
- In language schools and vacation courses;
- In adult education, providing stimulating material for reading and discussion.

The worksheets

This teacher's book contains eight photocopiable worksheets for each title, as well as a test.

The majority of the worksheets are linked to one specific article in that title, although there are always a couple which refer to the whole title.

At the top of each worksheet, there is a clear reference to its links with:

- The article (or whole magazine) it is based on;
- Vocabulary area(s);
- Grammar area(s);

The activities in the worksheets are designed to be done by students working individually, in pairs or in small groups. They are flexible, and can be varied to suit individual teaching and learning contexts.

The more open worksheets, those referring to the whole content of the magazine, also involve management skills and group dynamics.

Many of the worksheet activities have a variety of possible answers, but where these are specific, they are included in the answer keys on pages 141-146.

The tests

The aim of these tests is to encourage the students to look back at the articles in order to check facts, notice details and identify specific information to answer the questions. They are not designed as memory tests. The answers are also included in the answer keys.

The audio CDs

Each of the two cds contains recordings of selected articles from specific titles. These form a short audio magazine to accompany each title.

CD A: beginner, beginner plus and elementary levels (*People, places, animals, sports, festivals, environment.*)

CD B: pre intermediate and intermediate levels. (*Communication, entertainment, consumers, travel and tourism.*)

These audio magazines provide material for 'listening for pleasure'. They have been designed to provide extensive listening practice rather than for intensive listening comprehension tasks. Their aim is to help bring the articles alive, to add variety and to aid comprehension.

The voices include British and American English, as well as a number of non-native speakers. Each audio magazine thus contains a range of listening styles which match the textual and visual variety of the printed material.

The audio scripts for each CD are included from page 147 of this teacher's book. Note that phrases from the text version which are unsuitable for an audio version, e.g. "Read this" or "now read on" have been omitted.

The audio material for each topics title always contains the following items:

- Welcome! (abbreviated) and goodbye.
- Page 3 article.
- Chatrooms and goodbye.

In addition, various other articles gave been recorded following these criteria:

- They lend themselves to listening (e.g. Songs, conversations, texts involving multiple speakers).
- The articles are long and having an audio version will help students understand the text.

The articles which have been recorded are indicated by a 🎧 symbol in the specific notes for using that title. They are listed below.

CD A

Track	Article
People	
1.	*Welcome!
2.	Personal identity
3.	A song to a special person
4.	*Chatrooms and goodbye
Places	
5.	*Welcome!
6.	My dream place
7.	Song: a strange place
8.	*Chatrooms and goodbye
Animals	
9.	*Welcome!
10.	Feet talk!
11.	It's a dangerous world!
12.	Animals attract tourists
13.	An animal song
14.	*Chatrooms and goodbye
Sports	
15.	*Welcome!
16.	Sport: to do or to watch?
17.	The price of sport
18.	The two sides of sport
19.	*Chatrooms and goodbye
Festivals	
20.	*Welcome!
21.	Let's begin with the new year
22.	*Carnival in august
23.	'Family' festivals
24.	Festival raps, songs and rhymes
25.	*Chatrooms and goodbye
Environment	
26.	*Welcome!
27.	My environment
28.	The food chain
29.	Natural disasters
30.	*Chatrooms and goodbye

CD B

Track	Article
Communication	
1.	*Welcome!
2.	Hello!
3.	The story of english
4.	English travels east
5.	Teen speak
6.	*Chatrooms and goodbye
Entertainment	
7.	*Welcome!
8.	It's festival time!
9.	*What strange music!
10.	*Music opens doors
11.	*Music sells!
12.	*The story of a group: franz ferdinand
13.	*Chatrooms and goodbye
Consumers	
14.	*Welcome!
15.	Let's go shopping!
16.	Ad-speak
17.	Consumer hot topics: obesity
18.	Getting rid of the calories
19.	Problem solving
20.	*Chatrooms and goodbye
Travel and Tourism	
21.	*Welcome!
22.	Travel? Why?
23.	What's it really like?
24.	Venice: Italy
25.	Living with tourism
26.	A travel story: Part I
27.	A travel story: Part II
28.	*Chatrooms and goodbye

*** Only Part Of The Article Recorded For Maximum Audio Impact.**

Topics

B. Using Macmillan Topics: **Generic Ideas**

All the titles in the macmillan topics series contain many of the same features. These ideas can thus be used with any topics title. Choose the ones that are most motivating for your students. Be selective!

1. Jigsaw reading

Many of the articles look quite long, but these are normally divided into several short sections, usually with a section heading. This means that the students can be asked to read just one section at a time.

Another way of handling these articles is through jigsaw reading. Each student, or small group of students, chooses to read just one section. They become the 'experts' on the information in that section. Thus a genuine information gap is created between the 'experts' and the 'non-experts'. The information exchange can then be done in different ways:

- The 'experts' tell the 'non-experts' what they have read. These then read that section themselves and check whether the information they have been given is correct.
- The 'experts' give the others deliberately false information, which they check as before.
- The 'non-experts' prepare questions to ask, using the section heading to guide them.

2. Browsing

The first thing to do with any title is to give the students time to look at it. Ask them to flick through it, just as they would with any magazine, pausing at any pages that attract their attention, and getting a general, subjective 'feel' for it. Time spent on this is worthwhile, as it will help them realize that this material is very different and that reading it will be a pleasure, rather than something to be afraid of.

Suggestions

• While-browsing

Give the students sufficient time to look through the title and find the most interesting-looking article (without actually reading it). Notice their reactions – this will guide you in selecting what to use first with them.

• Post-browsing

Ask for their personal reactions to the material. Is it what they expected? What is different from other reading material they have used? Does it resemble anything they read in l1 magazines or websites? Encourage them to exchange opinions.

3. Covers and cover lines

The front cover of each title is a visual expression of its topic. At the side, there is a list of some of the articles it contains. These explore different aspects of the topic.

Suggestions

• Brainstorming (whole class or in groups)

Ask the students to say what the visual images suggest to them. Ask them to suggest other possible images to illustrate the topic. They can bring examples to the next lesson. Without reading the titles, they can suggest what range of articles they would expect to find in a magazine on this topic.

• Speculation

Read out the list of titles (or write these on the board). Ask the students what they think each one will be about. Some of the titles are self-explanatory, while others are more ambiguous. Discuss their different suggestions. They can keep a note of these and compare them later with the actual articles. (You may prefer to do this activity using the full contents list from page 1.)

• Follow up

Ask the students to design a similar cover and list of articles for a magazine on this topic.

4. Letter! (Page 1)

This serves as an introduction to the topic of the specific title. It discusses this in a general way and present the various aspects of it which are covered by the articles. It is the equivalent of the editorial in a magazine. The language is direct, addressing the reader personally. There are also reminders about the mini-projects the students can do while exploring the topic.

Suggestions

• Pre-reading

Check and pre-teach any unfamiliar language in the letter. Ask the students what they would include in a similar introduction.

• Reading

Ask the students to read the letter and make a note of the specific points the author mentions. Let them compare their notes with each other. Make a list of these on the board.

• Post-reading

Discuss the points they agree and disagree with. Then ask them to write a similar letter to introduce this topic (individually, in pairs or groups).

5. Contents (page 1)

The titles repeat those listed on the front cover. Some articles are one-page, while others occupy two pages.

Suggestions

• Speculation

Ask the students to choose one title and to guess what they expect it to be about. They should also guess what pictures it may have with it. They write a note of this.

• Checking

They turn to their chosen article and compare the content with their notes.

• Follow up

When they read the article, they decide whether the title

is suitable for it. If not, they should suggest others. Discuss these with the whole class.

6. Check it out (page 2)

This page summarises the useful and specialist vocabulary associated with the general topic. It provides the students with a basic resource for reference and gives them a core set of vocabulary for their vocabulary notebooks.

In addition, this page can be used from time to time for:

- Dictionary work
- Reference skills
- Language awareness activities (word building and cognates).

There are additional ways of using 'check it out' on page 11.

7. Websites and references (page 2)

The topic-related references are to websites rather than to print material because of the problems of availability for the students and the suitability of the language level. They should be encouraged to suggest their own relevant print and website resources for the topic (l1 and l2) and keep these updated.

Suggestions

• Activity

Ask the students to check out the websites and to report back on them.

• Follow up

Ask them to add their own suggestions, both immediately and while they are using the title. They can devise a 'quality rating' for each address, highlighting such items as clarity, ease of use, attractiveness, interest, etc.

8. Word files (on each page with the article)

These boxes contain the key vocabulary items from that article, ie those which are essential for an understanding of the text. They are listed alphabetically. At the bottom of the box, signaled by flags, are the American English and British English equivalents of certain words. This highlights the wide range of varieties of english which students will encounter outside the classroom.

Suggestions

• Pre-reading (whole class, group, pair or individual)

Ask the students to identify the word file items in the text and to use the context and the pictures to check the meaning.

• Reading/post reading (whole class, group, pair or individual)

Ask the students to note any other unfamiliar words in the article. They can work out the meaning from the context and pictures and then write similar word file explanations for their vocabulary notebooks.

9. Titles (each article)

As noted in 3 above, some of the article titles are literal, while others follow the style often used in magazines and are more ambiguous (e.g. *Feet talk!*). The visual appearance of each title has been chosen to reinforce its meaning and to echo the style and content of the article (e.g. Serious, factual, funny).

Suggestions

• Language focus

Check if the students understand the meaning of the title. Discuss whether it is appropriate for the article. Why (not)?

• Design focus

Discuss the design features in the same way.

• Follow up

Ask the students to make up their own titles and design styles for the article once they have read it. Compare and discuss their ideas.

10. Mini-projects (on each page with the article)

These mini-projects are designed to relate the content of each article to the students' own lives. Some of these are research ideas - things to find out by talking to other people, or by using text and internet resources or their own experience. Others are practical follow-up activities, using the ideas in the articles. Many of them also link with other school subjects and thus support crosscurricular work and clil contexts.

These mini-projects are optional and are designed so that the students can do them on their own, or working with others. They may choose to do only a few of them. The best results of these mini-projects can be collected and used for a class exhibition at the end of the term.

Suggestions

• In-class

You can use the ideas for discussion as a post-reading activity.

• Out of class

The students can do these mini-projects in their own time, record their results, and bring these to show or discuss in the lesson. They may then choose to work further on the projects, perhaps combining with another person or pair.

11. Visual design and illustration (each article)

The design style of each article has been chosen to resemble those used in magazines. This reinforces the content and style of the article. This integration of text, page design and illustration presents the students with something that looks familiar, even if it is written in a foreign language, thus helping their motivation and comprehension. The visual design reinforces and highlights the meaning.

Suggestions

• Discussion

The students discuss their first impressions of the page. Can they suggest adjectives to describe it (e.g. *Exciting*, *modern*, *confusing*, etc.)? Let them group these into positive and negative judgements. Do they all agree? What is the overall class impression?

Encourage them to discuss whether the content of the article is reinforced (or not) by the design, e.g. *Typeface*, *colour*, *page layout*.

• Intercultural connections
They can look for articles or photos about similar topics and ideas in local l1 magazines. Ask them to bring these to the class and analyse similarities and differences.

12. Quiz: do you know? (Page 14 or 22)

This page is designed to be dipped into at any time, or when they have finished working with the title. The quiz questions focus partly on vocabulary extension and consolidation (word boxes and matching activities) related to the topic. There are also more general puzzles and general knowledge quizzes, often using details from some of the photos used in the articles.

Suggestions
• Quiz show or test
You can use this section:
- For fun
- As part of a class 'quiz show', with the students competing in teams
- As an informal test activity

• Follow up
Ask the students to write their own quiz questions in groups, using these ones as a model. Emphasise the need for clarity and precision when writing their questions. Encourage them to try out various versions before deciding on the final one. They can then give them to another group or class to do.

13. Projects (page 15 or 23)

This page presents arrange of projects designed to appeal to different students. Some are very factual, while others are more creative. They take varying amounts of time to complete and involve different numbers of students. The aim is to give them the chance to extend their reading in a practical way and to work with others. As these projects involve some kind of presentation, they also give the students practice in organizing their ideas and choosing an effective way of presenting them.

As with the mini-projects, many of these more extended ones link with other school subjects and are ideal for crosscurricular and clil work.

14. Chatrooms and goodbye (page 16 or 24)

Most of the articles are written in factual styles (description or narrative), but these chatroom exchanges introduce some informal 'written dialogue'. They are examples of the kind of language the students can find in internet chatrooms, closer to spoken english.

Suggestions
TEENS CHAT
• Reading aloud (pairwork)
The dialogues can be used for paired reading aloud. Encourage the students to identify the emotions underlying each person's utterances (*surprise*, *indignation*, etc) and to try to express these through their voices (*stress and intonation*).

• Writing dialogues (pairwork)
The students can continue the written exchanges, each person adding one line at a time, as in a chatroom. These can then be read aloud.

• Discussion
The ideas can be discussed, noticing any cultural differences from the students' own experiences.

FUN CHAT/ CAN YOU BELIEVE IT? (Not always included)
These two sections contain jokes and visual comments linked to the overall topic. Many of them provide opportunities for noticing and discussing intercultural differences and similarities. They are also intended as a 'fun' ending.

• Discussion
The students discuss and intercultural points.

• Follow up
Ask them to find similar items from their own culture and to present these as alternative endings.

GOODBYE!
This note from the author is similar in style to the letter in page 1 and can be treated in the same way.

Appendix: Ten ways to use the **Check it out page**

NOTE: These ideas are based on the animals title, but the activity types can be applied to any of the titles in the macmillan topics series.

1 Student vocabulary books

Aim: To individualise vocabulary learning.
Activity: Encourage the students to keep a personal topic-centred word book. They use it to add new words as they come across them. They can use the lists on page 2 as a core, to start them off. When they find a new word or phrase that they want to add (perhaps from their coursebook), they can decide how best to show these. They can illustrate them, add translations into l1, and/or write sentences to contextualise them.

2 Dictionary meanings (Monolingual Or Bilingual Dictionaries)

Aim: To select the appropriate meaning in a dictionary entry.
Activity: Ask the students to look up one of the words from page 2 in their dictionary. E.g. *Mouse*. How many meanings are given? Which is the most relevant in this case?

3 Dictionary annotations (Monolingual Or Bilingual Dictionaries)

Aim: To use all the information that a dictionary gives about a word.
Activity 1: Ask the students to choose one of the words from page 2 and to look it up in their dictionary. What extra information are they told about it?
E.g. *Pet* (macmillan english dictionary)

/pet/ Noun C **.	It's a countable noun, with common Frequency.
/pet/ Adj.	It always comes before a noun.
/pet/ Verb	It is pronounced in the same way as a Noun, adjective or verb.

Activity 2: Ask them to discuss which dictionary information is most useful. They can also devise their own systems to use in their word books.

4 Word families.

Aim: To show that it is often easier to learn 'families' of words.
Activity: Choose one of the words from page 2. Write it on the board. E,g.

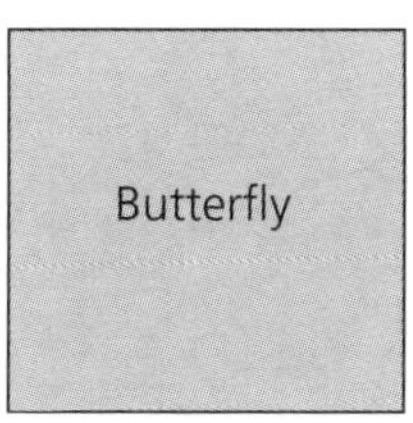

Ask the students to draw a word-family diagram, adding appropriate words from the page. They can compare their diagrams with another pair or group. Alternatively, this can be done as a whole-class activity on the board.

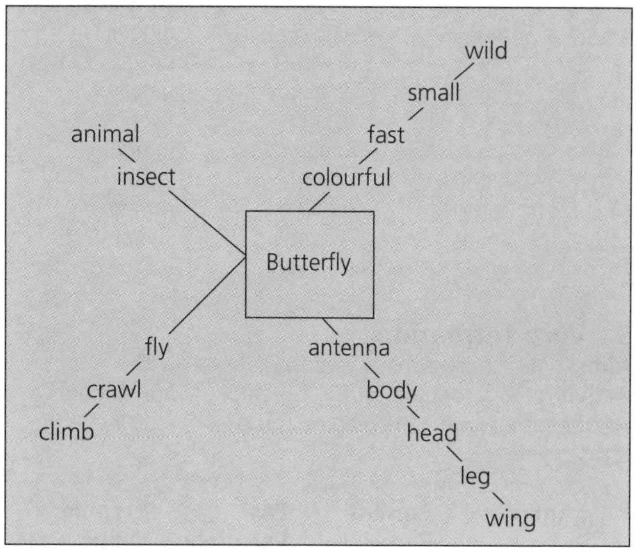

They can add other appropriate words now, or later.

5 Opposites

Aim: To expand vocabulary through word association.
Activity: Ask the students to group the words on page 2 into opposites. E.g. *Big/small.*

6 Collocation

Aim: To make common connections between words.
Activity: Ask the students to choose a group of animals from the lists (e.g. Birds). Working individually, in pairs or groups, or as a whole class on the board, they focus on the parts of the body for that group. They think of all the adjectives that could be used with them. E.g.

Noun	**Adjective**
eye	bright/small/shining ...
beak	sharp/open/pointed ...
feather	brown/ long/ soft ...

7 Cognates and 'false friends'

Aim: To identify cognates and be aware of 'false friends'
Activity: Ask the students to choose one 'family' of words from page 2 (different groups could choose different ones). They underline the words that are cognates with l1. Are there any differences of spelling or pronunciation? They also notice if there are any 'false friends'.

8 Word Formation

Aim: To notice connections in word formation.
Activity: Work with the list of descriptive words, or the verbs. If suitable for the age of your students, ask them to suggest or find out associated grammatical groups. They then notice any patterns, e.g. The nouns end in *–er*.

E.g.	**Verb**	**Adjective**	**Noun**
	climb	climbing	climber
	crawl	crawling	crawler
	dig	digging	digger
	dive	diving	diver
	eat	edible	eater
	fly	flying	flyer
	jump	jumping	jumper
	kill	killing	killer
	run	running	runner
	swim	swimming	swimmer
	walk	walking	walker

9 Verb formation

Aim: To notice patterns in verb formation.
Activity: If appropriate for the level/age of your students, ask them to suggest the present and past participles of the verbs on page 2.

E.g.	**Infinitive**	**Present Participle**	**Past Participle**	**Irregular Simple Past**
	Climb	Climbing	Climbed	-
	Crawl	Crawling	Crawled	-
	Dig	Digging	-	Dug
	Dive	Diving	Dived	-
	Eat	Eating	-	Ate
	Fly	Flying	-	Flew
	Jump	Jumping	Jumped	-
	Kill	Killing	Killed	-
	Run	Running	-	Ran
	Swim	Swimming	-	Swam
	Walk	Walking	Walked	-

10 Writing definitions

Aim: To relate meanings and lexical items.
Activity 1: Give the students a filled-in crossword puzzle frame using the words on page 2 (or write it on the board). Ask them to write clues for the words in it.

E.g.

B	U	D	G	E	R	I	G	A	R
				A					A
				G					B
				L					B
				E					I
									T

Across
1. A pet bird. It's very colourful.
2. (Etc.)

Down
1. A fierce bird. It has sharp claws.
2. An animal with long ears.
3. (Etc.)

Activity 2: working in pairs or groups, the students make up cross words for each other, using the words on page 2.

Teacher's Notes: **PEOPLE**

Ideas for use

This title contains a lot of ideas and information connected with different kinds of people and their lives. It encourages the students to observe and record details about other people and to relate these to themselves and their own environment.

Crosscurricular links: Art and Design; Current issues; Geography; History; Languages and Literature.

Don't forget! Look carefully for the People Focus mini-projects with each article. You will find more general ideas to use with all the titles in the *Topics* series on pages 13-15 of this Teacher's Book.

Cover and contents

Encourage the students to browse through *People* and to look at the range of articles, illustrations and design styles.

Speculation. Ask the students to speculate about the people on the cover. Who are they? Where are they?

Discussion. What do these photos on the cover suggest? Are they a good depiction of the topic, *People*? Ask the students to suggest other possible images for the cover.

Page 1 – Letter 🎧

The letter introduces the general topic. It reminds students that reading is only the first step and that these articles can also be a springboard for project work and research.

It also draws attention to the website as an interactive place for students to exchange their own photos and information. See the People Focus icon.

Discussion. Which titles are easy to understand (e.g. People and clothes)? Are any of them more difficult (e.g. Personal identity)? Encourage the students to guess what the articles are about and to flick through the pages to check this.

Page 2 – Check it out

See page 16 for different activities to use with this reference page.

The students may be able to suggest more English words connected with people for each section. Encourage them to keep Word Books where they add new vocabulary under section headings as they come across it.

✏ **Worksheet 1**
Vocabulary – Family relationships
Grammar – Verb *to be*
Content – L1

Page 3 – Personal identity 🎧

The dialogue presents the idea that all of us play many different roles in life at the same time.

Warm up. Ask the students to think of the different roles that people play, e.g. student, daughter or son, brother or sister, boyfriend or girlfriend. Brainstorm the various roles and relationships in the class and write these on the board.

Read and discuss. Ask the students to read the article. See if they agree or disagree with the statements from it.

Photo focus - groupwork. In groups or pairs, ask the students to speculate about the two people in the photos. Ask each group or pair to write a mini-profile of the two people. The groups compare their ideas.

Stereotypes. Discuss the meaning of 'stereotype' with the class. Ask them to find some adjectives in the article that often apply to three groups of people.

Brainstorm other stereotypical adjectives that often apply to these (or other) groups of people.

Discussion. Focus on the idea of stereotypes for different nationalities. Who uses them? Why?

People Focus. Prepare for this activity by returning to the various roles and relationships the class suggested in the Warm up. Discuss the best way of illustrating these for one person in a diagram or mind map.

✏ **Worksheet 2**
Vocabulary – Describing people
Grammar – Adjective + noun, Verb *to be*
Content – Art, Design, L1

Page 4 – My life: past, present and future

This article looks at three of the different ways people use to record their lives:

- Diaries describing daily events.
- Blogs for interaction with other people.
- Records of 'favourite' things over a specific period of time.

Warm up. Ask the class to suggest the different methods that people use to record personal events. Write these on the board. Find out which of these they use.

Writing/Guessing activity. The students copy the 'Favourite things' headings onto a piece of paper. They can add two or three more categories of their own. They fill it in for themselves, but do not show this to anybody. Collect all the pieces of paper. The students take it in turns to pick one piece of paper. They try to guess who wrote it.

Page 5 – Heroes

This article presents the idea of three different types of heroes – historical or national figures, local or everyday heroes, and personal heroes.

Warm up. Ask the class the four questions at the top of the page. Try to get them to define what a hero (or heroine) is for them. They can even suggest examples.

Read and discuss. National heroes.
Ask the students to read this section. Do they agree that these people are heroes? Why (not)?
Which people would they suggest for this category from their country? Do they all agree?

Local heroes. The cutting from the newspaper describes something a 'local hero' did. After they have read this section, ask the students for examples of similar stories in the newspaper or on TV.

Personal heroes. Do they agree that there are these two kinds of personal heroes: famous people and people you know and admire?

Groupwork. In groups, the students focus on one of these types of heroes. Are there any more heroes that fit in this category?

Worksheet 3
Vocabulary – Likes and dislikes
Grammar – Present simple, Verb *to be* + adjective
Content – L1, Maths

Pages 6 and 7 – I have a voice!

This two-page article describes a real event in July 2005: an international meeting of young people organised by UNICEF to coincide with the G8 world leaders' meeting.

Warm up. Write these words on the board:

discussion   politicians   summit meeting   workshop

Ask the students to suggest possible meanings for them. Encourage them to use dictionaries.

Then do the same with these two acronyms:

G8   UNICEF

Finally, ask them to look at the title of the article and the photos on Pages 6 and 7. What do they think that 'I have a voice!' means in this context?

Finding facts. Ask the students to look at the 'parallel' information at the top of Page 6.

Establish that there were two overlapping conferences: the G8 leaders' summit at Gleneagles and the C8 one for young people 20 kilometres away.

They then read the next two sections, which are just about the C8 conference. Ask them to find out:
The organisers: (UNICEF)
Three topics: (HIV/Aids, access to education, poverty)

Discussion. What other problems in the world affect young people? Are any of these a problem in your country?

Reading for information. Ask the students to read the next two sections about the people who attended the C8 conference, and their preoccupations.

Out-of-class. Ask the students to find all these countries in an atlas and to group them into continents.

Continent	**Countries**
Africa	(Guinea, Lesotho, Sierra Leone)
Asia	(Bhutan, Cambodia, Yemen)
Europe	(Britain, France, Germany, Italy, Moldova, Russia)
Americas	(Bolivia)

Which continent are all these G8 countries in? (Europe).

Note: The other members of the G8, whose leaders were at the politicians' summit, are Canada, Japan and the USA.

Page 7 – Photo and words.

Ask the students to look at the photo on Page 7 and to read the text. In small groups, find the answers to these questions. Who is the man? What is his normal work? What is his special work? Where do the group go to relax?

Speculation. Before they read the final section (The Manifesto), ask the students to guess what topics might be in it. Remind them of the concerns expressed on Page 5 and the countries where the students come from.

Read and check. The students look at the eight topics in the manifesto and compare these with their own ideas.

Discussion. Discuss the ideas in the Manifesto – including the sentences at the end about the future.

Do they think this C8 meeting was a good idea? Will the politicians take notice? Finally, is 'I have a voice!' a good title?

Writing. In groups, the students think about similar problems that are important for them. This is part of the People Focus mini-project. Then design and write a similar poster about their concerns.

Worksheet 4
Vocabulary – Countries, Continents, languages
Grammar – Present simple
Content – Art, Design, Geography, History, L1

Pages 8 and 9 – Statues

This factual article on two pages presents a different aspect of the topic, people: their representation as statues.

Warm up. Do a brainstorming with the class on any statues they have seen, either in books or magazines or in real life. Write these on the board.

Brainstorming. Ask the class to look at the photo on Page 8 of the Statue of Liberty. How much do they know about it? What can they find out about it?

Photos and words. Ask the students to look at the big photo across both pages, as well as the smaller ones on Page 8, and then to read the sections about Religious statues and Different cultures.

Warm up. Ask the students if they have seen any modern statues, or ones made from unusual materials.

Read and discuss. Ask the students to read the sections on Page 9. They compare these examples with any that they suggested in the Warm up. Which statue do they like best?

Worksheet 5
Vocabulary – Describing appearance
Grammar – Frequency adverbs
Content – Art, Design, Geography, History

Page 10 – People and clothes

This article discusses the 'pros and cons' of wearing uniform. It is presented in a school context, but many of the opinions apply to other types of uniform as well.

Warm up/Brainstorming. What do the class think about uniforms? What are the good and bad points about them?

Discussion. Do the students agree with the opinions in the article? Which ones are most persuasive?

Writing. The students write a sentence in support or against uniforms to express their own personal opinions.

People Focus. There are lots of different types of school uniform. Which of the ones here do the students prefer? How many different designs can they find?

Page 11 – Time for a change!

This article looks at the different ways that people change their appearance.

Warm up. Ask about the different ways that people change their appearance, e.g. clothes, make-up, tattoos, hairstyles. Discuss what the reasons are for changing, e.g. age, fashion.

Tastes change. Ask the students to read this section and then to answer the questions for themselves. What clothes, music or hobbies did they like last year? And this year?

Changing bodies. Which photos illustrate the ideas in this section? Which ones show traditional body decoration? Which ones show 'fashion'?

People change. Out-of-class. Ask the students to find photos of themselves at different ages. What changes most?

Discussion. Ask the class to look at all the photos and choose a word or phrase to describe each one, e.g. funny.

Page 12 – Happy Birthday!

This article discusses important personal anniversaries – Name Days and Birthdays – as well as significant ages in different cultures. Which are more important in your culture?

Read and reply. Ask the students to read the balloons about Birthdays and Name Days. Ask them to answer the questions in them. Then they compare their replies.

Discussion. Write the ages 12-21 on the board. What can you do at various ages in your country?

Read and compare. Ask the students to read about significant birthdays in Britain (the green balloon). What is the same or different in your country?

People focus. You can prepare for this with a whole class brainstorming activity.

Worksheet 6
Vocabulary – Dates, Months, Season
Grammar – *Can* + verb
Content – Geography, History, Maths

Page 13 – A song to a special person

This Beatles song is very well known. It is written partly in French and English. It can for discussing relationships between people from different cultures.

Focus on words. Ask the students to find the sentences and phrases (in English) that show how difficult communication can be.

Discussion. What other communication problems can there be between people (e.g, age, culture, distance)?

Page 14 – People quiz: do you know?

Family fun. This gives practice in family relationships, but is also meant to be fun.

Parts of the body. The students can make up similar picture quizzes using photos cut out of magazines.

Page 15 – Projects

Ask the students to read all the projects carefully in order to decide which ones are interesting for them.

Encourage the students to also review and present the things they have been doing in the various People Focus mini-projects.

Page 16 – Chatrooms

Teens chat. Ask the student to read the exchange and look at the two photos. What's Anna's problem?

Follow up. Ask the students to find other animal statues.

Worksheet 7
Vocabulary – Describing illustrations
Grammar – General
Content – Art, Design, L1

Worksheet 8
Vocabulary – Opinions
Grammar – Present simple
Content – Art, Design, L1, Maths

Title review. The students can do a review to help inform other people. This can be of the whole magazine, or of specific articles.

Test Worksheet
The aim of the test is to encourage the students to look back through the articles in order to check facts, notice details and find specific information to answer the questions.

Extra teacher's resources

The websites listed on Page 2 are worth visiting for further information.

Oxfam: www.oxfam.org.uk/coolplanet
UNICEF: www.unicef.org.uk/youthvoice
WWF: www.wwf.org

People Worksheet 1

References: **Check it out** - Page 2

Focus:

Vocabulary Family relationships
Grammar Verb *to be*
Content L1

Activities

1. Family names

Who's this? Unjumble these four family members. Write their names on the lines.

MRETHO ______________ THRAFE ______________

NMAGETHRDOR ______________ RRAFHEANGTD ______________

2. Same people, different names

Write your four names on the first line at the top of the columns.

________	____________	______	________________________
________	____________	______	________________________
________	____________	______	________________________

Now write these variations in the correct column.

Dad	Daddy	Grandad	Grannie
Grandma	Grandpa	Mum	Mummy

3. Family members

Find nine family members in this word box.

C	M	K	D	G	C	O	U	S	I	N
P	A	O	F	R	Y	C	J	O	Y	A
N	U	T	B	A	H	Q	I	R	B	Z
V	P	Z	U	N	C	L	E	G	Q	E
G	R	A	N	D	M	O	T	H	E	R
S	H	U	I	F	O	S	R	W	J	L
I	J	N	E	A	T	D	L	P	K	A
S	H	T	I	T	H	G	W	F	C	B
T	F	A	T	H	E	R	S	E	V	D
E	X	K	W	E	R	X	U	T	L	F
R	N	G	B	R	O	T	H	E	R	M

4. Draw a family tree for your family.

Put in relationships, names and ages.

People Worksheet 2

References: **Personal identity** - Page 3

Focus:

Vocabulary Describing people
Grammar Adjective + noun, Verb *to be*
Content Art, Design, L1

Activities

1. Describing you
Here are some words to describe people's appearance.

SHAPE OF FACE:	fat	long	short	thin		
COLOUR OF EYES:	black	blue	brown	green	grey	pink
SHADES OF HAIR:	blonde	dark	fair			
TYPE OF HAIR:	curly	long	short	straight		

Look in the mirror. What can you see? Complete the box.

Eyes	Mouth
Eyebrows	Ears
Nose	Face
Cheeks	Hair

Exchange your Worksheet with a partner. Are your personal descriptions accurate?

2. Secret descriptions
Choose a person in the class. Write their description here. Keep their name a secret.

Eyes	Mouth
Eyebrows	Ears
Nose	Face
Cheeks	Hair

Exchange Worksheets with a partner.
Who is the person? She/He is ______________. Are you correct?

3. Describing people: personality
Look at the words to describe personality on Page 2 (Check it out).
Which words describe you? Which words describe your best friend? Write them here.

ME	MY BEST FRIEND

4. Describing people: appearance and personality
Write three sentences to describe your appearance and your personality.

NAME: ______________________________
a. ______________________________
b. ______________________________
c. ______________________________

Do the same about your best friend.

NAME: ______________________________
d. ______________________________
e. ______________________________

People Worksheet 3

References: **My life: past, present and future** – Page 4

Focus:
Vocabulary Likes and dislikes
Grammar Present simple, Verb *to be* + adjective
Content L1, Maths

Activities

1. Favourite things

What are your favourite things now? Write your 'Top Three' in these categories.

	NUMBER ONE	NUMBER TWO	NUMBER THREE
Fashion idea			
TV programme			
Music group/CD			
Sports star			
Other favourite things			

2. Giving reasons: likes

Why do you like them? Give your reasons. e.g. I like Franz Ferdinand because they're fun.
Use the words in the box to help you.

cool	different	exciting	fun	modern

a. ______________________________
b. ______________________________
c. ______________________________
d. ______________________________
e. ______________________________

3. Giving reasons: dislikes

Now write five sentences about the things you don't like. Give your reasons.
e.g. I don't like small watches because they're old-fashioned.
There are some negative words in the box.

boring	noisy	old-fashioned	uncomfortable	ugly

a. ______________________________
b. ______________________________
c. ______________________________
d. ______________________________
e. ______________________________

4. Analysing likes and dislikes

Do a class survey to discover the top three likes and dislikes.
Write down your results.

References: **I have a voice!** - Pages 6 and 7

Focus:

Vocabulary Countries, Continents, Languages
Grammar Present simple
Content Art, Design, Geography, History, L1

Activities

1. Rich and poor countries.

There are 13 countries in the article. Find 12 of them in this wordbox.

B	J	R	N	R	U	S	S	I	A	Y
C	A	M	B	O	D	I	A	O	F	E
G	S	O	A	G	T	E	Z	U	W	M
U	E	L	Y	R	F	R	A	N	C	E
I	D	D	S	N	U	R	P	B	E	N
N	Q	O	K	O	Q	A	G	O	J	B
E	L	V	I	T	A	L	Y	L	M	H
A	N	A	H	C	B	E	H	I	A	U
L	E	S	O	T	H	O	T	V	X	T
X	G	E	R	M	A	N	Y	I	D	A
M	I	V	I	F	C	E	L	A	K	N

What's the missing country? ____________

2. Countries and continents.

The C8 students are from four different continents.
Write down the names of their countries in each continent.

Continents	Countries
Africa	
Americas	
Asia	
Europe	

Check with the article and put a ring round the G8 countries.
Which continent are these countries in? ____________

3. Discovering more.

Work in a group. Choose one of the countries from 2 and fill in the table below.
Use an atlas or the Internet to help you.

Country ____________________

Capital ____________________

Main language(s) ____________________

Other information ____________________

____

____

____

____

____

People Worksheet 5

References: **Statues** – Pages 8 and 9

Focus:

Vocabulary Describing appearance
Grammar Frequency adverbs
Content Art, Design, Geography, History

Activities

1. Describing statues

Where are these statues?

Brazil	Easter Island	New York
a beach	a cold place	a garden

a. They have big heads. ____________
b. It's on a mountain over a city. ____________
c. They're on a beach. ____________
d. It's French – but it's in a different country. ____________
e. It's cold! ____________
f. It has green hair. ____________

2. Checking information

Is this information true or false? Check with the article and circle T or F.

a. Statues can tell us about different cultures. T F
b. Statues are always of famous people. T F
c. Religious statues are always in churches. T F
d. The statues on Easter Island are small. T F
e. Some statues are frightening. T F
f. Artists always use stone or marble for statues. T F
g. Hot sun is bad for some statues. T F
h. Some statues are a symbol of a city or country. T F

Correct the false information here.

____
____
____
____

3. Materials

Match the materials with the descriptions.

fibreglass	marble	metal	mud
plastic	stone	terracotta	wood

a. It's very heavy. It comes out of the earth.
b. Another heavy material. It's often white. It shines in the light.
c. It's usually dark red or brown. This material comes from the earth, too.
d. This material is very heavy, too. It's often grey or brown. It's very strong.
e. It comes from trees.
f. This modern material is usually very light.
g. Another modern material. It's very light and strong. There's glass in it.
h. A natural material from the earth. It's heavy and dark brown.

4. Your statue

Design a statue. Decide the person, material(s), size and place.

PHOTOCOPIABLE

References: **Happy Birthday!** - Page 12

Focus:

Vocabulary Dates, Months, Season
Grammar *Can* + verb
Content Geography, History, Maths

Activities

1. Checking and comparing information

When can people do these things in Britain? Write the ages here.

	AGE in Britain	AGE in my country.
a. Work on Saturdays for five hours.		
b. Work for 35 hours a week in the school holidays.		
c. Finish full-time education.		
d. Get married if your parents agree.		
e. Get married if your parents don't agree.		
f. Ride a motorbike.		
g. Drive a car.		
h. Vote in European or national elections.		

When can you do these things in your country? Find out and write the ages above.

2. Collecting information

You can work in a group or with a partner.
Choose a month. Do a class survey. Who has a birthday in this month? Who has a name day?
Write their names here.

MONTH: ____________________

BIRTHDAYS	NAMEDAYS

3. Analysing and presenting information

Design a graph, pie chart or bar chart to show this information.
Which months have the maximum birthdays? When are the top name days?
Decide the best way to present this factual information about your class.

People Worksheet 7

References: **All**

Focus:

Vocabulary Describing illustrations
Grammar General
Content Art, Design, L1

Activities

1. People and words

Here are some words for the pictures in 'People'.
Write the article or page number in the right-hand column.

WORDS	ARTICLES
a. 'Wow! This is exciting!'	
b. 'That's a great hairstyle!'	
c. 'Don't move! Say cheese!'	
d. Are these animals real?	
e. A fine moustache!	
f. Look - Ewan and friends.	
g. 'Is that really me?'	
h. How about a swim?	
i. 'I love you!'	
j. 'You look great!'	
k. A famous detective.	
l. Shakespeare today.	

2. Writing words

Choose 3 photos. Write a speech bubble, a 'thinks' bubble or a title for each photo.

PAGE	ARTICLE	WORDS
—	______________	______________________________
—	______________	______________________________
—	______________	______________________________

3. Comparing words

Compare your ideas with other people. Choose the best words for all the photos.
Make a class poster with the top ideas.

References: All

Focus:

Vocabulary Opinions
Grammar Present simple
Content Art, Design, L1, Maths

Activities

1. Making choices

Look at all the pages and articles again. Which are your favourites?
Write your top three choices here.

NUMBER ONE.	Page:_______	Title _________
NUMBER TWO.	Page:_______	Title _________
NUMBER THREE.	Page:_______	Title _________

Compare your choices with other people.

2. Giving reasons

What are the reasons for your choices? Complete these sentences.

a. I like Number ONE because it's ___________
b. I like ___________
c. ______________________

3. Class survey

Count the class votes for every article.
Which article is the class 'Number One'? _______________
Which is the 'Number Two'? _______________
And 'Number Three'? _______________

Make a poster with the top three titles. Under each title, write all the reasons. E.g.

CLASS ______________________	OUR FAVOURITE 'PEOPLE' PAGES		
	NUMBER ONE	NUMBER TWO	NUMBER THREE
	______________	______________	______________
NUMBER OF VOTES:	______________	______________	______________
REASONS:	______________	______________	______________
	______________	______________	______________
	______________	______________	______________
	______________	______________	______________

PHOTOCOPIABLE

People Test Worksheet

Name: ____________________

Total Points (1 per question) ____________

1. Look through People. Identify these articles. Write the page number and the title.

a. There are pictures of a lot of statues.
   Page ________ Title ____________________
b. You can read about different kinds of diaries.
   Page ________ Title ____________________
c. This article is about special days for different people.
   Page ________ Title ____________________
d. Young people send their ideas to politicians.
   Page ________ Title ____________________
e. What clothes do people want to wear at school?
   Page ________ Title ____________________
f. One person, several identities.
   Page ________ Title ____________________
g. People on the beach.
   Page ________ Title ____________________
h. A 'green' person.
   Page ________ Title ____________________
i. Two languages, but good communication.
   Page ________ Title ____________________
j. Read some Shakespeare!
   Page ________ Title ____________________

2. Are these statements true or false? Check them with the articles and circle T or F.

a.	Page 1	The picture at the top is the same as the picture on the cover.	T F
b.	Page 2	There is a special section about the family in Check it Out.	T F
c.	Page 3.	This article is about cosmetics.	T F
d.	Page 4.	The article is about famous people.	T F
e.	Page 5.	Ordinary people can be heroes.	T F
f.	Page 6.	An 11-year old girl is a radio presenter.	T F
g.	Page 10.	All these people like to wear school uniform.	T F
h.	Page 11.	Some people paint designs on their hands.	T F
i.	Page 12.	In England, it is legal to marry at 18.	T F
j.	Page 16.	These statues are very old.	T F

3. What is the English word for these things?

a. Your personal identity. ____________________
b. An interactive diary on the Internet. ____________________
c. Another word for 'courageous'. ____________________
d. Your 'grannie' is your .... ____________________
e. People often wear these clothes at school. ____________________
f. A special day for people with the same name. ____________________
g. 'Mom' in American English, but .... In British English. ____________________
h. A 'teen-speak' word for 'favourite' ____________________
i. The sand near the sea. ____________________
j. The individual character and identity of a person ____________________

Teacher's Notes: **PLACES**

Ideas for use

This title includes a lot of ideas and information about different kinds of places. It often looks at these places from unusual angles. It encourages the students to observe and record details about places in their own environment.

Crosscurricular links: Art and Design; Geography; History.

Don't forget! Look carefully for the Places Focus mini-projects with each article.

You will find more general ideas to use with all the titles in the *Topics* series on pages 25-27 of this Teacher's Book.

Cover and contents

Encourage the students to browse through *Places* and to look at the range of articles, illustrations and design styles.

Warm up. What different places do they know the names of in English? What do they know about each one? Which are their favourite places?

Discussion. What do the photos on the cover suggest? Are they a good depiction of the topic, *Places*? Ask the students to suggest other possible images for the cover. You can use the pictures to discuss the various categories of places, e.g. indoor, outdoor, personal, public.

Page 1 – Letter 🎧

The letter contains a series of statements about the content. It also draws attention to the website as a place for students to exchange their own information.

Make sure that the students understand (and can identify) the Places Focus icon.

Discussion. Which titles are easy to understand (e.g. My dream place)? Are any of them more difficult (e.g. Connecting places)? Encourage the students to guess what the articles are about.

Page 2 – Check it out

See page 28 for different activities to use with this reference page.

The students may be able to suggest more places in English for each section. Encourage them to keep Word Books for adding new vocabulary.

✎ **Worksheet 1**
Vocabulary – Places + adjectives
Grammar – Adjective + noun (collocation)
Content – Art, L1

Page 3 – My dream place 🎧

The article contains descriptions of two contrasting 'dream places'. It can be used for a jigsaw reading activity.

Warm up. Brainstorm 'dream places' with the class. Focus on personal places, such as the students' rooms at home. Get their suggestions for colour, size and furnishings.

Finding information. The students can choose to read either the first or second description. Write these headings on the board and ask to copy them into their notebooks.

SIZE COLOUR SHAPE FRIENDS SPECIAL FEATURES

Then ask them to read 'their' section and find the relevant information for each heading. Make sure they understand what a 'special feature' is, e.g. a password to enter a room. They write this information in their notebooks.

Information exchange. The students work in pairs with someone who chose the other description. They ask and answer questions about the two rooms. Then they read the 'other' description to check the information their partner gave them.

Pictures and words. Ask the students to look carefully at the illustrations of the two rooms. Do they fit the verbal descriptions well? Do they think the boy's description is serious or a joke? Why? Finally, the class can vote on which room most of them prefer.

Places focus. Encourage them to think about their dream rooms. These can be as fantastic as they want. You may like to brainstorm their ideas first.

✎ **Worksheet 2**
Vocabulary – Describing rooms
Grammar – Adjective plus noun (collocation)
Content – L1

Pages 4 and 5 – Doors: going out and coming in

This is a two-page article, but it is divided into short sections which can be read one at a time or used for jigsaw reading and information exchange activities. The idea is that doors can signify different emotions and events.

Warm up. Ask the students to think of a number of different doors they have seen and to choose an adjective to describe each one. Write their suggestions on the board and then group these into categories. e.g. colour, shape.

Describing doors: pictures and words. Ask the students to look at the photos of doors on these two pages and to choose an adjective from the list on the board, or using their own ideas, to describe each one. Compare these suggestions. Notice how the same picture may suggest different things to different people.

Discussion. The students read the text on Page 4. Notice the questions in paragraph 3. Ask them to choose one of the doors and answer those questions for it. They compare their ideas. The first section on Page 5 describes some of the different materials that doors are made from. The second paragraph describes some of the different emotions that are aroused by different doors and situations.

Groupwork. In groups, the students focus on one of these ideas. They read the relevant section carefully and then think of other examples of doors that illustrate the ideas in it. If they do photos or drawings, these can act as preparation for the Places Focus mini-project.

Worksheet 3
Vocabulary – Adjectives (colour, shape, size)
Grammar – Adjective + noun + Present simple
Content – Art, L1

Pages 6 and 7 – Places to live, work and play

This is an article about different places and their uses. It focuses on ways in which their design and architecture are linked to their function.

Warm up. Write these words on the board:

HOUSES SCHOOLS OFFICE BUILDINGS

Ask the students to think of typical buildings in their city or region for each of the three categories. Collect their ideas to build a group of words to describe each of these typical buildings.

Out-of-class. Ask the students to copy the words for one of these groups, and to find a building of that type. They can draw or photograph it. Ask them to bring their pictures to the next lesson and suggest any extra words that can be used to describe it. The class then decides if they agree with the two first sentences at the top of Page 6.

Photos and words. The students look at the photos on Pages 6 and 7. Without reading the text, they try and decide which of these four categories each building can be put in. Compare their ideas in groups or on the board.

DOMESTIC (HOME) EDUCATIONAL PUBLIC OTHER

What's this place? In pairs or small groups, the students read this section and try to answer the questions about the four buildings.

Do they like these buildings? Why (not)? Do they know of similar public buildings? Do they like them?

It's not all fun. Do the class know of people who live in mobile homes and move around. What are the pros and cons? Do they agree with the opinion in this paragraph?

Remember! Do the class know of any homeless people?

Information collecting. Divide the class into groups or pairs. Half of them read the section 'Different climate, different buildings' in the left-hand column, and the others read 'Home or tourist attraction?' in the right-hand column. In their groups or pairs, they think of buildings that they know which are tourist attractions. Why are these interesting? Is it because of their design? Does this depend on the climate or weather?

Worksheet 4
Vocabulary – Places for living, Working and leisure, Weather
Grammar – Present simple
Content – Art and Design, Geography, L1

Pages 8 and 9 – Connecting places: bridges

This factual article on two pages presents the idea of bridges as connections between places and different groups of people.

Warm up. Do a brainstorming with the class on bridges they know.

See how many examples of these each person can write down within an agreed time. Then write the results on the board. For each one, decide:
- What it connects (i.e. what is on each end of it?).
- What it goes over (river/road/railway/countryside).
- Who uses it.

You can rank the bridges they have suggested in order of:
- importance
- age
- amount of traffic

There are photos of six bridges on Page 8. Ask the students to look at the photos and read the names of each bridge. Which ones do they recognise?

Read and remember. Ask the students to read the texts about these 6 bridges. Then they close their magazines. Read these sentences about the bridges aloud – the first person to give the name of the bridge. its city and country correctly wins a point. You can play this in teams.

This bridge opens for ships. *(Tower Bridge)*
There are shops on this one. *(Ponte Vecchio)*
A lot of tourists walk over this bridge. *(Charles Bridge)*
This is a very sad bridge for some people. *(Bridge of Sighs)*
It's the symbol of an important city. *(Sydney Harbour Bridge)*
People travel to work over this bridge every day. *(Rio-Niteroi Bridge)*

NOTE: The bridge in the big background photo is the Bay Bridge, San Francisco.

Using information. The two bridges on Page 9, Millau and Gateshead, are very modern. Ask the students to read the descriptions of both of them. Then they put the information under the same headings as in the Warm up activity.

This activity is preparation for the mini-project in the Places Focus.

Bridges as symbols. Ask the students to read this section. Do they know any bridges that have been destroyed or damaged? Can they guess where this bridge is? Why is it an important symbol for people? (Mostar, in Bosnia. It was built in 1566 and was destroyed in the Bosnian War in 1993. It used to connect two communities, Muslim and Croat. It was rebuilt and reopened in July 2004 as a symbol to reconnect the two communities.)

Worksheet 5
Vocabulary – Cities, Countries, Geographical features
Grammar – Present Simple
Content – Geography

Pages 10 and 11 – Connecting places: tunnels

This two-page article also looks at ways of connecting people and places, but this time under the ground.

Warm up. As with the previous article, ask the students to first of all think of tunnels that they know, and consider their purpose.

Discussion. The whole class should read the introductory paragraph on Page 10 and decide if they agree with the last two sentences. How do they feel in a tunnel and on a bridge? Are these feelings different? Collect as many adjectives to describe these feelings as possible and write them on the board.

Groupwork/Out-of-class. In groups, the students choose one of these five sections and suggest examples of the kind of tunnel in it from their own experience. They should find out as many facts about each tunnel as possible and present these to the class.

Page 12 – Animal places

This article looks at the kind of places that animals live in.

Warm up. Ask the students to suggest the names of some animals in English. Write these on the board. Then ask where these animals normally live, e.g. in nests, in caves, under trees.

Discussion. The students read the three sections and decide the advantages and disadvantages of each type of 'home'.

Page 13 – Strange places: a song

This Beatles song describes a fantasy place.

Warm up. Focus on the three questions at the top of the page. The students check their answers.

Vocabulary. You may want to ask for suggested meanings for these words and phrases:

aboard	on a ship
band	music group
a life of ease	a good way to live
Everyone one of us has all we need.	We have everything that we want

Song. The song has a strong rhythm. Encourage the students to sing or clap with it.

Discussion. Ask for suggestions for songs about strange places. This is preparation for the Places Focus activity.

Worksheet 6
Vocabulary – Colours
Grammar – General
Content – Art, Design, L1, Music

Page 14 – Places quiz: do you know?

1. The students can cut photos of places out of magazines and use them in a similar way to make a quiz.
2. The students can make up similar quiz questions about places.

Page 15 – Projects

Ask the students to read all the projects carefully in order to decide which ones are interesting for them.

These projects can be done in groups, pairs or individually. Some of them may link with those done in other subjects, e,g. History or Geography.

Encourage the students to also review and present the things they have been doing in the various Places Focus mini-projects.

Page 16 – Chatrooms

Teens Chat. This exchange discusses the meanings behind the names of many places – dates, famous people or events.

Follow up. Ask the students to suggest or find out the 'story' behind some of their local places.

Discussion. Do they agree that the names of places connect with school subjects? Which ones?

Worksheet 7
Vocabulary – Describing illustrations
Grammar – Adjective + noun
Content – Art, Design, L1

Worksheet 8
Vocabulary – General
Grammar – General
Content – Art, Design, L1

Title review. The students can do a review to help inform other people. They can agree their own criteria, or you can put a framework on the board for them to copy.

Test Worksheet
The aim of the test is to encourage the students to look back through the articles in order to check facts, notice details and find specific information to answer the questions.

Extra teacher's resources

These websites are worth visiting for further information.

Educational: www.kidport.com
BBC young people: www.bbc.co.uk/cbbcnews
Wildlife: www.wwf.org
Design: www.technologystudent.com
Bridges: www.gateshead.gov.uk
Buildings: www.GreatBuildings.com

Places Worksheet 1

References: **Check it out** – Page 2

Focus:
Vocabulary Places + adjectives
Grammar Adjectives + noun (collocation)
Content Art, L1

Activities

1. Different places

Unjumble the words. Write the names of the places.

PLACE		ARTICLE	PAGE
OMOR	______________		
LENTUN	______________		
ENST	______________		
LANAC	______________		
ELOH	______________		
EDGRIB	______________		
THOLE	______________		
AREPO OSHUE	______________		

Now find a picture of each place in your magazine. Write the page number.
Then write the title of the article.

NOTE: Some places are on two pages.

2. Describing places: adjective + noun

Here are 8 adjectives from Check it out. Match each adjective with a place from your list.
Choose two other adjectives and places in (i) and (j).

	ADJECTIVE	PLACE
a.	ancient	______________
b.	beautiful	______________
c.	dark	______________
d.	exciting	______________
e.	historical	______________
f.	modern	______________
g.	new	______________
h.	public	______________
i.		______________
j.		______________

Compare your list with a partner. What are the differences?

3. Inside places and rooms

Draw a plan of your apartment or house here (use an extra page if necessary).
Write the names of the rooms and the 'inside places'.

References: **My dream place** – Page 3

Focus:
Vocabulary Describing rooms
Grammar Adjective + noun (collocation)
Content L1

Activities

1. Describing rooms

Complete these descriptions of the two dream rooms. Use these nouns. Don't look at the article!

colour (x2)	friends	notice	password	room (x2)
shape	size	walls	website	window

GIRL
The girl wants a big _______ with a big _______. Her favourite _______ is blue, so she wants blue _______. The special feature is a big _______ on the door. It says 'Private'. Her _______ can come in, of course.

BOY
He wants a virtual _______. It's on a _______. He can change the _______, the _______ and the _______. His friends have a _______ to enter it.

Now compare your descriptions with the article on Page 3. Are they correct?

2. A different room

Read about a different room. Then answer the questions about it.

'My dream room is very modern. It's really cool.
It has white walls, a white ceiling, a white floor…
It's like a white box. The cupboards are white, too – and really big!
I can hide all my stuff in them. So my room is always tidy!

The furniture is black. My computer, DVD player and TV are all silver.
It's really 'Hi-tech'. Well, that's my dream. '

a. What colour is the furniture? ______________________________
b. What things are white? ______________________________
c. What colour is the technical equipment? ______________________________
d What's special about the cupboards? ______________________________
e. Why is this good? ______________________________
f. What four adjectives describe this room? ______________________________
g. What is like a white box? ______________________________

3. Write three sentences about your dream room here.

a. ____
b. ____
c.. ____

PHOTOCOPIABLE

Places Worksheet 3

References: **Doors going out and coming in** – Pages 4 and 5

Focus:
Vocabulary Adjectives (colour, shape, size)
Grammar Adjectives + noun + Present simple
Content Art, L1

Activities

1. Identifying doors

This is a diagram of the doors on pages 4 and 5.

a

b

c

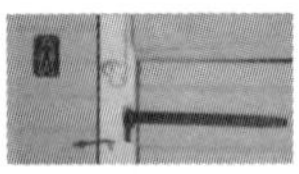
d

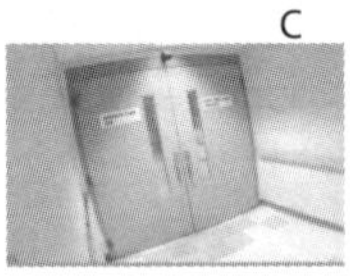
e

f

g

h

i

j

Compare it with the photos in the article.
Write the colour, shape and size of each of the doors in this table. Add any special features.

DOOR	COLOUR	SHAPE	SIZE	SPECIAL FEATURE
a.				
b.				
c.				
d.				
e.				
f.				
g.				
h.				
i.				
j.				

2. Where am I?

Match the descriptions and the places. There are several possible answers.

a. This place has a very strong door.
b. You can see through this door.
c. This door goes round and round.
d. 'I don't want this door to open!'
e. 'I want to go through that door!'

3. Write a sentence to describe a door in your school. Don't say where it is!

Places Worksheet 4

References: **Places to live, work and play** – Pages 6 and 7

Focus:
Vocabulary Places for living, Working and leisure
Weather
Grammar Present simple
Content Art, Design, Geography, L1

Activities

1. What's the purpose?
Look at the photos in the article. Find these places.

art gallery	caravan	doorway	hotel
house	opera house	parliament building	yurt

What do people do in them? ('To play in' means for leisure activities.)
Write the places in the correct columns. Some places have several purposes.

LIVING	WORKING	PLAY (LEISURE ACTIVITIES)

Compare your decisions with a partner. Are they the same?

2. Categorising places
Look at the places in Check it out on Page 2 again. Are they for living, working or leisure?
Write them in this chart.

LIVING	WORKING	LEISURE ACTIVITIES

Then think of other places to put in the chart.

Places Worksheet 5

References: **Connecting places: bridges** – Pages 8 and 9

Focus:
Vocabulary Cities, Countries, Geographical features
Grammar Present simple
Content Geography

Activities

1. Countries and cities

Complete this chart with the cities and the names of the bridges in the article on Pages 8 and 9.

COUNTRY	CITY	BRIDGE
Australia		
Brazil		
Czech Republic		
England		
England		
France		
Italy		
Italy		

2. Bridges and water

Four of these bridges go over rivers. Which bridge crosses each river?

RIVER	BRIDGE
Arno (Italy)	
Thames	
Tyne	
Vltava (Czech Republic)	

Four bridges go over different natural features. What are they?

NATURAL FEATURE	BRIDGE
canal	
harbour	
sea	
valley	

One bridge is the 'odd one out' – it doesn't go over water. Which bridge?

3. A local bridge

Choose a bridge in your town or region.
What does it go over? What places does it connect? What colour is it? How long is it?

Write some sentences about it. Don't put its name!
MY BRIDGE:

a. ______________________ c. ______________________

b. ______________________ d. ______________________

Exchange worksheets with a partner. What's the bridge? This bridge is ______________________

References: **A strange place** – Page 13

Focus:
Vocabulary Colours
Grammar General
Content Art, Design, L1, Music

Activities

1. Finding information
Look carefully at the song. Find this information.

a. The type of ship.
b. Its colour.
c. The colour of the sky.
d. The colour of the sea.
e. Who lives on the ship?
f. Who lives next door?
g. Who begins to play music?
h. What word means 'on the ship'?

2. Using information
Imagine you are on the ship too.
What is good about it? What's funny? Who is with you? Where are you?
Write an email or postcard to a friend about your trip.

3. Your own song
Write a song or poem of your own about a strange place. Think about where the place is, who lives there and what colour it is.

Places Worksheet 7

References: **All**

Focus:
Vocabulary Describing illustrations
Grammar Adjective + noun
Content Art, Design, L1

Activities

1. Groupwork
Work in a group.
Look through the magazine again. The photos and references are from a lot of different countries. Are there similar places in your town or country? What local photos can you suggest?

Discuss your ideas and agree the best choice. Write them in the right-hand column.

ARTICLE	LOCAL PLACES
My dream place.	
Doors: going out and going in	
Places to live, work and play	
Connecting places: bridges	
Connecting places: tunnels	
Animal places	
A strange place	
Teens Chat: names of place	

Compare your ideas with another group.

2. Choose an adjective to describe each of your examples.
Write them next to your suggestions.

PLACE	ADJECTIVE

References: **All**

Focus: **Vocabulary** General
Grammar Art, Design, L1
Content General

Activities

1. Making choices

Look at all the pages and articles again. Which are your favourites?
Write your Top Three choices here.

NUMBER ONE.	Page: ________	Title________________
NUMBER TWO.	Page: ________	Title________________
NUMBER THREE.	Page: ________	Title________________

Compare your choices with other people.

2. Giving reasons

What are your reasons for your choices? Complete these sentences.

a. I like Number ONE because it's ________________
b. I like ________________
c. ________________

3. Class survey

Count the class votes for every article.

Which article is the class 'Number One'?
Which is the 'Number Two'?
And 'Number Three'?

Make a poster with the top three titles. Under each title, write all the reasons. E.g.

CLASS ____________ OUR FAVOURITE 'PLACES' PAGES

	NUMBER ONE	NUMBER TWO	NUMBER THREE
NUMBER OF VOTES:	________	________	________
REASONS:	________	________	________
	________	________	________
	________	________	________

Places Test Worksheet

Name: ______________________________

Total Points (1 per Question) __________

1. Look through *Places*. Identify these articles. Write the page number and the title.

a. There are pictures of a lot of doors.
Page ________ Title ______________________

b. You can read about animals' homes.
Page ________ Title ______________________

c. This page is about a kind of ship.
Page ________ Title ______________________

d. These things go under the ground.
Page ________ Title ______________________

e. Connections up in the air.
Page ________ Title ______________________

f. A virtual room.
Page ________ Title ______________________

g. A blue place.
Page ________ Title ______________________

h. A strange, round house
Page ________ Title ______________________

2. Are these statements true or false? Check them with the articles and write T or F.

a. Page 2. There are no websites for Bridges.. . T F
b. Page 3. The girl loves blue. T F
c. Page 4. The article about 'Doors' is on two pages.. T F
d. Page 5. You can't see through a glass door. T F
e. Page 7. Houses in Amsterdam are all on busy streets. T F
f. Page 8. There are shops on the Bridge of Sighs. T F
g. Page 9. The length of the Millau Bridge is 3 kilometres. T F
h. Page 10. There are no metro systems in Athens and Rome. T F
i. Page 11. You can see ancient tombs and monuments under the city of Rome. T F

3. What is the English word for these things?

a. A special word to enter a place. ______________________
b. The way into a place. ______________________
c. The adjective for a person with no home. ______________________
d. A walker. ______________________
e. A person on a bicycle. ______________________
f. A place for a dead person. ______________________
g. A bird's home. ______________________
h. The opposite of 'inside'. ______________________

Teacher's Notes: **ANIMALS**

Beginner plus

Ideas for use

This title includes a lot of information about different kinds of animals. It encourages the students to observe and record details about them. It also includes articles relating to conservation and the environment.

Cross curricular links: Science; Geography.

Don't forget! Look carefully for the Animal Detective mini-projects with each article. You will find more general ideas to use with all the titles in the *Topics* series on pages 37-39 of this Teacher's Book.

Cover and contents

Encourage the students to browse through *Animals* and to look at the range of articles, illustrations and design styles.

What different animals do they know the names of in English? What do they know about each one? Which are their favourite animals?

Discussion. What do the photos on the cover suggest? Are they a good depiction of the topic, *Animals*? Why (not)? Ask the students to suggest other possible images for the cover. You can use the pictures to discuss the various categories of animals, e.g. birds, fish, insects, mammals, reptiles. Ask the students to suggest examples of animals in English for each group.

Page 1 – Letter

The letter contains a series of questions about animals. You may like to discuss these in L1 with the students. They will serve as a general 'warm up' for the topic and help to show what aspects really interest each person.

Make sure that the students understand (and can identify) the Animal Detective icon.

Discussion. Which titles are easy to understand (e.g. Pets Corner)? Which are more difficult (e.g. WWF)? Encourage the students to guess what the articles are about and to flick through the pages to check this.

Page 2 – Check it out

See page 40 for different activities to use with this reference page.

Worksheet 1
Vocabulary – Animals
Grammar – Adjective + noun
Content – Science

Page 3 – Feet Talk!

Identify some of the parts of human feet (heel, sole, toes). Ask the students to compare the four different types of birds' feet. What can each bird do? How do its feet help it?

Footprints. Do this as a quiz. The students can work individually or in pairs.

Animal Detective. Discuss where they will find the information and how they will present it.

Out-of-class. Ask the students to find pictures of birds with these types of feet and to bring them to class. They can group them into categories, e.g. Birds that can swim. Birds that can run fast. Birds that can climb trees. Birds that can catch other animals.

Worksheet 2
Vocabulary – Parts of the feet
Grammar – *Can* for ability + action verbs
Content – Science

Page 4 – It's a dangerous world!

You can use a jigsaw reading activity with this article. Divide the class into three groups. Each group reads one of the three sections. They then become the 'experts' and tell the others about it. The other groups check the information by reading the text.

The students can also collect information about 'their' animal group and bring relevant photos to class.

Discuss the dangers mentioned in the Conservation Spot. Do they know of other problems for animals? How can people help with these?

Animal Detective. Help the students to choose their animal. Discuss where they can find the information.

Out-of-class. The students can collect pictures and information about different animal families (see Page 5, or about the three animals shown here.

Worksheet 3
Vocabulary – Domestic animals
Grammar – Present simple
Content – Science

Page 6 – Birth, life and death

Check whether the students are familiar with the concept of 'metamorphosis' and these life cycles from their Science lessons. If not, use the photos to explain the stages.
Ask the students if they are afraid of any animals, e.g. spiders, mice, snakes. Discuss what is scary about them.

Out-of-class. If there is a stream or lake nearby, the students may be able to observe the various transformations from frogspawn to tadpoles to frogs. They could keep a diary and record each stage.

Worksheet 4
Vocabulary – Frog/butterfly metamorphosis
Grammar – Present simple
Content – Science

Page 7 – A working life

Discuss the difference between wild animals, pets and working animals. Ask for examples in English of each group.

Ask the students to read either the top section or the one about dogs. Is there any information that is new for them? Are there any similar facts they could add?

What other working animals can they suggest? What do these animals do?

Pages 8 and 9 – WWF across the world

Encourage the students to look at the page design and photos. Check what they know about WWF. Point out the panda logo.

There is a lot of information here, but it is presented in clear, factual language. Do not let the amount of text destroy the students' interest and curiosity.

Focus first of all on the four question-and-answer lines at the top of Page 9. Discuss this information. Is it new for the students? Do they know of any other organizations like WWF?

Next, look at the three sections below on Pages 8 and 9:

- WWF Brazil, tourism and turtles on Page 8.
- WWF Thailand and educational projects on Page 9.
- WWF Scotland and sea animals on Page 9.

The students can choose one of these sections to read and explore further. It may be more productive for them to do this in pairs or small groups.

Animal Detective. Page 8. Check that the Projeto Tamar website is still active, and that they will understand the English version.

Out-of-class. If the students are excited by this article, encourage them to find out about other animal conservation organizations and, especially those in your area. They may know people who take part in them.

Animal Detective Page 9. There may be other animals in danger that the students would prefer to find out about.

Worksheet 5
Vocabulary – Animals, Environment
Grammar – Present simple
Content – Geography, Science, History, Art, Design

Page 10 – Pets' corner – Popular pets

The article opens with some slogans about some popular pets. Check the students can identify the four animals in the photos – rabbit (bunny), dog, cat, budgerigar (budgie). Check they know the other three animals in the slogans – goldfish, hamster, guinea pig.

Find out what pets the students have. Which are the most popular/unusual ones?

Discuss the meaning of the six adjectives in the slogans – crazy, daft, ga-ga, hysterical, grumpy, happy.

Encourage the students to make up similar slogans about their pets, e.g. 'Mad about a mouse!'

Discuss the implication of the warning, 'A pet is for life, not just for Christmas!' This warning reminds people that owning a pet is a long-term responsibility.

Discuss the 'pet care' phrases in the white box. Which ones are important for their pets?

In the quiz, the students have to find a piece of advice for each pet. Do they think these are good ideas? Can they suggest others for looking after specific pets properly?

Page 11 - Pets' corner – Our pets in the wild

This article is written in note form, like a lot of scientific articles. It shows how present-day pets and domestic animals have developed from their origins as wild animals. The comments about the original habitat, behaviour and food are still relevant to ways of caring for pets in that group.

Ask the students if any of this information is new or surprising for them. Do they know other similar links between wild and domestic animals?

Worksheet 6
Vocabulary – Personal habits
Grammar – Present simple
Content – Geography, Science

Page 12 – Animals attract tourists!

This article is written in a humorous way, but it also raises a serious question about the exploitation of animals for tourism. You may like to discuss this in relation to tourism and animals in your country.

What does Hamish think about tourists? The students can make up 'think bubbles' for the photographs.

Identify the souvenirs that are linked to Hamish (biscuits, chocolates, soap). What other animal souvenirs could be sold?

Look at the notice 'BEWARE OF HAMISH'S HORNS'. What sort of warning notice could be written about tourists?

Page 13 – An animal song

This is a traditional song which exists in different versions.

Ask the students to identify the animals in the picture and to count them. How many different varieties are there? (Eleven: bees, butterflies, elephants, hippopotamuses (hippos), kangaroos, monkeys, parrots, rabbits, snakes, tortoises/turtles, zebras.)

Discuss what food each type of animal eats. Which ones are carnivores? Which ones can stay with other animals?

After they have heard the song, encourage them to read it aloud and/or sing it. It has a strong rhythm which they can tap out. Different groups can read out or sing different sections.

Page 14 – Animal quiz: Do you know?

1. Compare these animal proverbs with those in your culture. What animals often appear in proverbs (e.g. cats, monkeys, elephants)?
2-5. The students can make up a similar quiz about animals.

Page 15 – Projects

Ask the students to read all the projects carefully in order to decide which ones are interesting for them. Find out which are the most/least interesting for this class and if any of them just interest one person.

These projects can be done in groups, pairs or individually. Some of them may link with those done in other subjects, e,g. History or Science.

Encourage the students to also review and present the things they have been doing in the various Animal Detective mini-projects. If appropriate, these can form a class end-of-term exhibition.

Page 16 – Chatrooms

Fun chat. Are there similar animal sayings in your culture? If so, the students can draw similar cartoons for them.

Teens chat. Discuss the problems people often have with their pets, e.g. goldfish die, mice escape, cats kill birds.

Can you believe it? Ask the students to write a caption for the photo, e.g. 'That's a lovely coat!', or a 'think bubble'.
Encourage them to bring unusual photos of animals to class.

Worksheet 7
Vocabulary – Animals
Grammar – Adjective + noun
Content – Geography, Science

Worksheet 8
Vocabulary – Describing animals
Grammar – Present simple, Adjective + noun
Content – Geography, Science

Title review. The students can do a review to help inform other people. This can be of the whole magazine, or of specific articles. They can agree on their own criteria, or you can put this framework on the board for them to copy and adapt.

CRITERIA	ARTICLE	STARS	COMMENTS
Interest			
Information			
Design			
Photos			
Animal Detective			
Other			

Test Worksheet
The aim of the test is to encourage the students to look back through the articles in order to check facts, notice details and find specific information to answer the questions.

Extra teacher's resources

These websites are worth visiting for further information. They all have links to other relevant sites.

WWF: www.wwf.org
BBC young people: www.bbc.co.uk/cbbcnews
HWDT: www.hwdt.org

Animals Worksheet 1

References: **Check it out** – Page 2

Focus:

Vocabulary	Animals
Grammar	Adjective + noun
Content	Science

Activities

1. Animal Names

Look at this list of animals and complete their names.

	Colour (s)	Page (s)
B _ _ _ _ _ _ _ Y	______	______
C _ _ _ _ O	______	______
D _ _ _ _ Y	______	______
E _ _ _ E	______	______
F _ _ G	______	______
H _ _ _ E	______	______
O _ _ _ _ _ H	______	______
R _ _ _ _ T	______	______
S _ _ _ E	______	______
T _ _ _ R	______	______
W _ _ F	______	______
Z _ _ _ A	______	______

Now find a picture of each of these animals in your magazine.
What colour is it? What page is it on? Write the number in the right-hand column.

Note: Some animals are on several pages.

2. Describing Animals

Here are eight adjectives from Check it out. What animal goes with each adjective?

Adjective	Animal	Adjective	Animal
a. aggressive	______	e. herbivorous	______
b. big	______	f. pet	______
c. carniverous	______	g strong	______
d domestic	______	h. wild	______

Compare your lists with a partner. What are the differences?

3. Parts of the body

Look at the five types of animals.
Notice the names for the parts of the body.

Now choose a different animal. It can be a bird, a fish, an insect, a mammal or a reptile.

Draw the animal here. Label the parts of its body.

PHOTOCOPIABLE

Animals Worksheet 2

References: **Feet Talk!** – Page 3

Focus:

Vocabulary	Parts of the feet
Grammar	*Can* for ability + action verbs
Content	Science

Activities

1. Find the bird

Find the names of some birds in this word box. They are horizontal and vertical.

W	O	O	D	P	E	C	K	E	R
A	S	C	U	F	S	L	X	A	O
S	T	S	C	S	W	S	D	G	D
D	R	D	K	D	A	D	D	L	Y
P	I	G	E	O	N	D	D	E	M
H	C	V	R	N	N	E	S	K	G
L	H	R	R	I	A	N	D	X	I

2. Look at their feet!

Put these birds into the correct columns. It depends on their feet!

Flexible feet	Sharp claws	Skin	Toes at back and front

3. What can they do? Answer the questions and give reasons.

a. Which birds can swim well? _______ and _______

Why? Because they have ____ between their toes.

b. Which bird can hold food in its feet?

____

Why? Because it has __________________

c. Which birds can find insects in trees __________

Why? ______________________________

d. Which birds can run very fast? ____________

Why? Because their feet are ______________

4. Which animals?

Look at the footprints on Page 3. Write the name of the animals here.

1. ______________________ 2. ______________________

3. ______________________ 4. ______________________

5. ______________________ 6. ______________________

5. Over to you – observation and deduction

Now observe an animal. Draw its foot and its footprint here.
What can your animal do? Write a sentence about it.

____

____

Animals Worksheet 3

References: **Families** – Page 5

Focus:
Vocabulary Domestic animals
Grammar Present simple
Content Science

Activities

1. Domestic Animals

Use the information in the article to identify these animals.

a. It eats fish and drinks milk. ______________

b. It wags its tail and barks. ______________

c. It's a big animal, but it eats grass. You can ride on it. ______________

d. It gives us milk. ______________

e. Its coat makes warm clothes for us. ______________

f. It 'quacks' to communicate. ______________

g. A big, white bird with a long neck. ______________

h. We eat the eggs from this bird. ______________

2. Different Generations

Young animals often have special names. Unjumble the parents' names and discover the relationships. Draw a little picture of the animals to help you remember the names.

	Puzzle name	Young Animal	Adult Animal	Picture(s)
a.	WOC	calf	______________	
b.	NHE	chicken	______________	
c.	NAWS	cygnet	______________	
d.	CKUD	duckling	______________	
e.	ERSHO	foal	______________	
f.	ESOOG	gosling	______________	
g.	TAC	kitten	______________	
h.	PEESH	lamb	______________	
i.	OGD	puppy	______________	

3. Trick Questions

a. What do we call a young goat? ______________

b. What's the slang word for a young person? ______________

References: **Birth, life and death** – Page 6

Focus: **Vocabulary** Frog/butterfly metamorphosis
Grammar Present simple
Content Science

Activities

1. What's this?

Complete the words, then draw a little picture of each one.

Name	Pictures
B _ _ _ _ _ _ _ Y	
C _ _ _ _ _ _ _ _ _ R	
C _ _ _ _ _ _ _ S	
F _ _ G	
T _ _ _ _ _ E	

2. Now use your words to complete these sentences.

a. The ______________ lays her eggs in some water.
b. ____________________ protects the eggs with jelly.
c. Young ______________ come out of the eggs. Their legs grow.
d. Finally, the ____________ become ______________________ .
e. The ____________ comes out of the egg. It eats a lot and becomes big and strong.
f. A ________________ becomes a ______________________ .
g. The ________________ opens and a ____________ comes out.

3. Choose butterflies or frogs. Write a sentence to describe each stage in its developement.

Animal ________________

Stage 1 ____

Stage 2 ____

Stage 3 ____

Stage 4 ____

Animals Worksheet 5

References: **WWF** – Pages 8 and 9

Focus:
Vocabulary Animals, Environment
Grammar Present simple
Content Geography, Science, History, Art, Design

Activities

1. WWF Brainstorm

Work on your own, with a partner or in a group.

Did you know that WWF means 'World Wildlife Fund'?

Now write down as many facts about the WWF as you can. Give yourselves a time limit.
Don't look at the article first!

____

____

Compare your facts with other people.

2. WWF Facts

Don't look at the article. Can you answer these questions?
Write the answers and then check with the information at the top of page 9. Were you correct?

a. Is the WWF national or international? ________________

b. Where does it operate? ________________

c What does it defend? ________________

d. What is its logo? ________________

e. How does it use the phrase 'For a living planet'? ________________

3. Group investigation: WWF experts

Work in a group. Investigate WWF work in one of these countries: Brazil, Thailand or Scotland. If the group is too big, make several groups.

First, find this country on a world map. What do you know about its geography and history?
In a notebook, make a 'country file' of information. Refer to this to understand the WWF work.

Now read your part of the article and find the answers to these questions.

a. What animals does WWF protect there? ________________

b. What are the special dangers for these animals? ________________

c. What special programmes does WWF organise there? ________________

d. Who can take part in the programmes? ________________

e. Where can you get more information? ________________

4. Group presentations

Present all the relevant information about WWF in that country to the class. Design a poster or a website with facts and pictures. Ask and answer questions about it. You are the experts!

Animals Worksheet 6

References: **Our pets in the wild** – Page 11

Focus:
Vocabulary Personal habits
Grammar Present simple
Content Geography, Science

Activities

1. What's this?
Choose one of the animals. Use the information to answer these questions about it.

a. How long does it live? ____________________

b. Which countries does it live in? ____________________

c. What type of countryside does it like? ____________________

d. What does it eat? ____________________

e. How does it behave? ____________________

2. Use your answers to write a description of your animal in the wild. Use the Present Simple.

Name: ____________________

Description:

It ____________________

____

____

____

____

3. Now choose one of the other animals. Write three sentences about it to use in an Animal Quiz. e.g. hamster. It eats plants and seeds. It lives in Northern Syria. It likes mountains.

a. ____________________

b. ____________________

c. ____________________

Either:

Exchange Worksheets with a partner. Guess each other's animals.

Or

Have a Class Quiz. Read out your clues. Guess all the animals.

Animals Worksheet 7

References: **Check it out** – Page 2

Focus:
Vocabulary Animals
Grammar Adjective + noun
Content Geography, Science

Activities

1. Look through the articles .
Write down the names of all the animals that live in your country or region.

____

____

2. Compare your list with a partner.
Do you agree? Change your list if necessary.

____

____

____

3. Now find all the 'foreign' animals. Write their names here.

Animal	Country/Countries
______	______
______	______
______	______

4. Find out where these animals live. Use your general knowledge, reference books or the Internet. Write the countries in the second column above.

5. Research Activity*
Choose one animal from the magazine. Find out about it. Write the results here.

Animal: ______________________________

Country/countries: ______________________________

Habitat (e.g. forest, mountains): ______________________________

Size: ______________________________ Colour: ______________________________

Food: ______________________________

Special details (e.g. It can climb trees. It goes to sleep in the winter.) ______________________________

6. Follow up activity
Use your information to make a poster about your animal. Present it to the class. Answer their questions about the animal.

Note: For these activities, you can work alone, with a partner, or in a group.

Animals Worksheet 8

References: **All**

Focus:
Vocabulary Describing animals
Grammar Present simple, Adjective + noun
Content Geography, Science

Activities

1. Look through your magazine. Choose one photo of an animal. Remember its name, the article and the page number. Keep this information secret!

2. Answer these questions about your animal here.

a. What colour is it? ____________________

b. Is it a bird, a mammal, a reptile or a fish? ____________________

c. Where does it live? ____________________

d. What does it eat? ____________________

e. How does it move? ____________________

One special extra fact: ____________________

3. Identify and check
Exchange Worksheets with a partner. Read the sentences and identify your animals. Check the facts in your magazine. Write the animal's name, the article and the page number here. Exchange your Worksheets again. Correct?

Animal: ____________________

Title of article: ____________________ Page number: __________

4. Additional activity
Write a factual description of your animal here and illustrate it.
You can use your descriptions to make a class Animal Facts poster.

Name: ______________________________

Total Points (1 per question) __________

1. Look through *Animals*. Identify these articles. Write the page number and the title.

a. There are pictures of elephants, donkeys and dogs.
   Page ________ Title ______________________________
b. You can read about good and bad parents.
   Page ________ Title ______________________________
c. This article is about 'metamorphosis'.
   Page ________ Title ______________________________
d. This animal doesn't like sandwiches!
   Page ________ Title ______________________________
e. Feet give us information about animals.
   Page ________ Title ______________________________
f. Zebras and stick insects hide from their enemies.
   Page ________ Title ______________________________
g. Think before you buy a pet!
   Page ________ Title ______________________________
h. A beautiful peacock butterfly.
   Page ________ Title ______________________________
i. Its logo is a panda.
   Page ________ Title ______________________________

2. Are these statements true or false? Check them with the articles and circle T or F.

a. Page 3. Woodpeckers have four toes. T | F
b. Page 4. Lizards are very dangerous. T | F
c. Page 5. Swans teach their kids to swim. T | F
d. Page 6. Frogs have long tails. T | F
e. Page 7. Huskies work all through the year. T | F
f. Page 8. Turtles lay their eggs in the sea. T | F
g. Page 10. Oxygen is important for goldfish. T | F
h. Page 11. Hamsters live in groups in the wild. T | F
i. Page 16. Horses wear coats in Britain in the winter. T | F

3. What is the English word for these things?

a. The mark from a foot on wet ground or snow. ____________________
b. Snakes are in this category of animals. ____________________
c. These animals have black and white stripes. ____________________
d. A baby swan. ____________________
e. A baby frog. ____________________
f. American slang word for a 'friend'. ____________________
g. A male cow. ____________________
h. A ship full of animals (in a song). ____________________
i. The animals on the front and back covers. ____________________

Teacher's Notes: **SPORTS**

Ideas for use

This title explores different sports from the point of view of both participants and spectators. It also looks at some sports-related topics such as sponsorship and exploitation. It encourages the students to think critically about the topic in relation to themselves and to other people.

Crosscurricular links: Art; History; Geography; L1 Language and Literature; Music; Science; Technology.

Don't forget! Look carefully for the Sports Detective mini-projects with each article. You will find more general ideas to use with all the titles in the *Topics* series on pages 49-51 of this Teacher's Book.

Cover and contents

Encourage the students to browse through *Sports* and to look at the range of articles, illustrations and design styles.

Discussion. What do the photos on the cover suggest? Are they a good depiction of the topic, *Sports*? Why (not)? Ask the students to suggest other possible images for the cover. You can use the pictures to discuss the various types of sports and also the relative attractions of taking part in and watching sport.

Page 1 – Letter 🎧

The letter contains a series of questions about sport. You may like to discuss these in L1 with the students. They will serve as a general 'warm up' for the topic and help to show what aspects really interest each person.

Make sure that the students understand (and can identify) the Sports Detective icon.

Discussion. Which titles are easy to understand (e.g. The Olympic Story)? Which are more difficult (e.g. Sport: import/ export)? Encourage the students to guess what the articles are about and to flick through the pages to check this.

Page 2 – Check it out

See page 52 for different activities to use with this reference page.

✎ **Worksheet 1**
Vocabulary – Sports places and people
Grammar – Present simple
Content – Sports

Page 3 – Sport: to do or to watch? 🎧

This article presents different personal views of doing or watching sport under six different headings:

Way of life	Travel	New Skills
Excitement	Health	TV Addict

Pre-reading. Check whether the students understand the meaning of these phrases. Ask them to think of ways in which each one might be linked with sport.

They can imagine they are going to interview one (or all) of the people quoted. They should write down a question they would like to ask, e.g. 'How do you practise your sport?', 'Is playing sport good for you?', 'What new sports can you watch on T.V.?'.

Reading and speaking. You can then use the article for a jigsaw reading activity. Each student becomes a spokesperson for one of the six viewpoints. The others use their questions to interview them. Encourage them to add questions and ideas of their own.

✎ **Worksheet 2**
Vocabulary – Personal habits
Grammar – *Wh-* questions, Present simple
Content – Sports

Pages 4 and 5 – The Olympic Story

This article is in two parts. The first part (Page 4) is about the Olympic Games in Greece (Ancient Greece, the 1896 revival, the 2004 Games). The second part (Page 5) is about Special Olympics: the Paralympics and the Winter Olympics.

Warm up. Discover what the students know about each of the five topics, or can find out about them.

Discussion. Ask the students what they remember about the last Olympics, Winter Olympics or Paralympics, or anything they know about the next event(s).

Pages 6 and 7 – Marathon and marathons

While they are reading it, ask them to make a note of any new or surprising information. Encourage them to use these notes as a basis for finding out more about marathons.

Groupwork/Writing. The students use the information in the article and their own ideas to make up a marathon quiz, working in groups. They can use Wh- questions or True/False statements, e.g. 'Where is Marathon?' (in Greece/ near Athens) or 'Marathon is a real place' (True)/ 'All modern marathons are in big cities' (False). They can then test their quizzes on other groups.

Save the rhino. After reading this section, the students can tell the class about any other animals that are in danger, e.g. whales, tigers.

✎ **Worksheet 3**
Vocabulary – Numbers
Grammar – Present Simple
Content – History, Geography, Maths

Pages 8 and 9 – The A-Z of sport

The text is presented like a board game. It includes a number of different sports. The introductory text presents the idea that some sports are national, regional or local, while others are international. Some sports may start as a local activity, but then spread to other places because of historical reasons, maybe because of emigration or colonization.

Discussion. Identify the sports on the board. Are the students familiar with all of them?

Discuss which sports may belong to specific places and the reasons. This may be because of climate, e.g. ice hockey in Scandinavia, Russia, Canada and parts of the U.S. It may also be because of geography, e.g. downhill skiing in the mountains.

Reading. Ask the students to read about the 13 sports on the board and to notice the training tips for each. They decide if they agree with these tips.

Speaking quiz. The texts can be used for a quiz. One person gives a clue, e.g. Wind and a lot of water are important for it (windsurfing). The others guess the sport. A variation is to ask Yes/No questions about them.

Vocabulary 1. There are 26 letters here, but only 13 sports are described. The students work in groups to suggest sports for the empty squares. They may need to use a dictionary to help them find the names in English. This is also a good way of practising spelling with the English alphabet. Here are some suggestions for most of the 'missing' letters.

This is also a preparation for the Sports Detective activity.

A	Archery	O	Orienteering
C	Canoeing	Q	Quoits
E	Equestrian	U	Underwater swimming
G	Gymnastics	Y	Yachting
H	Hang-gliding		
K	Karate		
M	Mountain biking		

Vocabulary 2. They can also suggest alternative sports for the filled squares.

B	Badminton, Basketball, Bobsleigh, Boxing, Bungee jumping
F	Fencing
I	Ice skating
L	Lacrosse
P	Pentathlon, Punting
R	Rowing, Rugby
S	Skating, Skiing, Squash
T	Tae kwon do, Tennis
V	Volleyball
W	Weight lifting, Wrestling

Writing. The students each choose one sport and write their own Training Tip for it. Then they ask the others/a partner to guess which sport their tip relates to.

Board game. You can use the board here, or ask the students to copy it onto a larger piece of card. They play the A-Z game in groups, with a dice and counters. They begin on the 'A' square and try to arrive at 'Z' first. When they land on a square, they must give an extra fact about the sport, or mention a new sport beginning with that letter. If the answer is correct, they move forward one square.

Worksheet 4
Vocabulary – Different sports, Alphabet
Grammar – Present simple, Imperatives
Content – Art, Design, Sports

Page 10 – The price of sport

Ask the students to look at the pictures and guess what the article is about. (It discusses some ways in which workers are often exploited to produce cheap sports clothing and souvenirs.)

Warm up. Ask the students to suggest sports items where the logo helps them to be sold to the public, e.g. football shirts, baseball caps. Do they have any such items? Do the prices increase before a big event or match?

Vocabulary. You can use this as an opportunity for a general review of sports clothing vocabulary, e.g. trainers, cap, gloves, sweatshirt.

Asian worker quotation. Ask the students to imagine working in this way. Do they know other examples of exploitation like this?

Note: The 40+ page Oxfam report, 'Play Fair at the Olympics', gives a number of case studies of this kind and suggests a Code of Practice for sports organizations and sportswear companies. You can download the PDF file from www.playfairolympics.org (3.9 kb.).

Writing. Ask the students to design a sports logo for a piece of clothing and to describe it: colour(s), shape, symbol, slogan, etc.

Page 11 – The beautiful game

The article gives factual information about leading football players from different continents.

Warm up. Discuss the differences between club teams (The players can be any nationality) and national teams (The players must be from that country). Ask them to name other players who play in 'foreign' club teams.

Use the photos to identify the players. Do the students know any more facts about them? Do they still play for the same clubs?

Speaking/Writing quiz. Use the factual information to make up a quiz. e.g. 'He's English but his club team's Spanish' (David Beckham). You can do this as an oral whole-class activity, or the students can write questions and play in groups.

Discussion. Ask the students which international players they would choose for a similar article. They can try to convince each other of the best choices. This can be a preparation for the Sports Detective activity.

Page 12 – The two sides of sport

This article presents some positive and negative attitudes towards sport. This is especially important in a class where some people do not like sport.

Before they read it, ask the students to each think of one positive and one negative thing about sport. List these on the board. Are any aspects positive for some people and negative for others? When they read the article, they should check whether any of these ideas are mentioned in it.

Writing. They use the ideas in the article and their own to write a questionnaire about personal attitudes towards sport. They can administer these to each other or to another class, and analyse the results, e.g. the most common negative or positive views and the % of people who think the same.

Worksheet 5
Vocabulary – Likes and dislikes
Grammar – Present simple, Asking questions
Content – Sports

Page 13 – Sport: Import/export

This article shows how some sports have started in one country, or within one group of people, and then moved to other places.

Use the photos to identify the three sports (judo, cricket, polo). Check what the students know about each one (or can find out).

You can use the first three sections for a jigsaw reading activity with three groups. Encourage them to find out more about the other two sports through questions and answers (this could be done through interviews with the 'experts' from another group).

The final section is about spectators and travel. You can use it for discussion about where the students have travelled for sports reasons (or would like to travel to).

Discussion. Ask the students to find out about other sports that have travelled in this way. e.g. rugby.

Worksheet 6
Vocabulary – Countries and continents, Sports
Grammar – Present simple, Asking questions
Content – History, Geography

Page 14 – Sports quiz: Do you know?

Puzzle pictures. The students can make up similar quizzes, using parts of photos from magazines and newspapers.

Page 15 – Projects

Ask the students to read all the projects carefully in order to decide which ones are interesting for them. Find out which are the most/least interesting for this class and if any of them just interest one person.

These projects can be done in groups, pairs or individually. Some of them may link with those done in other subjects, e.g. History or Science.

Encourage the students to also review and present the things they have been doing in the various Sports Detective mini-projects. If appropriate, these can form a class end-of-term exhibition.

Page 16 – Chatrooms

Fun Chat: Olympic Games

Ask for suggestions of other unusual or new Olympics sports, or suggest sports which should be included. The official website, www.olympic.org, has lists of past and present recognized Olympic sports.

Can you believe it? Encourage the students to find photos or cartoons of other unusual sports.

Teens Chat. They can make up similar dialogues about their attitudes towards sport and then read them aloud, conveying their feelings through the intonation.

Worksheet 7
Vocabulary – Action verbs
Grammar – Present continuous
Content – Art, Design, L1

Worksheet 8
Vocabulary – Sports
Grammar – Describing sports
Content – Art, Design, Sports

Title review. The students can do a review to help inform other people. This can be of the whole magazine, or of specific articles. If it helps you can put this framework on the board for them to copy and adapt.

CRITERIA	ARTICLE	STARS	COMMENTS
Interest			
Information			
Design			
Photos			
Sports Detective			
Other			

Test Worksheet

The aim of the test is to encourage the students to look back through the articles in order to check facts, notice details and find specific information to answer the questions.

Extra teacher's resources

These websites are worth visiting for further information.

Olympics: www.olympic.org
Sportswear: www.plasyfairolympics.org
BBC young people: www.bbc.co.uk/cbbcnews

PHOTOCOPIABLE

Sports Worksheet 1

References: **Check it out** – Page 2

Focus:

Vocabulary Sports places and people
Grammar Present simple
Content Sports

Activities

1. Sports word box: sports verbs

Find some sports verbs in the word box. The words are horizontal and vertical.

C	E	L	E	B	R	A	T	E
O	Q	O	W	N	Z	V	R	K
M	E	S	U	P	P	O	R	T
P	R	E	A	Q	T	U	L	C
E	E	Y	H	I	T	W	I	H
T	R	A	I	N	G	J	P	E
E	W	T	S	C	O	R	E	E
P	R	A	C	T	I	S	E	R

How many horizontal words? How many vertical words?

Now match five of the verbs with these nouns.

	NOUN	VERB
a.	SCORER	____________
b.	SUPPORTER	____________
c.	WINNER	____________
d.	LOSER	____________
e.	CELEBRATION	____________

2. Football or tennis?

Look at the two groups of words on Page 2. Write the answers in the correct column.

		FOOTBALL	TENNIS
a.	They play the sport here.	____________	____________
b.	This person controls the match.	____________	____________
c.	The players need these to win!	____________	____________
d.	Two positions in football.	____________	____________
e.	Tennis players hit the ball with this.	____________	____________

3. People in sports

Find these names in the list in Check it out on Page 2.

		PERSON
a.	This person runs or jumps.	____________
b.	This person wants to win.	____________
c.	This person watches the events.	____________
d.	This person supports a team.	____________
e.	This person describes an event for T.V.	____________
f.	This person gives advice to players.	____________
g.	A group of sports people.	____________
h.	A group of players and spectators.	____________

References: **Sport: To do or to watch?** – Page 3

Focus:
Vocabulary Personal habits
Grammar *Wh–* questions, Present simple
Content Sports

Activities

1. Personal views

Match the opinion and the heading

Excitement	Health	New Skills
Travel	TV Addict	Way of Life

a. 'I live near the beach, so I do it every day'
b. 'You can see lots of sports – at home!'
c. 'I feel really good after a game.'
d. 'You can go to some great places!'
e. 'Win or lose? You never know!'
f. 'I can do lots of new things this year.'

2. Interview questions

Complete these questions for each person. Use the words in the box.

how	what	where	why (x3)

a. AJ ________________ do you live?
b. JL ________________ do people feel self-confident?
c. LM ________________ do you watch TV?
d. MO ________________ travel to watch sports events?
e. PH ________________ do you feel after a game of tennis?
f. TY ________________ is your favourite sport?

3. Interview answers

Exchange worksheets with a partner. Answer the questions here.

a. AJ ________________
b. JL ________________
c. LM ________________
d. MO ________________
e. PH ________________
f. TY ________________

Now interview each other with your questions and answers.

Sports Worksheet 3

References: **Marathon and Marathons** – Pages 6 and 7

Focus:

Vocabulary Numbers
Grammar Present simple
Content History, Geography, Maths

Activities

1. Facts and figures

What do these figures represent? Look at the article on pages 6 and 7 to find the information.

Dates

490 BC ______________________
1896 ______________________
1970 ______________________

Numbers

25 ______________________
55 ______________________
300 ______________________
10,000 ______________________
25,000 ______________________
40,000 ______________________

Distances

42 kilometres ______________________
226 kilometres ______________________
240 kilometres ______________________

2. The numbers game

Work in groups. One person says one of the numbers. The others give the information. The first person with a correct answer wins a point.

3. Famous people

Match the people and their description.

a. Fauja Singh
b. Pheidippides
c. Spiridon Louis

A famous Greek postal worker
A 93-year-old marathon runner
A famous Ancient Greek runner

4. How far is 42 kilometres?

Find a map of your town or area.
Calculate 42 kilometres on it. Choose a good route for a marathon. Remember, hills are difficult!
Draw the marathon route here.
Mark any difficult places. Write the reason.

Compare your ideas.

PHOTOCOPIABLE

References: **A – Z of Sport** – Pages 8 and 9

Focus:

Vocabulary Different sports, Alphabet
Grammar Present simple, Imperatives
Content Art, Design, Sports

Activities

1. Sports brainstorm

What are the names of some sports in English? Write their names next to their first letter.

SPORTS ALPHABET

A	J	S
B	K	T
C	L	U
D	M	V
E	N	W
F	O	X
G	P	Y
H	Q	Z
I	R	

Look at the article on Pages 8 and 9. Compare your list with this. Add more sports to your list. You can find more ideas on different pages of this magazine.

2. Describing sports

Identify these sports in 'The A-Z of Sport'.

a. You enter the water in a special way.
b. You jump a long distance
c. You 'dance' on the ice.
d. You do tricks on a board.
e. You move very fast on the water.
f. You play on a table.
g. You want to throw your opponent.
h. You hit a ball and run round four places.

Now choose three of 'your' sports from your list. Write similar descriptions of them. Exchange Worksheets with a partner. Guess the sports.

a.
b.
c.

3. Group Investigation: Sports experts

Work in a group. Look at 'your' sports on the lists. Write instructions for training for these sports. Each person chooses one of the sports. Research it. Find out about its history. What are the rules? Who are the champions? Where is it popular?

4. Group Presentations

Present your information on a poster or website. Use colours and pictures.

Sports Worksheet 5

References: **Two sides of sport** – Page 12

Focus:

Vocabulary Likes and dislikes
Grammar Present simple, Asking questions
Content Sports

Activities

1. Positives and negatives

Do you like sports? What about other people?

Think of one thing you like about sports and one thing you don't like. Write these in the box.

My attitude to sports

Positive:

Negative:

Now interview three other people. Ask 'What do you like about sports?' 'What don't you like about sports?' Write their names and their opinions here.

Other attitudes to sports

Positive:

Name:

Name:

Name:

Negative:

Name:

Name:

Name:

2. Comparing opinions

Look at the 'positive' and 'negative' opinions in your data. Are any of them positive for one person and negative for somebody else? What are the differences?

3. Categorising opinions

Look at the article on Page 12. It mentions four positive areas and four negative areas.

POSITIVE:	Social effects	Lifeskills	Fashion	Fun
NEGATIVE:	Training	Drugs	Isolation	Violence

Do your opinions follow these catagories too? Are there different categories?
Group your opinions under similar headings.

References: **Sport: import export** – Page 13

Focus:

Vocabulary Countries and continents, Sports
Grammar Present simple, Asking questions
Content History, Geography

Activities

1. Identifying places

Write these places on the world map. Use an atlas to help you.

a. Argentina	b. Australia	c. China	d. England
e. India	f. Iran	g. Ireland	h. Japan
i. New Zealand	j. Pakistan	k. Sri Lanka	l. the USA
m. the West Indies			

2. Read the article on page 13 about cricket, polo and judo.

Where do these three sports begin? Where are they played now? Write the information here.

SPORT	BEGINS IN...	GOES TO....
Cricket:		
Polo:		
Judo:		
(Other)		

Can you think of another 'travelling sport'? Add the information.

3. Local sports

Choose a sport in your country or region. Present information about it.

COUNTRY/REGION:
SPORT:
PLACE (field, indoors, etc):
PLAYERS (number in a team):
EQUIPMENT:
OTHER COUNTRIES:
OTHER INFORMATION:

Sports Worksheet 7

References: **All**

Focus:
Vocabulary Action verbs
Grammar Present continuous
Content Art, Design, L1

Activities

1. Action pictures

Find your favourite action photo in the magazine. Remember the page number. Don't tell anyone!

What's happening in it? What are the people doing? What clothes are they wearing? Write three secret sentences about it here, using the Present Continuous.

a. ______________________________

____

b. ______________________________

____

c. ______________________________

____

Exchange worksheets with a partner. Read the descriptions and guess the page numbers. Find the photos. Is your partner's description a good one?

2. What are they thinking?

With your partner, write 'think bubbles' for the people in your photos.

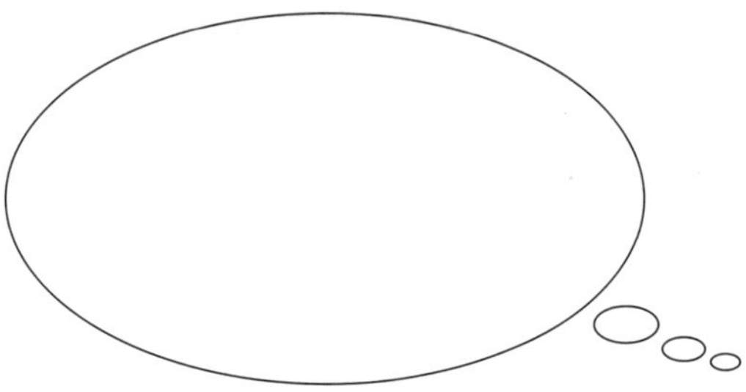

3. Descriptions

Choose a different photo and write a description of it here. You can work alone or with other people.

____

____

____

____

PHOTOCOPIABLE

References: **All**

Focus:
Vocabulary Sports
Grammar Describing sports
Content Art, Design, Sports

Activities

1. Types of sports

Here are six categories for different sports. Can you think of other categories?

In a team	Individual	International	Local
Popular	With a ball	____________	____________

Compare your ideas.

2. Categorising sports

Look through all the pages of *Sports*. Look carefully at all the photos and the articles.
Put each sport into one of your categories.

Now think of other sports for your categories. Your lists on Worksheet 4 can help you.

3. Using the ideas

Make a class list of categories and sports.
Use this to design a poster or website on the class 'Sports Overview'. Make up a slogan for it.

Sports Test Worksheet

Name: ______________________________

Total Points (1 per question) ______________

1. Look through *Sports*. Identify these articles. Write the page number and the title.

a. There are photos of famous football players..

Page ________ Title ______________________________

b. You can see an old Greek temple.

Page ________ Title ______________________________

c. This article contains six different opinions about sport.

Page ________ Title ______________________________

d. You can be a good athlete at 93, too!!

Page ________ Title ______________________________

e. A place with a famous name for runners

Page ________ Title ______________________________

f. Think about the workers!

Page ________ Title ______________________________

g. Good practice with the English alphabet

Page ________ Title ______________________________

h. It is very hot there

Page ________ Title ______________________________

2. **Are these statements true or false? Check them with the articles and circle T or F.**

a.	Page 3.	There are lots of different sports on T.V..	T F
b.	Page 4.	Women compete in the Ancient Olympics.	T F
c.	Page 5.	The sports in the Paralympics have different rules from those in the other Olympics	T F
d.	Page 7.	Live animals take part in city marathons.	T F
e.	Page 9.	Tables are useful in one sport.	T F
f.	Page 10.	A lot of sportswear comes from Asia.	T F
g.	Page 11.	Footballers always play in their home country.	T F
h.	Page 12.	Sports help people to be part of a group.	T F
i.	Page 13.	Only people in England play cricket.	T F

3. **What is the English word for these things?**

a. A person who loves sport and supports a team. ______________

b. A person who watches a sports event. ______________

c. A big building for sports events. ______________

d. A sports competition for people with special problems. ______________

e. The British English word for 'vacation'. ______________

f. Another verb for 'to practise' a sport. ______________

g. To enter the water in a straight line. ______________

h. People often wear these clothes to play or watch sport. ______________

i. People make this vocal noise to encourage their team. ______________

j. The best player or competitor. ______________

Teacher's Notes: **FESTIVALS**

Elementary

Ideas for use
This title includes a lot of information about different kinds of festivals all over the world. It encourages the students to think about those in their own country and to learn about those of different cultural groups there and elsewhere. It also relates festivals to beliefs and values and develops intercultural awareness.

Crosscurricular links: Art and Design; History; Geography; L1 Language and Literature and other languages; Music.

Don't forget! Look carefully for the Festival Eye mini-projects with each article. You will find more general ideas to use with all the titles in the *Topics* series on pages 61-63 of this Teacher's Book.

Cover and contents
Encourage the students to browse through *Festivals* and to look at the range of articles, illustrations and design styles.

Discussion. What do they associate with the festivals in the cover titles – New Year, Carnival and Family Festivals?

Discuss what the words, photos and the general look of the cover suggest to them (e.g. fun, movement, excitement). You may like to build up a Festivals word and ideas map on the board.

Page 1 – Letter
What different kinds of festivals are the students familiar with (national, religious, local, family, etc.)? After reading the letter, they can suggest examples of festivals in these categories that they celebrate themselves. Are there any differences between members of the class? What are the reasons (cultural, religious, etc.)? Remember that these differences may be sensitive for some students.

Make sure that the students understand (and can identify) the Festival Eye icon.

Discussion. Which titles are easy to understand (e.g. Chinese New Year)? Which are more difficult (e.g. Life and Death) ? Encourage the students to guess what the articles are about and to flick through the pages to check this.

Page 2 – Check it out
See page 64 for different activities to use with this reference page.

Ask the students to check the Festivals Calendar. Have any festivals that are important to them been left out? Which ones? Should these be included? They can design a revised Festivals Calendar.

Worksheet 1
Vocabulary – Festivals, Celebrations, Countries, Nationalities
Grammar – Adjectives
Content – Geography, History

Page 3 – Let's begin with the New Year!
Discuss what they think the photo shows. Do they think it is a good illustration for an article about New Year?

Discuss New Year. Do the students celebrate it? When? How? (This is preparation for the Festival Eye mini-project.)

Discussion. Is any of this information about dates new or surprising for the students? The article mentions two different ways of celebrating New Year in one place (Rio de Janeiro). One involves a lot of noise and fireworks, while the other is more spiritual. Do they know of other examples like this (e.g. Christmas in many places). What about other ways of 'saying goodbye' to the old year?

Out-of-class. Ask them to find and bring pictures and information about other New Year celebrations.

Worksheet 2
Vocabulary – Dates
Grammar – Future time: *going to* and *will*
Content – Geography, History, L1

Page 4 – Chinese New Year
Check what the students know about this celebration. If they belong to a Chinese community or have friends who do, then they can add extra information to the article.

The article mentions special festival food. Discuss what the students eat on New Year's Eve. Do different families eat different things? (This is preparation for the Festival Eye mini-project.)

Groupwork. They can discuss and design a special New Year's Eve menu to contain their favourite food and drink.

Worksheet 3 (also for Page 5)
Vocabulary – Celebrations
Grammar – Present simple for description
Content – Geography, History, L1

Page 5 – Scottish New Year
This article contains a lot of factual information. Ask the students to find out the information on the next page.

Bad weather. Ask them to read this section. What was the message for 100,000 people at the end of 2003? (Sorry. No party tonight. Come back next year!)

Worksheet 3 (also for Page 4)
Vocabulary – Celebrations
Grammar – Present Simple for description
Content – Geography, History, L1

The name for New Year's Eve in Scotland.	(Hogmanay)
What time it gets dark there in December.	(Before 4pm)
A symbol of warmth.	(A piece of coal)
What represents food.	(A piece of biscuit)
The name for a big fire in the open air.	(Bonfire)
The kind of things that people throw into the fire.	(Old things)
The city with the longest New Year's party.	(Edinburgh)
The number of days for this party.	(4 days)

Pages 6 and 7 – Festival food

Recipes. (Pancakes and Gingerbread). Discuss what kinds of pancakes the student know. What are their favourites – sweet or savoury? Do they know how to make them? Are their recipes different from the ones here? Do the same with gingerbread recipes.

Ask the students to choose one of the four festivals (Pancake Tuesday, Bonfore Night, Thanksgiving, Christmas Eve). They read about it and, in groups, use the information to design an invitation to a meal on that day.

If they celebrate any of the festivals at home, do they eat the same things as the article describes, or different? What are their favourite things?

Out-of-class. The best test of comprehension is to try out the two recipes! Check the ingredients first. Are there any things that they could not find easily?

Worksheet 4
Vocabulary – Food, Cooking
Grammar – Giving instructions
Content – Geography, History, L1

Pages 8 and 9 – Your Carnival

This article is on two pages. Ask the students to look at them and suggest adjectives to describe their appearance, e.g, fun, mysterious, exciting, beautiful. What words do they associate with Carnival? Are these the same?

Do a jigsaw reading activity on Carnival in these places. Ask the students to decide which Carnival they would prefer to take part in. What are their reasons?

Writing/Groupwork. Ask them to look carefully at the ten photos on Page 9. Get the to write speech bubbles, think bubbles or captions for each one. Let the class vote on the best ones.

Worksheet 5
Vocabulary – Carnival, Celebrations, Cities
Grammar – Descriptive language
Content – Art, Design, Geography, History

Page 10 – Carnival in August!

This article has four sections:
- General
- Facts
- History
- Music

Ask the students to suggest a title for each section.

Each student should write one quiz question about the article on a piece of paper. They fold this and put it into a container. Then they take it in turns to draw out a question. The person who wrote it must judge the correct answer and supply it if necessary. One point for a correct answer. They can also play this in teams.

Discussion. What do they know about West Indian music? What different types are there? Can they bring any CDs to class?

Page 11 – Life and death

Discuss the idea of a 'Day of the Dead'. Does it exist in your culture? Is it the same or different from the ones described here? In what ways?

Ask the students to look at the photo. Which of these words describe it best?
- funny
- scary
- horrible
- sad
- strange

Is there a better word to describe it?

Draw attention to the three colours used for the text area (black, white, orange). Do any of these represent life or death in your culture? Do these colours represent anything else?

Worksheet 6
Vocabulary – Describing emotions
Grammar – Describing photos and people, Invitations
Content – Art, Geography, History, L1

Page 12 – Family festivals

Ask the students to look at the four photos. Which one best represents a birthday? What about Valentines Day?

Check through the list of festivals with the students. Which ones are unfamiliar for them? Let them guess what these celebrate. Then they can do the quiz and check if they were correct.

Page 13 – Festival songs, raps and rhymes

Ask the students to look at the article and identify any examples that are unfamiliar for them.

Check through the language of each one with them in order to get a general idea of the meaning. Which examples exist in your culture or language? Are there any differences in the meaning or the music?

Listen to them in the audio magazine and encourage the students to sing or say them, beating out the rhythm.

Page 14 – Festivals quiz: do you know?

The content of the three multiple choice quiz sections is based on the content of Festivals.

If the students have read all the articles in Festivals already, they can do the quiz against time. If they have not, they can look through them to find the answers. This can be done individually or in teams.

Writing. They can use these quizzes as models for writing their own versions.

Page 15 – Projects

Ask the students to read all the projects carefully in order to decide which ones are interesting for them. Find out which are the most/least interesting for this class and if any of them just interest one person.

These projects can be done in groups, pairs or individually. Some of them may link with those done in other subjects, e,g. History or Science.

Encourage the students to also review and present the things they have been doing in the various Festival Eye mini-projects. If appropriate, these can form a class end-of-term exhibition.

Page 16 – Chatrooms

Teens Chat. What kind of place would the students choose to go to for a birthday meal?

Can you believe it?

Draw attention to the humorous tone of the messages – and the names.

Writing. They can write similar Valentine's messages. These can be as crazy as they like.

Worksheet 7

Vocabulary – Festivals
Grammar – General
Content – Art, Design, Geography, History

Worksheet 8

Vocabulary Festivals and customs
Grammar – Asking and answering Wh- questions
Content – Geography, History

Title review. The students can do a review to help inform other people. This can be of the whole magazine, or of specific articles. They can agree their own criteria, or you can put this framework on the board for them to copy and adapt.

CRITERIA	ARTICLE	STARS	COMMENTS
Interest			
Information			
Design			
Photos			
Festival Eye			
Other			

Test Worksheet

The aim of the test is to encourage the students to look back through the articles in order to check facts, notice details and find specific information to answer the questions.

Extra teacher's resources

This website is worth visiting for further information.

London Carnival: www.nottinghillcarnival.org.uk

Festivals Worksheet 1

References: **Check it out** – Page 2

Focus:

Vocabulary Festivals, Celebrations
Countries, Nationalities
Grammar Adjectives
Content Geography, History

Activities

1. Festival nouns

Look at the list on page 2. Write the nouns below.

	NOUN
a. This group of people play music	
b. A big fire	
c. People cover their faces with this	
d. A line of people walking in a festival	
e. These make bright lights and loud noises	
f. The date every year of a past event	
g. These two things give light	
h. This person makes music	
i. A moving platform with actors and dancers	

2. Describing festivals

Look at the group of adjectives on page 2. Which Festivals photos can they describe? Write the page number(s) beside each one.

	PHOTO ON PAGE
a. beautiful	
b. colourful	
c. exciting	
d. fantastic	
e. happy	
f. local	
g. national	
h. noisy	
i. political	
j. religious	
k. sad	
l. traditional	

Compare your list with two other people. Are your ideas the same or different?
Which photos have several different adjectives to describe them?

3. Famous festivals

Look at the list of festivals. Group them under these headings:

RELIGIOUS	NATIONAL	INTERNATIONAL

Compare your lists. Add more festivals from your country and culture.

References: **Let's begin with the New Year** – Page 3

Focus:

Vocabulary	Dates
Grammar	Future time: *going to* and *will*
Content	Geography, History, L1

Activities

1. Collecting information

When is New Year this year? Write the dates here.

Country and culture	**Date**
In our country	______________
Chinese New Year	______________
Indian New Year	______________
Jewish New Year	______________
Muslim New Year	______________
Other	______________

Now check your facts with the article. Were you correct?

2. New Year resolutions

The New Year is 'a time of optimism'. People often make New Year Resolutions. What are you going to do next year? Write three resolutions here.

Next year, I'm going to ______________

I'm also going to ______________

Finally, ______________

3. New Year predictions

What will happen next year? Make some predictions. They can be serious or funny.

I will ________________________________

My best friend ________________________________

My family ________________________________

(3 famous people) ________________________________

____

____

The world ________________________________

Compare your predictions with other people. Who is optimistic? Who is pessimistic? Then agree a prediction for your class. Write it here:

____

____

____

Festivals Worksheet 3

References:	**Chinese and Scottish New Year** – Pages 4 and 5
Focus:	**Vocabulary** Celebrations **Grammar** Present simple for description **Content** Geography, History, L1

Activities

1. Finding information

Read the two articles. Complete these facts.

CHINESE NEW YEAR

a. Chinese New Year lasts for ____________ days.
b. Shops and offices are closed for _____ days.
c. On the last day of the old year, people ________________.
d. At New Year, young people receive ______________ from their parents.
e. It's bad luck to kill _____________ at New Year.
f. The food is often ____________________.
g. During the celebrations, there are a lot of ________________.
h. People carry the _____________ symbol of the new year.
i. On the last day, there is a Festival of ______________________.
j. It's a big holiday in many parts of ______________________.

SCOTTISH NEW YEAR

a. Hogmanay is the _________ night of the year.
b. A stranger with a piece of coal is a symbol of ___________ luck.
c. This represents __________________________.
d. Biscuits represent __________________________.
e. Whisky represents __________________________.
f. People throw __________ things onto a bonfire.
g. These represent the ________________________________.
h. The party in Edinburgh goes on for ____________ days.
i. 2003 was a bad year because the ___________ became very strong.
j. The authorities said '__________________________________!'.

2. Making choices

Which festival do you prefer? Give three reasons.

I prefer _________________________ because
a. ____
b. ____
c. ____

Find a person with a different preference. Try and convince them to change their opinion.

3. Describing your New Year

Write a similar description of New Year in your culture. Mention some of these things:

celebrations	clothes	families	fireworks
food	good luck	music	symbols

References: **Festival Food** – Pages 6 and 7

Focus:
Vocabulary Food, Cooking
Grammar Giving instructions
Content Geography, History, L1

Activities

1. Food for four festivals

Match the food, the festival and the country.

Fish	Gingerbread	Goose	Mince Pies	Pancakes
Panettone	Pumpkin Pie	Sausages	Sweet potatoes	Turkey
Bonfire Night	Christmas	Mardi Gras	Thanksgiving	Britain
Central and Eastern Europe	France	USA	Italy	

FESTIVAL	COUNTRY/COUNTRIES	FOOD

2. Crosscultural comparisons

What about your country? Do you celebrate these festivals? If so, what do you eat? Is it the same in all the regions? Are there any local specialities? Tell us here!

FESTIVAL	COUNTRY/REGION/PLACE	FOOD

3. Recipes

Read the recipe for making pancakes. It uses lots of verbs. Choose the best verb to complete these instructions.

add	pour	leave	cook	spread	melt
keep	beat	put (x2)	make	eat	whisk

a. ________ the ingredients in a bowl.
b. ________ the eggs and the milk.
c. ________ the eggs and milk to the mixture.
d. ________ the mixture with a wooden spoon.
e. ________ it for an hour.
f. ________ a piece of butter.
g. ________ a little of the mixture into the pan.
h. ________ the other side.
i. ________ the pancake on a plate.
j. ________ butter, sugar and lemon juice on it.
k. ________ the pancake warm.
l. ________ more pancakes.
m. ________ them quickly!

Now write the instructions for making one of your festival foods. Check them out with a partner.

Festivals Worksheet 5

References: **Your Carnival, My Carnival, Whose Carnival?** – Pages 8, 9 and 10

Focus:
Vocabulary Carnivals, Celebrations, Cities
Grammar Descriptive language
Content Art, Design, Geography, History

Activities

1. Carnival brainstorm
Don't look at the article. Answer these questions.

a. What does the word 'carnival' come from?
b. What does this mean?
c. When did it begin?
d. When is it?
e. What do people do during it?

Look at the first paragraph of the article. Check your facts.

Choose one of the photos in balloons on Page 9 and invent a slogan for it.
Write it here:

Compare your slogans with the whole class. Choose the best ones for each photo.

2. Carnival facts: places
The article mentions several carnival cities in Europe and the Americas. Write their names here.

COUNTRY	CITY/CITIES/REGION
Argentina	
Brazil	
Canada	
France	
Italy	
USA	

What about Britain? Check out the information on Page 10.

CITY:	AREA:	MONTH:

Now find these cities in an atlas.

3. Group Investigation: Carnival experts
Choose one of the carnival cities and find out more about it. e.g. population? climate? music?

Present your city and its carnival to the class. Use photos and text in a poster or on a website.

References: **Life and Death** – Pages 11 and 12

Focus:
Vocabulary Describing emotions
Grammar Adjectives, Invitations
Content Art, Geography, History, L1

Activities

1. Describing photos

Look at the photo on Page 11. Which of these adjectives describe it best? Tick the boxes. Add your own choice.

❏ funny ❏ horrible ❏ interesting ❏ sad ❏ scary ❏ strange

Now look at the photo of people on Page 12. Do the same.
❏ emotional ❏ false ❏ sentimental ❏ sweet ❏ warm..

Compare your choices with a partner.

2. Remembering the dead

Read the article on Page 11 and find this information:

a. In this country, people remember the dead in April. ____________________
b. People often dress up as witches here. ____________________
c. In this country, people provide food for their ancestors. ____________________
d. You can eat sweets like skeletons here. ____________________

3. Celebrating the living

Look at the list of celebrations on Page 12. What dates do you celebrate during the year? Is it 'personal' or 'public'?

Fill in this calendar for each month and write Personal or Public beside each event.

MONTHS	CELEBRATION	TYPE

4. Invitation to a festival

Choose one of these celebrations (including the ones on Page 11).
Plan a party for it. Decide what food and decorations to have.
Write an invitation to it. Use suitable colours.

Festivals Worksheet 7

References: **All**

Focus:
Vocabulary Festivals
Grammar General
Content Art, Design, Geography, History

Activities

1. Look through Festivals. Choose one of the events in it.

2. Design a website, an ad or a poster to attract people to this festival.
You can work in pairs or in groups. First of all, discuss and agree the important features of the festival, e.g.

- date ______
- place(s) ______
- main focus ______
- main events. ______

3. Then decide the following:

- what factual information to include.
- what kind of picture best expresses the character of this festival.
- a title or 'slogan' to attract people.

4. Organise an exhibition of the results. Vote on the most effective design.

Festivals Worksheet 8

References: **All**

Focus:
Vocabulary Festivals and customs
Grammar Asking and answering *Wh-* questions
Content Geography, History

Activities

1. Verbs
Look at the verbs in the Check it out section (Page 2). Check you know the meanings.

2. Write 5 or 6 wh- question words here.

____

____

3. Make up 3 questions. Use some of these question words, and appropriate verbs relating to festivals.
Consult the magazine while writing your questions.

a. Question: ______________________________

____

b. Question: ______________________________

____

c. Question: ______________________________

____

4. Exchange questions with another pair or group.
Answer each question correctly, and also put the page number where you can find the information.

a. Answer + page: ______________________________

____

b. Answer + page: ______________________________

____

c. Answer + page: ______________________________

____

5. Check your answers with each other.

PHOTOCOPIABLE

Festivals Test Worksheet

Name: ______________________________

Total Points (1 per question) ______________

1. Look through *Festivals*. Identify these articles. Write the page number and the title.

a. There is a picture of a person in a black hat and coat, with a brown bag.

Page ________ Title ______________________________

b. You can try out a recipe for pancakes.

Page ________ Title ______________________________

c. This article is about West Indian culture in London.

Page ________ Title ______________________________

d. They don't eat meat in this festival, but they clean their houses.

Page ________ Title ______________________________

e. Chocolates, roses and a big cake..

Page ________ Title ______________________________

f. Two pages of celebrations for a special festival in two continents.

Page ________ Title ______________________________

g. One festival – different dates!

Page ________ Title ______________________________

h. Bonfires and bad weather (often) = this festival.

Page ________ Title ______________________________

2. Are these statements true or false? Check them with the articles and circle T or F.

a.	Page 3. The new year always begins on 1st January.	T F
b.	Page 4. Young people receive gifts of money at Chinese New Year.	T F
c.	Page 5. In Scotland, New Year is in the winter..	T F
d.	Page 6. Pancake Day and Mardi Gras – two different festivals.	T F
e.	Page 7. Bonfire Night is a religious festival	T F
f.	Page 8. It's always hot and sunny at Carnival	T F
g.	Page 8. People in Venice wear masks at Carnival.	T F
h.	Page 10. A lot of West Indians live in London.	T F
i.	Page 11. Halloween was originally a festival to remember dead people.	T F
j.	Page 12. You can celebrate Valentine's Day twice if you travel!	T F

3. What is the English word or name for these things?

a. The New Year festival in Scotland. ______________________

b. An important U.S. family festival in November. ______________________

c. Traditional songs from Trinidad. ______________________

d. The past generations of your family. ______________________

e. The French name for Carnival. ______________________

f. The year 2006 in the Chinese calendar. ______________________

g. A calendar that follows the moon. ______________________

h. No one can see your face behind this. ______________________

i. The forty days between Carnival and Easter. ______________________

Teacher's Notes: **ENVIRONMENT** Elementary

Ideas for use

This title examines the environment and the place of the individual in it. It also looks at natural resources such as water and energy. It shows how the various elements of the environment are inter-related. The students are encouraged to think critically about a the topic in relation to themselves and other people, and to discuss practical solutions.

Cross curricular links: Geography; Health Education; History; Science and Technology.

Don't forget! Look carefully for the Environmental Eye mini-projects with each article.

You will find more general ideas to use with all the titles in the Topics series on pages 73-75 of this Teacher's Book.

Cover and contents

Encourage the students to browse through *Environment* and to look at the articles, illustrations and design styles.

Discussion. What do the photos on the cover suggest? Are they a good depiction of the topic *Environment*? Why (not)? Can they see the person in the large photo? Why is a person included? (The environment is about people as well.)

You can use the pictures to discuss the various aspects of the environment, e.g. air and water, or urban and rural.

Ask the students to suggest other possible images for the cover to reflect the topic.

Page 1 – Letter 🎧

The letter contains a series of questions about the environment. You may like to discuss these in L1 with the students. They will serve as a general warm up for the topic and help to know what aspects really interest each person.

Make sure that the students understand (and can identify) the Environmental Eye icon.

Warm up. What articles or topics would the students expect to find in a magazine about the environment? Write their suggestions on the board. They can then compare their ideas with he contents here.

Discussion. Which titles are easy to understand (e.g. My environment)? Which are more difficult (e.g. Making a difference)? Encourage the students to flick through the pages and to guess what the articles are about.

Page 2 – Check it out

See page 76 for different activities to use with this reference page.

✏ **Worksheet 1**
Vocabulary – Environmental verbs and nouns
Grammar – Present simple/Present continuous
Content – Geography, Science

Page 3 – My environment 🎧

Discussion. Ask the students to identify the various jigsaw puzzle pieces. Discuss why these are represented as interlocking items. Ask them to suggest other components of the environment that could be depicted here as well.

Writing and Design. Ask the students to look at the 'arrows' diagram which shows various parts of the environment centred on 'ME'. They can design similar diagrams of interconnections based on themselves for their own environment. Compare the different versions.

Discussion. The second part of the article describes the positive and negative results of an environmental change (a new road). Are there similar examples in your local environment? Which effects are positive and which are negative?

✏ **Worksheet 2**
Vocabulary – Cities and traffic
Grammar – Cause and effect
Content – Science

Pages 4 and 5 – Using water

This double-page article is in two parts. It is written in a factual style.

The first, on Page 4, looks at some of the ways we use water in three different areas.

The second part, on Page 5, gives some examples of different areas of the world with too much or too little water. It suggests some possible courses of action.

Discussion. Do a brainstorming with the class on water in the environment. Ask questions such as:
Where does water come from?
How do we use it?
Why is it a problem?

✏ **Worksheet 3**
Vocabulary – Environmental verbs and nouns
Grammar – Cause and effect
Content – Science

Pre-reading. The students work in groups. Before reading the article, they choose one of these areas: Domestic, Agriculture, Industry, and discuss how water is used in it. They make a list of their ideas.

Checking information. They read the relevant section on Page 4 and compare their ideas with the statements.

Sharing information. The groups tell each other about any new or surprising information they found in the article relating to 'their' section. The others can ask questions.

Warm up. Write these four problems on the board. Ask the students to suggest how any of these affect them, with as many concrete details as possible. They then compare these with the ones in the article.

The right kind of water. They read this section to find the answers to these questions:

Why can irrigation be bad for grapes?
(Salt is bad for grapes. Irrigation increases the level of salt in the soil, so irrigation is bad for the grapes.)
What is the solution to the problem?
(To find a new type of grape.)

Page 6 – The food chain

Warm up. Find out what the students know about the food chain. Ask them to suggest some links in it, e.g:

Grass > Cows > Milk > Humans
Flowers > Bees > Honey > Humans

Who can make the longest chain?

Photos and text. Ask the students to look at the photos before reading the article and to speculate about the chain they illustrate. Write these key words on the board to help them:

plant deer lion eagle mushroom

Finding information. Ask the students to read the text and find out what these 'links' do.

Producers.	*They produce their own energy.*
First-level consumers.	*They eat producers to get energy.*
Second-level consumers.	*They eat first-level consumers to get energy.*
Third-level consumers.	*They eat second-level consumers.*
Decomposers.	*They consume dead things.*

Writing. Ask the students to write and illustrate their own account of the food chain, using the article as model, but adding their own examples and details.

Worksheet 4
Vocabulary – Food, animals, plants
Grammar – Sequencing
Content – Science

Page 7 – Humans and the natural world

This article describes ways in which humans and animals can affect each other. It uses whale-watching as the example.

Warm up. Ask the students what they know about whale-watching. e.g. Who does it? Why?

Reading and checking. Ask them to read the first paragraph to check their ideas. They then, in their notebooks, summarise possible problems for the whales.

Discussion. The section on killing whales may provoke a general discussion on the ethics of keeping and killing animals for food. This can include a discussion about vegetarianism. If this interests the students, they can do a survey on eating habits within their class.

Pages 8 and 9 – Making a difference

This two-page article describes a specific environmental and educational organization, the Hebridean Whale and Dolphin Trust (HWDT). This is based on the island of Mull off the west coast of Scotland. It provides educational programmes for primary and secondary schools in the area. It also does research into scientific environmental matters.

NOTE: 'The Hebrides' are the islands off the west coast of Scotland. 'The Highlands' are the whole of the north and west part of the country.

The first part of the article, on Page 8, left-hand column, describes research work with cetaceans (whales, dolphins and porpoises) which 'ordinary people' can take part in. The second part describes some educational projects done with primary and secondary school students.

Speculation. Ask the students to look at the photos on both pages and to speculate about the content of the article.

Discussion. Before they read the article, ask for their ideas about researching the environment.

How do scientists do research?
Is observation part of this?
What kinds of animal behaviour can be studied?
(e.g. migration patterns, feeding habits)
How do researchers usually record their results?
(e.g. taking photos, keeping an observation diary, collecting statistics).

Discuss what kind of animals they could observe and record in their environment.

They then read about the research done by HWDT and compare these ideas with their own.

Finding and checking information. Ask the students to read about the educational projects on Page 9 and find this information in this part of the article.

The length of minke whales.	*9 metres*
What animal eats plankton.	*whales*
The sounds that whales and dolphins make.	*clicks/whistles*

Discussion/writing. In groups, they discuss the kind of similar educational project they would like to do. Then they plan and write a programme for it.

Worksheet 5
Vocabulary – Environment
Grammar – Description
Content – Geography, Science

Pages 10 and 11 – Feeding the world

This article can be divided into different sections:

Introduction
GM crops
Fairtrade and specific examples (Page 11)

Reading for information. Ask the students to read these three sections and find out as much information as possible.

Discussion. Ask them to identify the products in the Fairtrade photo (chocolate, coffee, tea). Do they know where these are produced? Ask them to find out.

Discussion. Ask them to read Martin Luther King's statement at the top of Page 11. What does it mean? (We all depend on other people.) Do they agree with this? Why?

Game. Divide the class into two teams. They have two minutes to look at the table of countries and products. Then they close their books. A member of one team says a product, the other team must say where it comes from.

Writing. Ask the students to write a slogan or headline to summarise each section on this page.

Page 12 – Energy: where the wind blows

The article discusses some of the pros and cons of wind farms.

Warm up. Use the photos to establish what the students know about wind farms. The small photo shows a dragonfly – a small insect that flies very fast.

Finding information. Ask the students to read the article and find examples of positive and negative features of wind machines and wind farms. They can do this as a whole class, individually, in pairs or groups.

Discussion. Ask for suggestions of other natural forms of energy, e.g. Electricity from the sun. Car fuel from plants. What are the positive and negative aspects of these?

Writing. Are wind farms a good idea? The students prepare posters and slogans to express their opinions about this question and to convince other people. Then they vote on it.

Extra discussion. The class can also read about the school again and suggest other ways of saving electricity

Page 13 – Natural disasters 🎧

Warm up. Ask the students to name some natural disasters. e.g. avalanches, earthquakes, fires, floods, hurricanes, volcanoes. Write these on the board and then ask for examples of as many as possible e.g. The Asian tsunami in December 2004.

Discuss the parts of the world they associate with these events. What about their own country or region?

Comparing facts. The article presents the facts about hurricanes and floods in the same format. Ask the students to read and compare this information.

Writing. Ask the students to choose a natural disaster (real or imaginary) and to write a newspaper headline for it.

✏ **Worksheet 6**
Vocabulary – Earthquakes, hurricanes, floods
Grammar – Asking and answering *Wh-* questions, Present simple
Content – Geography, Science

Page 14 – Environment quiz: Do you know?

The students can make up a similar quiz about geographical features and places in one specific country or continent.

Page 15 – Projects

Ask the students to read all the projects carefully in order to decide which ones are interesting for them. Find out which are the most/least interesting for this class and if any of them just interest one person.

These projects can be done in groups, pairs or individually. Some of them may link with those done in other subjects, e.g. Geography or Science. Agree a timescale for doing the project and for presenting the results.

Page 16 – Chatrooms 🎧

Teens chat. The students can make up similar exchanges about weather superstitions.

Can you believe it?
This text on a sign in a park in India says: Your lungs are weak. Please do not smoke.
Writing. Ask them to make up similar unusual warnings.

✏ **Worksheet 7**
Vocabulary – Environmental concerns
Grammar – Asking for and giving factual information
Content – Geography, Science

✏ **Worksheet 8**
Vocabulary – Environment
Grammar – Descriptive language
Content – Geography, Science

Title review
The students can do a review to help inform other people. This can be of the whole magazine, or of specific articles. They can agree on their own criteria, or you can put a framework on the board for them to copy and adapt.

✏ **Test Worksheet**
The aim of the test is to encourage the students to look back through the articles in order to check facts, notice details and find specific information to answer the questions.

Extra teacher's resources

These websites are worth visiting for further information. They all have links to other relevant sites.

BBC young people: www.bbc.co.uk/cbbcnews
FAIRTRADE: www.fairtrade.org.uk
GREENPEACE: www.greenpeace.org
HWDT: www.hwdt.org
IFAW: www.ifaw.org
OXFAM: www.oxfam.co.uk/coolplanet
UNICEF: www.unicef.org
WWF: www.wwf.org

PHOTOCOPIABLE

Environment Worksheet 1

References: **Check it out** – Page 2

Focus: **Vocabulary** Environmental verbs and nouns
Grammar Present simple/Present continuous
Content Geography, Science

Activities

1. Environmental verbs

Use the verbs on Page 2 to complete these sentences.

a. New buildings often __________ the countryside.

b. Acid rain can __________ the water.

c. Scientists are ____________ new forms of energy.

d. There are several organisations to ____________ whales.

e. Industrial chemicals can __________ rivers and lakes.

f. When animals __________ their habitats, they often become extinct.

g. In the food chain, some animals ______ other animals for food.

h. The sea temperature is _____________ because of global warming.

i. The size of the big rain forests is ___________ every year.

j. Conservation groups often want to stop change and _______ things.

k. Environmental groups help to ______ the environment.

2. Disasters

Use the words on Page 2 for these natural disasters.

a. The water from rivers or the sea comes over the land. ____________________

b. In a hot, dry summer, there is a danger of these. ____________________

c. The earth shakes and buildings move. ____________________

d. There is no rain and plants die. ____________________

e. Violent weather with wind and rain. ____________________

f. People do not have enough food and often die. ____________________

3. Water

A lot of the words on Page 2 relate to water. Use these (and any others you know) to complete this Mind Map.

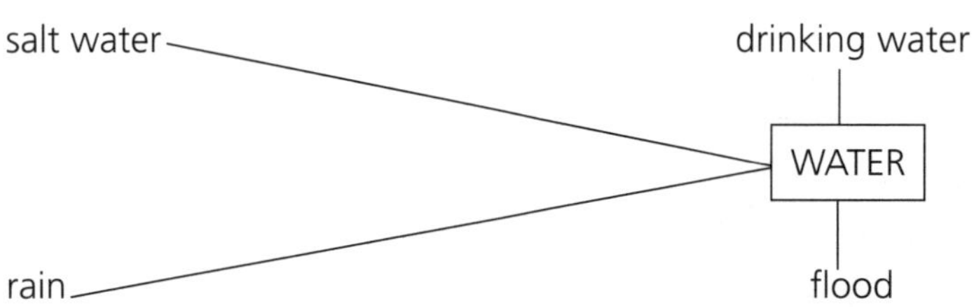

Compare your Mind Map with other people. How are they different?

References: **My environment** – Page 3

Focus:

Vocabulary Cities and traffic
Grammar Cause and effect
Content Science

Activities

1. Problems and solutions

Read the section 'Changes: positive or negative?'. Then use the phrases in the box to complete the sentences.

STAGE 1: THE PROBLEM

is full of fumes	move quickly
the doctors and hospitals are very busy	they get ill

a. There's too much traffic, so it can't ________________________.

b. Because of all the traffic, the air________________________.

c. People breathe in the traffic fumes, so ________________________.

d. Because people are ill, ________________________.

STAGE 2: A SOLUTION?

affects the food supply	can't find food
disappear from the countryside	the air becomes better
there is more pollution outside the city	they decide to build a big ring road
to move quickly round the city	use more chemicals on the crops

e. In order to solve the traffic problem, ____________

f. The new road allows the traffic ________________________.

g. Because the traffic moves quickly ________________________.

h. The new road attracts extra traffic, ________________________.

i. Farmers grow crops outside the city, so the new pollution ________________________.

j. To protect the food supply, farmers ________________________.

k. Many wild plants die, so animals ________________________.

l. As a result, wild birds and animals________________________.

2. Think about the your environment.

Write three 'cause and effect' sentences about it. Use 'so', because' and 'as a result'.

a. ________________________

b. ________________________

c. ________________________

Environment Worksheet 3

References: **Using water** – Pages 4 and 5

Focus:
Vocabulary Environmental verbs and nouns
Grammar Cause and effect
Content Science

Activities

1. Interpreting pictures

The theme of both articles is 'water in the environment'.
Look at the photos on Pages 4 and 5. What is their connection with the theme?

PHOTO	IT SHOWS	CONNECTION WITH THE THEME
1.		
2.		
3.		
4.		

2. Reinforcing the message

Write a caption for each photo. Reinforce their 'messages'.

a.____________________ b. ____________________

c.____________________ d. ____________________

3. Analysing requirements

Find the answers to these questions in the article on Page 4.

a. How much water does a person need every day? ____________________

b. What does fresh water become after we use it? ____________________

c. What are three domestic uses for water? ____________________

d. And three uses in agriculture? ____________________

e. What can countries with high mountains do with water? ____________________

f. According to the WHO, is most water used for agriculture, industry or domestic use? ____________

4. Identifying problems

Use the connectors 'so' or 'because' to complete these sentences.

a. There are floods __________ there is too much rain.

b. The level of rivers rise, __________ the water runs over the land.

c. In a drought, plants dies __________ there isn't enough water.

d. Chemicals kill plants and fish __________ they enter the water systems.

e Different countries have different priorities, __________ water can cause political problems.

Environment Worksheet 4

References: **The food chain** – Page 6

Focus:
Vocabulary Food, Animals, Plants
Grammar Sequencing
Content Science

Activities

1. The chain

Read the article on Page 6.
Now put these sentences in the correct order and connect them with the words in the box.

first	then	after that	finally

Some animals eat plants to get energy: they are first-level consumers.
Some animals and birds eat other animals – alive or dead: they're second or third-level consumers.
Plants are producers: they produce energy.
Some organisms consume dead plants and animals. They are decomposers.
This food returns to the earth. The cycle begins again.

____
____
____
____
____

2. Your food chain.

Think of three things you are eating or drinking today. Where do they fit in the food chain?
Write the links.

e.g. cheese ← milk ← cows ← grass

a. ______________________________
b. ______________________________
c. ______________________________

3. Dangers

What can be dangers for each step in these food chains? Are they natural or human dangers?

e.g. grass Natural: drought, flood, high temperatures, ...
Human: pollution, chemicals, ...

Write a 'dangers note' for each item and compare your ideas.

LINKS	DANGERS	NATURAL	DANGERS	HUMAN

Environment Worksheet 5

References: **Making a difference** – Pages 8 and 9

Focus:
Vocabulary Environment
Grammar Description
Content Geography, Science

Activities

1. Environment brainstorm

The title of this article is 'Making a Difference: the Hebridean Whale and Dolphin Trust.
Write down any words or ideas that this suggests.

____

____

Now look at the photos without reading the article. What do you think it will be about?
Discuss your ideas and make a note of them here.

____

____

Finally, write down the meaning of these phrases.

a. cetaceans______________________________
b. local communities______________________________
c. educational programmes______________________________

2. Environment facts

Read about HWDT's work. Find this information.

RESEARCH

a. The number of types cetaceans in this part of the Atlantic. ______________
b. What problems they can have with:
food, water, humans. ______________
c. Who helps the scientists with the research work. ______________
d. Where they record the facts. ______________
e. The number of cetaceans they can observe. ______________
f. The information they record. ______________

EDUCATIONAL PROJECTS

a. The two uses of the boat. ______________
b. The school subjects they study on the boat. ______________
c. Things the students can discover about a minke whale:
length, breathing, food, problem with the water. ______________

Read the description of the HWDT office at the bottom of Page 9. Now you have an idea of their work, write an ad for volunteers to join them next summer. Decide what skills are necessary. Include the necessary negative information about the work – bad weather, danger, small space.

References: **Natural Disasters** – Page 13

Focus:
Vocabulary Earthquakes, Hurricanes, Floods
Grammar Asking and answering *Wh*- questions, Present simple
Content Geography, Science

Activities

1. Parallel disasters

Read the article. Notice the questions and answers. Close your magazines. Choose either hurricanes or floods. Answer these questions for your topic.

DISASTER TOPIC:

What are they?	How do they affect people
Why do they happen?	What can people do?
Where do they happen?	

Check your answers with the article.

2. More disasters: earthquakes

Here are some facts about earthquakes. Write the same questions for each fact.

a. ______________________________

The earth's surface moves or shakes suddenly.

b. ______________________________

There are big 'plates' on the earth's surface which can move suddenly causing the earth to shake.

c. ______________________________

Where two or mores plates meet. China, Japan, the Philippines, the USA and Southern Europe are all danger zones.

d. ______________________________

In an earthquake, houses can fall and kill people. They can cause fires, big waves in the sea and floods.

e. ______________________________

Scientists can sometimes see the signs in advance. If that happens, they can warn people to leave their homes. But very often, there isn't enough time.

3. Finding out

What natural disasters can you remember?
Make a note of the type, the date and the country. Add any other important details.

NATURAL DISASTERS

TYPE	DATE	COUNTRY	OTHER DETAILS

Environment Worksheet 7

References: **All**

Focus:

Vocabulary Environmental concerns
Grammar Asking for and giving factual information
Content Geography, Science

Activities

1. Look through Environment and list all the articles which are relevant to your own environment.

2. Add any other local environmental activities that you can think of – include problems and successes.

3. Work in groups.
Choose one of these local issues and write a description of it for an international environmental website.

NOTE: You can use this guided writing frame.

PLACE:

ENVIRONMENTAL ACTIVITY:

PICTURES:

WHAT PEOPLE ARE DOING:

IDEAS FOR MORE ACTIVITIES:

References: **All**

Focus:

Vocabulary Environment
Grammar Descriptive language
Content Geography, Science

Activities

1. Look at the language in the Check it out section (page 2).
Check you know the meanings.

2. Look through *Environment* and choose your favourite picture.

3. In pairs or groups, make up good titles for these pictures.
You can use some of the specialist vocabulary from Page 2, or your own ideas. The aim is to produce a good title that sums up the pictures in just a few words..

e.g. 'Protect the ocean! ' (Front cover)
'Is wind power the solution?' (page 12)

4. An environmental horror story
Read this story. Can you suggest a solution?

<u>The place</u>
Gough Island is in the Tristan da Cunha group of islands in the South Atlantic. It's a small island: eight kilometres long and six kilometres wide.

<u>The characters</u>
They're not humans – the island is uninhabited. The main characters are huge mice and young birds.

<u>The background</u>
In the 19th century, ships used to stop there. The sailors took fresh water from the island – and mice went onto it from the ships. There was a lot of fresh food. Result? The mice got bigger and bigger! The island is now an important nesting place for birds.

<u>Albatrosses</u>
Albatrosses are one of the birds that nest on the island. These birds travel huge distances to look for food. Sometimes they leave the young birds for eight months!

<u>The problem</u>
The young birds sit and wait for their parents to return. A young albatross can be one metre tall, but it cannot fly. So it cannot escape, it can only turn round in the same place. The big mice like to eat young bird meat. They attack the young birds as they sit on the ground. Scientists calculate that these mice are killing around one million birds each year in the South Atlantic islands.

Source: BBC News Science report 25 7 05

Finally, think of a good title for the story.

Environment Test Worksheet

Name: ____________________

Total Points (1 per question) ____________

1. Look through *Environment*. Identify these articles. Write the page number and the title.

a. There are photos of floods and hurricanes.
Page ________ Title ____________________
b. You can see some cows sitting down.
Page ________ Title ____________________
c. This article is about energy.
Page ________ Title ____________________
d. Salt is bad for grapes!
Page ________ Title ____________________
e. This international organisation helps farmers
Page ________ Title ____________________
f. They're standing next to a whale.
Page ________ Title ____________________
g. Pieces in a jigsaw puzzle.
Page ________ Title ____________________
h. Who uses water?
Page ________ Title ____________________
i. B eats A. C eats B. Then D eats C.
Page ________ Title ____________________

2. Are these statements true or false? Check them with the articles and write T or F.

a. Page 3. Environmental changes are always positive. T F
b. Page 4. A person needs 19 litres of water every day. T F
c. Page 5. Politics sometimes cause water problems. T F
d. Page 7. Tourism is always bad for animals. T F
e. Page 8. Only professional scientists do research. T F
f. Page 10. Everybody likes GM crops. T F
g. Page 10/11. Fairtrade is good for producers and consumers T F
h. Page 12. Dragonflies produce energy. T F
i. Page 13. Hurricanes and typhoons are the same thing. T F
j. Page 16. Red sky at night is a good sign. T F

3. What is the English word for these things?

a. The bad gas from traffic or industry. ____________
b. Sea water. ____________
c. River water. ____________
d. Electricity from water energy. ____________
e. The British English word for a truck. ____________
f. This organism eats dead things. ____________
g. This enormous mammal lives in the sea. ____________
h. Very small plants and animals in the sea. ____________
i. To have no food. ____________

Teacher's Notes: **COMMUNICATION** Pre-intermediate

Ideas for use

This title includes a lot of information about different forms of communication – human, animal, spoken, written, non–verbal. It encourages the students to think about these in relation to both themselves and to other people. Communication between and within different cultures is discussed in order to develop intercultural awareness.

Crosscurricular links: Art and Design; Geography; History; L1 Language and Literature; other languages; Music; Technology.

Don't forget! Look carefully for the Checkout Spot mini-projects with each article.
You will find more general ideas to use with all the titles in the *Topics* series on pages 85-89 of this Teacher's Book.

Cover and contents

Encourage the students to browse through *Communication* and to look at the range of articles, illustrations and design styles.

Warm up. What different types of communication can the students suggest? e.g. speaking, writing, music, painting. What different methods do people use to communicate? e.g. sending emails, texting, phoning. What sometimes makes communication difficult? e.g. language. sympathy, distance.

Discussion. What do the photos on the cover suggest? Are they a good depiction of the topic, *Communication*? Ask the students to suggest other possible images for the cover.

Speculation. What can we guess about these two people? What is the situation? What is the girl saying? What tells us this? Collect the different ideas.

Cover titles. The student choose one title. What do they think the article will be about? They write a sentence about this and then turn to the article to check if they were correct.

Page 1 – Letter 🎧

Discussion. Focus on paragraph 3. What is 'teen speak'? (A special form of language that teenagers often use among themselves.) Do the students use this in their L1? What are its characteristics. e.g. special words, abbreviations, codes? Does it change often?

Make sure that the students understand (and can identify) the Checkout Spot icon.

Discussion. Which titles are easy to understand (e.g. The story of English)? Which are more difficult (e.g. Say it with flowers)? If you did not do this when looking at the front cover, encourage the students to guess what the articles are about and to flick through the pages to check this.

Page 2 – Check it out

See page 90 for different activities to use with this reference page.

Page 3 – Hello! 🎧

Warm up. Discuss the different ways that people greet each other in L1. How do these vary? e.g. formal, informal. How can you greet people without using words? e.g. shaking hands, kissing, waving. Which forms of greeting are normal in your culture? What do they depend on?

Pictures and words. The students look at the five cartoons and link these with the five non-verbal forms of greeting.

✏ **Worksheet 1**
Vocabulary – Greetings
Grammar – Present simple
Content – Languages

Pages 4 and 5 – Computer chat

This two-page article describes six forms of computer communication in factual language, using the same format and structure for each section.

Warm up. What do the students use computers for? Which are the most/least useful for them? Why?

Jigsaw reading. The students can read one section and then discuss the content with another group. They should notice the use of icons in each section to signal 'Positive' 'Negative' and 'Warning' . They can add their own ideas about 'their' section during the discussion.

Writing. The students write about their favourite computer use, using these sections as a model. Put together, these descriptions can form a class version of this article.

✏ **Worksheet 2**
Vocabulary – Computers
Grammar – Giving advice/instructions
Content – L1

Page 6 – Safe surfing

This article discusses the safety aspects of surfing the Internet and using Chatrooms.

Warm up. Discuss whether there are any problems with using the Internet. Has anybody had any bad experiences? Can they suggest any general advice?

Discussion. Ask the students to read the two sections of advice and then to say which they agree with and to add any personal suggestions or details. Do they think a safety code like this is a good idea? Why (not)? Can they think of other uses of a similar safety code? e.g. for films and TV programmes.

Checkout Spot. You can prepare for this by writing their 'Do/Don't' suggestions on the board.

Page 7 – TXT that MSG!

Warm up. Discuss how common texting is for the students. What kind of language do they use for it in L1? Is it like these messages? What are the advantages of texting? e.g. cheaper than talking on the phone, quick and easy, you can read the messages at any time. What are some of the disadvantages? e.g. It's disappointing if you don't get a reply, other people can read it, it becomes compulsive!

Discussion. Ask the students to read the last two paragraphs before deciding and discussing whether they agree with them. What are their reasons?

Writing. In pairs or small groups, they agree and write some rules for texting for their school.

Page 8 – Non-verbal communication: using the senses

This article, and the one on Page 9, describes different forms of non-verbal communication. They can be read together or separately.

Warm up. Ask for suggestions of signs that use pictures, colours or other non-verbal devices to communicate their messages.

Picture and text. Ask the students to look at the photos and decide what the message is and what type of signs they are.

This hill is very steep for lorries	Road sign.
An area to fix bicycles.	On a wall.
Stop!	Traffic light.
No smoking!	Public places.
Go left!	Road sign.
Stop!	Street sign.

Discussion. Decide if these signs are effective communication or not. Would words be better? Why (not)?

Finding information. Ask the students to read the article and discover:

How sounds are used to communicate urgent messages.
What kind of messages can be communicated through music.

✏ **Worksheet 3** (with Page 9)
Vocabulary – Communication
Grammar – Giving advice and warnings
Content – Languages

Page 9 – Non-verbal communication

Warm up. Ask the students how many ways they can communicate using parts of their body e.g. facial expression, nodding, hand gestures, etc. List these on the board.

Interpreting pictures. Ask the students to look at the two photos on the left. What messages do they communicate? What other gestures or facial expressions can the students suggest to communicate the same messages?

Pairwork. Ask the students to think of a message to communicate. They work in pairs or small groups and take it in turns to do this through gesture or facial expression. The other person guesses (and if possible reacts to) the message.

Discussion. Was the communication clear? How many variations can they find for each message? Do these depend on personality or culture?

Groupwork. After reading this section, the students work in groups and take it in turns to communicate different emotions through body language, e.g. fear, nervousness, tiredness, boredom, as a guessing activity.

Page 10 – Say it with flowers

Warm up. Find out what a red rose signifies in many cultures (I love you). Are there any other symbols for this message. e.g. hearts, kisses?

Checking information. Check that the students understand the phrases in the Hints Box before they read the article. These provide the answers to the questions about communication through colours, flowers and emoticons.

Discussion. Discuss the various meanings these symbols may have for different people and in different cultures. How many meanings can they suggest? This is preparation for the Checkout Spot activity.

Writing. The students send each other messages using signs, symbols. colours and emoticons. Are these easy to understand?

Page 11 – Mixed messages

This article is about personal problems in communicating clearly. The section on the left contains three real-life situations (from teenager magazines). The cartoon illustrates the third situation. The section on the right describes the problems whales may have with communication.

Warm up. Ask if any students have ever been misunderstood or failed to communicate easily. Were the consequences funny or serious? What happened? Why did the communication break down? They can compare their ideas with the suggestions in the Introduction to the article (paragraphs one and two).

Writing. After reading the three personal accounts, the students write a short piece of advice for each situation. Compare their suggestions.

Animals' problems. The students read this section to find the answers to these questions.

Which animals are having communication problems?	(whales)
What makes a lot of noise?	(tourists and boats)
What are the tourists doing?	(watching whales)
How are the whales solving the problem?	(by using pauses and communicating slowly)
What link does the article make between these animals and humans?	
(We use the same strategy when we communicate in noisy places.)	

Writing. Ask for suggestions for a more interesting title for this section.

Pages 12 and 13 – The story of English

This factual article is fairly long, but it is written in seven distinct sections. It is ideal for a jigsaw reading activity. Alternatively, you can ask the whole class to read just one or two sections at a time.

The words and phrases on Page 12.

Chutzpah (Yiddish).	To have strong confidence in yourself.
Gulag (Russian).	Prison.
Gung-ho (Chinese).	To be very enthusiastic about things that may be dangerous.
'I should worry!' (Yiddish).	An ironic comment.

The words and phrases on Page 13.

Step 5. These two lines are in Australian English. They come from a famous song, 'Waltzing Matilda'.

Step 6. Indian English words and phrases.

Angrez	English
Badmash	naughty
Jungli	uncultured, wild

Warm up. Ask what different types of English the students can think of. Why are there so many variations? What causes them?

Alternatively, write the questions from the top of Page 12 on the board as a framework for discussion. Let them see the answers after they have made their own suggestions.

Do they know of other languages that have different varieties? What about their own L1? What are the reasons for these variations?

Groupwork. Ask the students to work in groups. Each group reads one section. They make up three quiz questions about their section. Combine all the questions into a class quiz. They ask and answer them orally in the next lesson, without looking at the article. This can be done as a Quiz Show.

Discussion. After they have read the article, ask them to answer the question about History, Politics and Geography again. They can also suggest how and why other animals have moved from their country of origin and developed other forms, e.g. French, Spanish, Portuguese.

Writing and Design. Ask the students to look carefully at the visual design of these two pages. They then design a poster to show how another language has spread and developed – or a different design for English.

Worksheet 4
Vocabulary – Language
Grammar – Past Simple for narrative and description
Content – Art, Design, Geography, History, Languages

Pages 14 and 15 – Inventions: steps to better communication

This two-page article describes developments in inventions which help people to communicate. It is written in note form.

Telephones (Page 14) allow people to talk over distances, while flight (Page 15) allows people to travel physically across distances to different places. You can read both parts together, or treat them as separate articles.

Talking across distances. Do a class brainstorming on telephones. Who invented them? When? What could the early ones do? How did they operate? How did they change people's lives?

Encourage them to talk to older people to find out what phones used to be like (they only began to change around 1980).

Read and check. The students compare their ideas with the facts in the first part of the article. Point out that each new stage in their development results from the 'problem' in the previous stage.

Discussion. What are the different things a modern mobile phone can do? Write these on the board. The students then rank these for themselves, from 1 (top) to 10, in terms of usefulness. They compare their lists.

Let's go by air!. This part of the article describes stages in the development of flying in the same way as those in the development of telephones, ie each stage is an attempt to overcome the problems of the previous one. You can treat these in the same way as in the previous article.

Warm up. Discover what the students know or can discover about Icarus and Leonardo Da Vinci. Why are they relevant to an article about flying?

Read and check. The students read the first two paragraphs to check how these two people are connected with developments in flying.

Discussion. The students read the sections about the developments in balloons and planes. Is there anything here that surprises them? How would they answer the final question about developments in flying?

NOTE: Santos Dumont was an early Brazilian flyer who was a contemporary of the Wright Brothers. He lived in Paris at the beginning of the 20th century and loved flying. He had his own balloon which he tied to a lamp post when he went out to dinner! He was involved in the development of the first planes in France. He gave up his interest during the First World War – he was disgusted that flying was being used for war. The airport in Rio de Janeiro is named after him.

Research. Ask the students to choose one of the people or stages in development mentioned on these two pages and to find out more about them. Then they present their information to the class.

Checkout Spot. This activity can be expanded into a class project on communication developments which can be linked to work in other subjects such as Art and Design and Science.

Worksheet 5
Vocabulary – Telephones, Flying
Grammar – Past simple, Cause and effect
Content – Geography, History, Science

Page 16 – Secret communication

Warm up. Ask the students to describe any codes they know.

Read and check. Why do people use codes? In what circumstances? Collect the students' ideas and then ask them to read the Introduction (above the blue alphabet strip) and compare their ideas.

After this, they read each of the following four sections for information.

The Caesar code. The note on the left is in this code. Check if they can follow the instructions and decode it.
(I will go to Britain next summer. J.C.)

Encrypting. After reading this section, ask the students to find out this way of keeping credit card transactions safe.

Number codes. After they have read this, ask them to work out more complex versions. What information would the other person need to have in order to decode the message?

Long hair. Can they think of any other ingenious ways of hiding messages?

Page 17 – Teen speak

Warm up. Discuss why adults and teenagers often seem to have communication problems.

Read and discuss. The students read the first two paragraphs. Do they agree with the statements? Can they add other suggestions?

Groupwork. In pairs or small groups, the students read the four groups of words and phrases. They then try to work out the rationale behind them, in order to answer the two questions in the paragraph above (truncated words, diminutive endings)

Discussion. Discuss the L1 equivalent. What is its rationale? This is a preparation for the Checkout Spot.

Page 18 – Don't forget the animals!

The articles on this page and Page 19 describe some aspects of animal communication – animal-to-animal and animal-to-human. They can be read separately or together.

Warm up. Check what the students already know about the ways in which animals communicate with each other. Relate this to different species. Finally, brainstorm what they know about the way elephants communicate.

Read for information. Ask the students to read the article to find the answers to these questions, and to note where they find this information.

What do the older elephants teach the young ones?
(Life skills. Section 1)

What elephants do when one of the group dies?
(They stop by the body. Section 2)

What can they do with their feet?
(Listen. Section 3)

Why is this important?
(To keep in touch with the group. Section 3)

Page 19 – Animal communication: having fun

Discussion. When the students have read the article, they decide whether they believe the two stories.

Writing. They choose one of the stories and write newspaper headlines and a short report on it.

Pages 20 and 21 – From A-Z: the alphabet story

Warm up. Ask the students what they know or can find out about Western alphabets. Are they all the same? How have they developed? What about other ways of writing? Do they use letters or ideograms? Are they written from left to right, right to left, or vertically?

Reading for information. Ask the students to read the article and make a note of any new facts that they learn.

Writing. They use their notes to write five quiz questions about this alphabet. Collect all the questions and put them together to make a class quiz. The students then answer this without reading the article again. You can do this as an oral Quiz Show.

Worksheet 6
Vocabulary – Communication
Grammar – Past simple for narrative and description
Content – Art and Design, Geography, History, Languages

Page 22 – Communication quiz: do you know?

Animal communication. Making the various animal noises will help!

Colour links. They can discuss or find out about another culture.

American and British English. The students can make up a quiz with other groups of words.

Page 23 – Projects

Ask the students to read all the projects carefully in order to decide which ones are interesting for them. Find out which are the most/least interesting for this class and if any of them just interest one person.

These projects can be done in groups, pairs or individually. Some of them may link with those done in other subjects, e,g. History or Science.

Encourage the students to also review and present the things they have been doing in the various Checkout Spot mini-projects. If appropriate, these can form a class end-of-term exhibition.

Page 24 – Chatrooms 🎧

Teens chat. Are there any equivalents to these these jokes in the students' L1? Is there an equivalent to the saying 'Walls have ears'? Ask the students to tell or write similar jokes.

Can you believe it? Ask them to look carefully at the two photos. What English phrases can they find in each one? (Left photo: Tips here. Right photo: Handicrafts.)

Ask about the use of English or other foreign languages to attract tourists. Are there any funny examples?

✏ **Worksheet 7**
Vocabulary – Media
Grammar – Asking for information
Content – Art, Design, Maths

✏ **Worksheet 8**
Vocabulary – Ways of communicating
Grammar – Expressing ideas
Content – Art, Design

Title review. The students can do a review to help inform other people. This can be of the whole magazine, or of specific articles. They can agree their own criteria, or you can put this framework on the board for them to copy and adapt.

CRITERIA	ARTICLE	STARS	COMMENTS
Interest			
Information			
Design			
Photos			
Checkout Spot			
Other			

✏ **Test Worksheet**
The aim of the test is to encourage the students to look back through the articles in order to check facts, notice details and find specific information to answer the questions.

Extra teacher's resources

These publications and websites are worth consulting for further information.

Books

- Desmond Morris, *Peoplewatching*, Random House 2002. Like Desmond Morris' earlier books, this examines human body language through the eyes of an anthropologist.
- David Sacks, *The Alphabet*, Random House 2003. A fascinating account of how each letter in the Roman alphabet has developed over the centuries. Their sounds as well as their visual form are discussed.
- Melvyn Bragg, *The Adventure of English*, Hodder Headline 2003. This is a very readable account of how English has developed and spread around the world.

Websites
BBC young people: www.bbc.co. uk/cbbcnews
Newsround: www.news.bbc.co.uk/cbbcnews

Communication Worksheet 1

References: **Hello** – Page 3

Focus:
Vocabulary Greetings
Grammar Present simple
Content Languages

Activities

1. Greetings in English: verbal
Write five phrases to greet people in English here.

a. ______________________________

b. ______________________________

c. ______________________________

d. ______________________________

e. ______________________________

2. Greetings in English: non-verbal
Read the article (again). Write five non-verbal ways to greet people here.

a. ______________________________

b. ______________________________

c. ______________________________

d. ______________________________

e. ______________________________

3. Think of your culture. How do people greet each other in these situations?

a. You meet your best friend in the park.
YOU SAY:
YOU DO:

b.You see your aunt in the street.
YOU SAY:
YOU DO:

c. You are in the supermarket and you meet your head teacher.
YOU SAY:
YOU DO:

d.You go to a party. You meet a stranger. He/She is your age.
YOU SAY:
YOU DO:

e. (Invent a situation).
YOU SAY:
YOU DO:

Compare your ideas with the rest of the class.

Communication Worksheet 2

References:	**Computer Chat** – Pages 4 and 5	
Focus:	**Vocabulary**	Computers
	Grammar	Giving advice/instructions
	Content	L1

Activities

1. Computer language

Match the name and the description.

blogs	chat rooms	e-commerce
e-mails	search engines	surfing

a. A place where you can chat with other people. _______________

b. A quick and cheap way to send messages. _______________

c. A place where you can find website addresses for topics. _______________

d. An interactive diary. _______________

e. Visiting the internet. _______________

f. Buying and selling things from your computer. _______________

2. Choose carefully!

You want to do something. Which do you choose?

a. I want to buy a birthday present for my best friend. _______________

b. I'm researching a project for history. I'm looking for some good ideas! _______________

c. My sister's travelling in South America. I want to contact her. _______________

d. I can't remember the website address for this topic. _______________

e. I'm going to log onto the discussion about the environment. _______________

f. My sister's writing about her trip every day. There are photos, too! _______________

3. Give advice

Your friends are having some computer problems. Give them advice. Use the information in the article to help you.

a. 'Look at all this junk mail!'. _______________

b. 'I can't type quickly enough!' _______________

c. 'There's nothing new on this blog!' _______________

4. You and your computer

Which are the most/least useful things for you? Which are the most/least fun?
Are there any differences? Add any other favourite activities.

	USEFUL	FUN
Top activity	_______________	_______________
Bottom activity	_______________	_______________
Other favourite activities	_______________	_______________

Communication Worksheet 3

References: **Non-Verbal Communication** – Pages 8 and 9

Focus:
Vocabulary Communication
Grammar Giving advice and warnings
Content Languages

Activities

1. Picture messages

Look at the picture signs on Page 8. Match the correct message with each one. Where can you see them?

No smoking!	One way: go left	Stop! (x2)
This hill is very steep for lorries.		We repair bikes here.

Public place	Road sign (x2)	Street sign
Traffic lights	Wall picture	

	PICTURE	MESSAGE	LOCATION
1.			
2.			
3.			
4.			
5.			
6.			

2. Sound messages

What messages do these sounds communicate? Check your ideas on Page 8.

a. A non-stop bell inside a building.

b. Three short blasts on a whistle.

c. A siren on a fast car.

d. A favourite piece of music on a phone.

Check your ideas with the 2nd and 3rd paragraphs of the article on page 8.

3. Gestures

How do you give these messages without using words in your culture?
Write or draw some exmaples.

a.

b.

c.

d.

e.

f.

References: **The Story of English** – Pages 12 and 13

Focus:
Vocabulary Language
Grammar Past simple for narrative and description
Content Art, Design, Geography, History, Languages

Activities

1. Here are some words and phrases from the article. They are all used by English speakers. What other languages, countries or cultures do they represent?

	LANGUAGE, CULTURE OR COUNTRY
a. badmash	____________________
b. billabong	____________________
c. chutzpah	____________________
d. gulag	____________________
e. gung-ho	____________________
f. jungli	____________________
g. moose	____________________
h. swagman	____________________
i. tomahawk	____________________
j. wigwam	____________________
k. 'I should worry!'	____________________

Do you know any other words or phrases from any of these cultures?
Compare your ideas.

2. Without looking at the article, answer these questions.

a. Where did some English speakers go to in the 17th century? ____________
b. What type of English did they speak? ____________
c. Why did they go there? ____________
d. What important book in English did they take with them? ____________
e. Why did they need new words in their new country? ____________
f. Where did they find those new words? ____________
g. What new language began to develop as a result of these events? ____________

Check your answers with the introduction and Section 1 of the article.
Now think about these questions. Relate them to any language, not just English.

h. Why is Geography important too? ____________
i. What about Politics and Religion? ____________

Communication Worksheet 5

References: **Inventions** – Pages 14 and 15

Focus:
Vocabulary Telephones, Flying
Grammar Past simple, Cause and effect
Content Geography, History, Science

Activities

1. Phones facts

Check what you know about phones. Answer these questions before you read the article.

a. Who invented telephones? ______________________

b. When? ______________________

c. In which country? ______________________

d. What could you do with the first phones? ______________________

e. Why was this a great invention? ______________________

f. What was a 'minus point'? ______________________

Check your facts with the first part of the article.

2. Cause and effect

Look at the 'positive points' and 'problems' for each type of phone.
Notice how each new development solves the 'problem' of the earlier one.
Use the information to expand these sentences.

a. first phones/not mobile/but/speak from anywhere/mobile phones

____

b. not see/other person/ first mobile phones/ but/ send pictures/cameraphone

____

c. cameraphones/easy to steal/so/ phone crime/rising/many countries

____

3. Phones now

What can mobile phones do now? Make a list.
What would you like them to do in the future? What would your 'dream phone' be like?
Compare your ideas.

4. Flying: the debate.

There's a lot of discussion about cheap flights. They allow more people to travel, but more planes are bad for the environment.
Think of some positive and negative things about this and compare (and discuss) your ideas with the class. You can also choose one side of the argument, and try to convince other people.

References: **From A to Z: the alphabet story** – Pages 20 and 21

Focus:
Vocabulary Communication
Grammar Past simple for narrative and description
Content Art, Design, Geography, History, Languages

Activities

1. Alphabet questions

Answer these questions.

a. How many letters are there in your alphabet? ____________

b. How many letters are there in the English alphabet? ____________

c. Name two languages that use different symbols for the letters. ____________

d. Name one language that uses symbols for a word, not a letter. ____________

Check with the first part of the article on Page 20.

2. Roman Alphabet facts

Find the information to complete this table in Steps 1-3 on Page 21.

	Place	Date developed	Letters/changes
STEP 1			
STEP 2			
STEP 3			

STEP 4

Where did Portuguese and Spanish explorers take the alphabet? ____________________

Which other places did it travel to with explorers and emigrants? ____________________

What is the alphabet very useful for now? ____________________

Now use this information to draw the alphabet's journey on this map.

Communication Worksheet 7

References: **All**

Focus:
Vocabulary Media
Grammar Asking for information
Content Art, Design, Maths

Activities

1. Communication facts

Read this extract from a report about teenagers' communication.

What teenagers do online

Send or read e-mail:	89%
Visit websites about TV, music or sports stars:	84%
Play online games:	81%
Online news:	76%
Send or receive instant messages:	75%
Percentage of these who go online every day:	50%
Percentage who used it in 2000:	74%
Percentage of these who use instant messaging:	75%
Favourite features:	icons
Percentage who use the net now:	90%

Use this data to write a questionnaire about online use.
You can add different questions.

2. Administer your questionnaire to another group, or to a different class.

Report your findings and work out the percentages.

3. Survey design

Here is another survey about communication habits.

1. **News**
In a normal week, do you read a daily newspaper? YES NO

2. **Mobile phone calls**
In a normal day, how many mobile phone calls do you make?
None: Under 5: 6-10: 11-20: 21+:

3. **Text messages**
In a normal day, how many text messages do you send?
None: Under 5: 6-10: 11-20: 21+:

Design a form to use to collect this data. You need space for five replies (yourself, and four other people).
Answer the questions for yourself, and then ask four other people. Record the data on the form.
Share the results with the other groups and work out the percentages.

4. Comparing data

The original survey was done in the UK in September 2005. The organisers questioned 580 people aged between 14 and 21.
Here are the results. Compare them with yours.

The responses were:

1.	YES: 65%	NO: 43%	DON'T KNOW: 1%			
2.	None: 4% .	Under 5: 52%.	6-10: 26%.	11-20:11%.	21+:7%.	Other: 1%
3.	None: 3% .	Under 5: 32%.	6-10: 26%.	11-20:18%.	21+:20%.	Other: 1%

SOURCE: The Guardian Newspaper 7 October 2005.

PHOTOCOPIABLE

Communication Worksheet 8

References: **All**

Focus: **Vocabulary** Ways of communicating
Grammar Expressing ideas
Content Art, Design

Activities

1. Communicating

Look through your magazine.
Make a list of all the pictures of different forms of communication.
Decide what groups they fit into, e.g. 'people', 'machines', etc.
Summarise the groups here, adding the page reference.

GROUP	PICTURE DESCRIPTION	PAGE REFERENCE

Compare your groups with other people. Make any changes you want.

2. Reinforcing the message

Choose one picture from each of your groups. Invent a caption for it, to reinforce the message.

PHOTO
GROUP
CAPTION

PHOTO
GROUP
CAPTION
(etc)

3. Interpreting the topic

Look again at the different topics related to communication in the magazine.
Imagine you are the Editor of a new edition.
What other topics will you include? Will the articles be factual, humorous, 'personal interest', or ...?
How will you illustrate them?
Discuss your ideas with partner/in a group. Plan the content for this new issue.

TOPICS	TYPE OF ARTICLE	ILLUSTRATION

Finally, decide what you will put on the cover to express the idea of 'communication' visually.

4. The final word

Look at the cover. Decide what the person on the right is whispering.
Take it in turns to start a 'whisper chain' round the class. Each person whispers what they hear to the next person. The first person then says his/her original message out loud and the last person compares it with the one that they heard.
Was the communication good or did the message change?

Communication Test Worksheet

Name: ____________________

Total Points (1 per question) ____________________

1. Look through *Communication*. Identify these articles. Write the page number and the title.

a. There are two photos of people with laptop computers.
Page ________ Title ____________________
b. You can see different street signs.
Page ________ Title ____________________
c. This article is about an alphabet.
Page ________ Title ____________________
d. Feet are important for communication!
Page ________ Title ____________________
e. Let's thank Thomas Edison and Alexander Bell.
Page ________ Title ____________________
f. Adults may find this page useful.
Page ________ Title ____________________
g. Say 'I love you' with a flower.
Page ________ Title ____________________
h. It's not enough to know the word 'Hello'..
Page ________ Title ____________________
i. Communication isn't always easy.
Page ________ Title ____________________

2. Are these statements true or false? Check them with the articles and circle T or F.

a. Page 3. We can greet people with no words. T F
b. Page 4. There are no problems when we send emails.. T F
c. Page 5. A 'blog' is a personal diary on the Internet. T F
d. Page 7. Text messages do not use numbers.. T F
e. Page 9. Body language is the same in all cultures. T F
f. Page 11. Some animals can communicate through their feet. T F
g. Page 12. Mark Twain used Afro-American English in Huckleberry Finn.. T F
h. Page 13. There is only one correct form of English in the world now. T F
i. Page 16. We don't use codes in the modern world. T F

3. What is the English word for these things?

a. A 'virtual place' to meet other people. ____________
b. A person who looks for information on the Internet.. ____________
c. A green and red plant that symbolises Christmas in some countries. ____________
d. A person who goes to live permanently in another country. ____________
e. The old English word for 'you'. ____________
f. A phone with a screen to see the other person. ____________
g. A secret written language. ____________
h. To make an object or a person look different. ____________
i. A written symbol for an idea or an object. ____________

Teacher's Notes: **ENTERTAINMENT** Pre-intermediate

Ideas for use
This title explores different types of entertainment. It does this from the point of view of both participants (entertainers) and spectators. It also examines some entertainment-related topics such as sponsorship and the ideas which inspired specific films and pieces of music.

Crosscurricular links: Art and Design; Drama; Geography; History; Languages; Music; Science and Technology.

Don't forget! Look carefully for the Checkout Spot mini-projects with each article. You will find more general ideas to use with all the titles in the *Topics* series on pages 99-103 of this Teacher's Book.

Cover and contents
Encourage the students to browse through *Entertainment* and to look at the range of articles, illustrations and design styles. What different types of entertainment do they know the names of in English? What do they know about each one?

Discussion. What do the photos on the cover suggest? Are they a good depiction of the topic, *Entertainment*? Ask the students to suggest other possible images for the cover. You can use the large picture to discuss the various types of entertainment, e.g. theatre, films, music and the performers.

Speculation. What kind of music group is it? What type of music are they playing? Where?

Page 1 – Letter 🎧
The letter summarises the different aspects of entertainment covered in the articles.

Groupwork. Ask the students to choose the aspects of entertainment which sound most interesting to them. They can make a 'Top Three' list. This will serve as a general 'warm up' for the topic and help to show what aspects really interest each person.

Make sure that the students understand (and can identify) the Checkout Spot icon.

Discussion. Which titles are easy to understand (e.g. The story of a group)? Which are more difficult (e.g. Where do movies come from?). Encourage the students to guess what the articles are about and to flick through the pages to check this.

Page 2 – Check it out
See page 104 for different activities to use with this reference page.

Page 3 – It's festival time! 🎧
This article describes some of the background work and problem solving that goes into the organisation of a big festival.

Warm up. Ask for suggestions of different types of festival, e.g. music, dance, film, theatre. Find out if the students have been to any, either as spectators or performers. What do they remember best? Which of these memories are positive and which are negative?

Finding information. Ask if the students know anything about the four festivals mentioned here:
Glastonbury, Rock in Rio/Lisboa, Rock in the Park, Woodstock.

What can they find out? The websites listed on Page 2 may help them, while older people may give them information about Woodstock. What other famous music festivals do they know?

They compare their results and then decide which festival sounds most exciting. Which one would they like to visit?

Read and discover. Ask the students to read the article and find out what problems festival organisers have to consider in relation to these things.

crowds	security
food and drink	traffic
health and hygiene	weather

Groupwork. After they have read the final paragraph of the article, ask the students to plan their own ideal festival. They can do this in pairs or groups.

✏ **Worksheet 1**
Vocabulary – Festival organisation and content, Music styles
Grammar – Description
Content – Music

Page 4 – Festivals: more than the music
This article continues the idea that festivals are much more than the performances.

Warm up. Ask the students to look at the photo and the title. What does the picture make them think of? List their ideas on the board.

Read and find. Ask half the class to read about Glastonbury and the others to read about the Rock in Rio-Lisboa event. They should find and list all the special and/or non-musical aspects of the festivals that the article describes. These include:

Glastonbury
The festival raises money for charity.
Volunteers work at it.
One charity is responsible for providing and organising the showers and toilets.
Another charity provides a place to exercise and an organic café.
The programme includes discussions about the environment.
The Greenpeace people helped the organisers to clear up after the event.

Rock in Rio-Lisboa 2004
There were discussions about the state of the world.
There was a silence to promote world peace.
Famous musicians from different countries played together.

Page 5 – Behind the music

This article describes ways in which politics and social concerns often influence musicians. It uses two from Brazil, Gilberto Gil and Caetano Veloso, as the examples, but obviously the same considerations can be applied to people like Bob Geldof and Bono from U2, or other musicians the students may know.

Warm up. Ask the students what they know about Brazilian music. Have they heard of these two musicians?

Read and discover. The students choose one of the three sections of the article to read.
Caetano Veloso, Gilberto Gil, Exile
They look for the following information in their section.

Caetano Veloso
The name of his famous musical movement (with Gil and other musicians).
Why he had to leave his country.
What kind of festival he often attends now.
What he often speaks about at these festivals.

Gilberto Gil
His two present jobs (in 2006).
His diet.
His lifestyle now and in the past.

Exile
Where the two singers were born.
Where they went to.
A song which Veloso wrote when he as there.
The musical influences they took back to Brazil.

The students then tell the other groups what they have discovered.

Discussion. They all read the final section about Gil, music and society. Do they agree that music can connect the past, the present and the future?

Further discussion. Ask for suggestions of other performers who are also interested in social or political issues. Do they think that 'entertainment' and 'social issues' go well together? What pieces of music, poems or pieces of art show this? This is preparation for the Checkout Spot activity.

Worksheet 2
Vocabulary – Festivals, Poverty
Grammar – Past simple
Content – Current events, History, L1, Music

Pages 6 and 7 – What strange music!

This article describes an experimental theatre group in Vienna and their music.

Warm up. What type of music does the title suggest? What elements can be strange: the players, the instruments, the sound or something else?

Vocabulary check. Ask for the names of musical instruments in English. Write a list on the board. Then ask for the names of common vegetables. Write these on another part of the board. Is there any connection between the two lists?

The students then read the Introduction and the first three paragraphs of the article. They discover the link between the instruments and the vegetables.

Discussion. They read the rest of the article and discuss their answers to the final question.

Checkout Spot. Encourage the students to make their own 'instruments' to make strange music. They can experiment with recording this, altering the volume and speed to change the sound.

Worksheet 3
Vocabulary –Musical instruments, Vegetables, Sounds
Grammar – Giving instructions, Sequencing
Content – Music, Science

Pages 8 and 9 – The story of a group: the Beatles

Warm up. Check what the students know about the Beatles and their music. Write their suggestions on the board under these six headings:

names	their hits
city	their lives
first performances	other facts

Checking and recording facts. The students then read the article and check their ideas. Add new facts to the list, or make a mind map. e.g.

Discussion. Ask the students to look at each of the five section headings. Each one introduces the section and summarises the content. Ask them to read each title and section carefully. Can they suggest any better titles?

Writing/Groupwork. Ask the students to plan a similar article about a different music group. They should discuss and decide:

The section headings; The illustrations; The title

They write this outline on a piece of paper to show the plan of their article. Pin these up around the classroom. Compare and discuss the different approaches and ideas.

Pages 10 and 11 – Where do films come from?

This two-page article describes how some films are based on well known stories or books.

Warm up. Ask the students to suggest any examples which are based on such things. e.g. the Harry Potter films. How does the film differ from the original? What kind of things make this difference, e.g. visual medium, length, number of characters?

Has anybody seen the films shown here, *Troy* or *The Motorcycle Diaries*? If so, what did they think of them?

Troy. Brainstorm what the students know about the Trojan War.

Reading for information. Ask them to find the answers to these questions in the text. Read out one sentence and give them enough time to find the information.

Who wrote about the Trojan War?	(Homer)
When did he do this?	(In about 1000BC/3000 years ago)
Who fought in it?	(Greeks and Trojans)
Why?	(Paris, the Prince of Troy, ran away with Helen, the wife of the Greek King of Sparta)
Where did they fight?	(Outside the city of Troy)
How long did the war continue for?	(10 years)
Who suggested a clever trick?	(Odysseus)
What was the famous present to the Trojans?	(A big wooden horse)
What was inside it?	(Greek soldiers)
What happened to the city then?	(The Greeks burned it)

You can also treat these questions like a Quiz Show.

Discussion. Ask them to look at the last sentence: 'That's international entertainment!' Why is this film international?

(Greek – original story. German – director. Mexican, Maltese, British – locations. Bulgarian – singers.)

The Motorcycle Diaries. Discuss the meaning of 'icon'. (Originally it was a religious painting of a saint, especially in the Orthodox churches. It is now used for a picture of a person that is so widely recognised that it also symbolises a movement or idea.)

Can they think of people who have become icons? Brainstorm what the name 'Che Guevara' means to the class.

Read and correct. Emphasise that the article looks at two versions of this story: the book (Che Guevara's diary) and the film based on it. First of all, the students read the section about the book. They correct this faulty information.

This is a fictional story.	(It's a true story)
The two friends went to North America.	(They wanted to, but they didn't get there)
They rode a motorbike for the whole journey.	(It broke down so they had to hitchhike or walk)
They didn't do any work on the trip.	(They also worked in a leper colony)
The trip was not very important for the two friends.	(It changed their lives)
Guevara became famous as a result of this journey.	(He became famous when he went to Cuba)

Writing. Based on the correct information, the students write an advert for the book or the film.

Read and find. The students then read the section about the film and find this information.

Why was Alberto important for the film director? (He told him about the trip and showed him the photos from it)
What did Robert Redford do? (He encouraged the director to make the film)
What nationality is the film director? (Brazilian)
What other famous film did he make? (Central Station)
What language is used on the film? (Spanish)

Writing. Discuss the various aspects of a film that need to be considered in a film review, e.g. writing. directing. photography, acting. Then ask them to choose a film they have seen which has a story based on a book. They plan a review of it, covering the various aspects. They can give each one a star rating.

Worksheet 4.
Vocabulary – Films + Wars + Journeys
Grammar – Past Simple for narrative
Content – Geography, History, L1

Pages 12 and 13 – Music opens doors

Note: This article describes a music group whose name is the Amazon Youth Cello Choir. Although 'choir' is more normally used for a group of singers, the group is made up of young cellists. You can follow their progress on their website, www.acvapara.com

Warm up. Do a brainstorming with the class on the word 'Amazon'. What does it suggest to them? Use the questions and answers at the beginning of the article as a focus. Then compare their ideas with what one of the cello group says: 'They think there are wild animals in the streets here!'

Jigsaw reading. Divide the class into seven groups and ask each of them to read one of the seven sections. They then discuss their sections, asking and answering questions, before reading the whole article.

Writing. The students write an advert for a concert to be given by this group.

Worksheet 5
Vocabulary – Music
Grammar – Past simple for narrative
Content – Geography, Music

Pages 14 and 15 – Music sells!

This article is in two parts. The first part (Page 14) describes how a piece of music by Handel, who lived in the 17th and 18th centuries, was used by a famous jeans company in a recent advertising campaign. It describes the way 'old' music can attract attention to new products. The second part (Page 15) describes how many modern musicians and composers subsidise their serious work by recording commercial music.

Warm up. Do a class brainstorming on Handel and his music. Write any suggestions on the board.

Read and find. The students read this first part of the article to find the answers to these questions.

What is the full name of the man in the picture?	(George Frederick Handel)
What did he do to be famous?	(He composed music)
What nationality was he?	(German)
Where did he live for some of his life?	(In London)
What are some of his famous compositions?	(*The Water Music. The Messiah*)
When did he die?	(In 1759)
What is the image behind the text on these two pages?	(Jeans)

They compare their answers to the ideas they suggested in the brainstorming.

Discussion. After they have read the second part of the article, on Page 15, the students discuss the ideas in it.

Out-of-class. Ask the students to listen to the music in some TV or film adverts, and decide if it is modern or old. They should notice how the sound fits with the visual images, and with the 'message' of the advert.

Groupwork. The students plan TV adverts for a jeans advertising campaign. They decide what images and music to use. Each group presents their ideas and tries to impress the rest of the class that theirs is best. This can be done as a roleplay: rival advertising agencies presenting their projects to the company.

Pages 16 and 17 – The story of a group: Franz Ferdinand

This article describes a relatively 'new' group to contrast with a well known one like the Beatles (Pages 8 and 9). The students can monitor their activities and future growth through their websites, www.franzferdinand.co.uk and www.franzferdinand.org, as well as through the musical press.

The article is a collection of background information, quotations and photos, plus the words of part of one of their songs, *Auf Achse*.

Warm up. Before reading the article, brainstorm anything the class know about this group: the members, where they come from, their albums.

Read and find. Ask the students to read the article and find the answers to these questions.

The band's name is 'Franz Ferdinand'. Who was he?
Why did they choose this name?
How do we know they are good friends?
How do we know that they work hard?
Where did some of the group study?
Why does one of their songs have a German title?

Writing. In groups, the students write five Quiz Questions based on the article. They give these questions to another group to answer.

Discussion. Ask the students to look quickly at the article about the Beatles (Pages 8 and 9) and find some similarities or differences between the two groups.

Pages 18 and 19 – A recipe for making music

This article describes the various stages in composing and recording a piece of music. It is based on music produced acoustically rather than digitally – a form which is becoming popular again.

Warm up. Find out if the students know how music is mixed and recorded. Check they can recognise the instruments mentioned in the article:

acoustic guitar
bass guitar
drums
piano
saxophone

Writing. Each group writes a one-sentence reply to the question. They take it in turn to read these out. The class decides if they are accurate replies.

Page 20 – The (modern) circus is coming

This article describes ways in which modern circuses are different from traditional ones.

Warm up. Find out if the students have been to a circus. If so, what did they like/not like about it. If not, what do they know about circuses? Would they like to go? Why (not)?

People and Animals. Ask the students to read these two sections and find the circus performer who fits each of these descriptions.

They throw and catch objects.	(jugglers)
They 'fly' through the air.	(trapeze artists)
They make people laugh.	(clowns)
They can stand on their back legs.	(horses)

Modern developments. Ask them to read this section and find:

A country with a lot of theatre schools.	(France)
Two physical skills that circus students learn.	(dancing; playing musical instruments)
Two special circus skills that they learn.	(juggling; flying on the trapeze)
The name of a person who is training performers in Brazil.	(Pierrot Bidon)
His nationality.	(French)

Discussion. Are circuses cruel? Are modern circuses better than the old ones? Why (not)?

Page 21 – The clowns' story

This article describes the way in which clowns have developed in different parts of the world.

Warm up. Ask the students to identify the clown in the centre of the page (Charlie Chaplin). Find out if they know any other famous clowns. What about modern comedians and comics? Ask for suggestions. What do they do? e.g. tell stories, dance, tell jokes.

Writing. After they have read the article, ask the students to each write one factual question about it on a piece of paper. Fold these in half so that the questions are hidden. Put them into a container. The students take it in turns to draw out a question, read it aloud, and answer it. If they cannot, or give a wrong answer, the question is put back. One point for a correct answer.

Worksheet 6
Vocabulary – Circus, Clowns
Grammar – Describing people and actions
Content – History, L1, Music

Page 22 – Entertainment quiz: do you know?

Movie prizes. The students can choose one of these Film Festivals and find out who won the prizes at it this year.

Page 23 – Projects

Ask the students to read all the projects carefully in order to decide which ones are interesting for them. Find out which are the most/least interesting for this class and if any of them just interest one person. These projects can be done in groups, pairs or individually. Some of them may link with those done in other subjects, e,g. History or Science.

Encourage the students to also review and present the things they have been doing in the various Checkout Spot mini-projects.

Page 24 – Chatrooms

Teens chat. The students can make up similar exchanges about a new fashion accessory.

Can you believe it?. Ask about other unusual festivals they have seen. Where? What happened? Did they enjoy it?

Worksheet 7
Vocabulary – Entertainment
Grammar – Word order
Content – Art, Design, L1, Music

Worksheet 8
Vocabulary – Entertainment
Grammar – Present simple for descriptions
Content – Art, Design, Geography, History, L1

Title review. The students can do a review to help inform other people. This can be of the whole magazine, or of specific articles. They can agree their own criteria, or you can put this framework on the board for them to copy and adapt.

CRITERIA	ARTICLE	STARS	COMMENTS
Interest			
Information			
Design			
Photos			
Checkout Spot			
Other			

Test Worksheet
The aim of the test is to encourage the students to look back through the articles in order to check facts, notice details and find specific information to answer the questions.

Extra teacher's resources

These websites are worth visiting for further information.

Amazon cello project: www.acvapara.org
The Beatles: www.beatlesstory.com
Franz Ferdinand: www.franzferdinand.co.uk
Glastonbury: www.glastonburyfestivals.co.uk
Strange music: www.vegetableorchestea.org

Entertainment Worksheet 1

References: **It's Festival Time!** – Page 3

Focus:
Vocabulary Festival oganising and content, Music styles
Grammar Description
Content Music

Activities

1. Solving problems!

Find these words in the article. Why are they important for the festival organisers?

a. insurance
b. tickets
c. toilets
d. traffic
e. weather

2. Types of music

Look at the last paragraph. It mentions eight types of music.
Write them here and then add your favourite group or singer for each one.

	TYPE OF MUSIC	PEOPLE
a.		
b.		
c.		
d.		
e.		
f.		
g.		
h.		

Compare your ideas with other people.

3. Festival blog

Decide to be one of these people:

a. a festival organiser b. a performer c. a member of the audience

Write an entry for a festival blog as that person. It can be factual, funny, emotional ... or a mixture!

Share your blog entries with other people. Comment on the other entries.

Entertainment Worksheet 2

References:	**Festivals: More than the music** – Page 4 **Behind the music** – Page 5	
Focus:	**Vocabulary**	Festivals, Poverty
	Grammar	Past simple
	Content	Current events, History, L1, Music

Activities

1. Festival facts

Read about Rock in Rio-Lisboa (page 4) quickly and identify these people.

a. The Brazilian Minister for Culture who performed at the festival. ______________________

b. The Portuguese rock star who performed with him. ______________________

c. The author of the song they performed. ______________________

d. The ex-Beatle who was also there. ______________________

2. Festival values

Glastonbury and Rock in Rio-Lisboa both had a social agenda. Which festival...? Put G or R.

a. had debates on youth, social differences, technology and world peace? ☐

b. had places to exercise? ☐

c. organised discussions about GM crops? ☐

d. had a three-minute silence to promote world peace? ☐

e. helped promote work in Third World countries? ☐

Write about any other 'serious' things that happened at these festivals.

3. More musicians with a message.

Do you remember Live 8 in 2005? One of the organisers was the musician Bob Geldof. What do you know about him? Can you find out more?

a. What nationality is Bob Geldof? ______________________

b. What was the name of his group? ______________________

c. What event did he organise in 1985? ______________________

d. What did it do? ______________________

e. What famous song was part of this work? ______________________

f. What happened in 2005 at the same time as Live 8? ______________________

g. What is the slogan for Live 8? ______________________

h. What happened during the Live 8 event? ______________________

i. Another famous musician was one of the organisers. ______________________

What's his name, group and nationality? ______________________

Entertainment Worksheet 3

References: **What strange music!** – Pages 6 and 7

Focus:
Vocabulary Musical instruments, Vegetables, Sounds
Grammar Giving instructions, Sequencing
Content Music, Science

Activities

1. Musical instruments

Match the names and the instruments.

a. cello
b. drums
c. flute
d. guitar
e. maracas
f. trumpet
g. violin

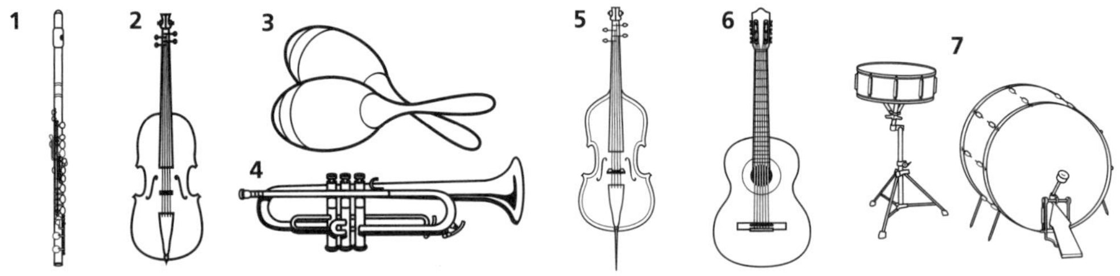

2. Vegetables

Match the names and the vegetables.

a. cabbage
b. carrot
c. cucumber
d. onion
e. peppers
f. pumpkin
g. tomato

3. Inventions

The musicians invent their instruments – the cucuphone is made from a cucumber. They say 'You can invent your own sound'.

Read the descriptions for making a carrot flute (Page 6) and the cucuphone (Page 7). Notice the words at the beginning of each new step.

First of all, … Then, … After this, …. Finally, ….

Design a new vegetable instrument. Write the instructions for making it here.
Plan the different steps. Connect them with the words and phrases above.

INSTRUCTIONS FOR MAKING A ………….

Finally, draw a picture of it and invent a name for it.

References: **Where do movies come from?** – Pages 10 and 11

Focus:
Vocabulary Films, War, Journeys
Grammar Past simple for narrative
Content Geography, History, L1

Activities

1. Find the story

Choose five recent films. Where do their stories come from? Are these original, history, biography, factual or fantasy? Make a note of them here.

	FILM	STORY TYPE
a.		
b.		
c.		
d.		
e		

2. Troy

Write down the things you already know about the Trojan War.
Now answers these question about it.

a. Who wrote about this war?
b. In the story, which armies were fighting?
c. What was the reason?
d. Where did they fight?
e. How long did the war go on for?
f. Who suggested a clever trick?
g. What was the famous present?
h. What happened to the city?

3. The Motorcycle Diaries

Read about the film and answer the questions.

a. Why was Alberto important for the director?
b. What did Robert Redford do?
c. Who was the director and what nationality is he?
d. What other famous film did he direct?

4. Film review

Choose one of these films, or another one of the same type. Write a review of it.
Plan the review carefully. Describe the different aspects of it (directing, acting, photography, music, etc.).

Entertainment Worksheet 5

References: **Music opens doors: The Amazon Youth Cello Choir** – Pages 12 and 13

Focus:
Vocabulary Music
Grammar Past simple for narrative, Asking questions
Content Geography, Music

Activities

1. Amazon Brainstorm
What do you know about the Amazon? Where is it? Which countries does it go through. How long is it? What is the country like? What cities are near it? What's the climate like?

2. Youth Cello Group Facts
The article is organised into eight sections. Look at one section at a time and find this information in it. Make notes.

The Place
a. Where is Belem?
b. What is the climate like in Belem?
c. What do some Brazilians think about the city?

The People
d. Where did Aureo first study the cello?
e. Where did he continue his studies?
f. When he returned to Belem, what did he do?
g. What did one student say about the cello?
h. What were the good things about being in the group?

The Problems
i. Why were the following things a problem for the students?
- cost
- time
- transport
- size

Overcoming Problems
j. What other problems did they have to overcome?

Success!
k. What did the group do after a few years?
l. Where did they do this?

A Lucky Meeting
m. Who met the group?
n. What did he decide to do?
o. What was in the programmes?
p. What did he give them?

Playing to the world
q. Who heard the programmes?
r. What were two results for the group?

The future
s. Is the future for the group good or bad? What do you think?

PHOTOCOPIABLE

Entertainment Worksheet 6

References: **The (modern) circus is coming** – Page 20
The clowns' story – Page 21

Focus:
Vocabulary Circus, Clowns
Grammar Describing people and actions
Content History, L1, Music

Activities

1. Clowns and circuses
Make a Mind Map with one of these words. Here are two examples.

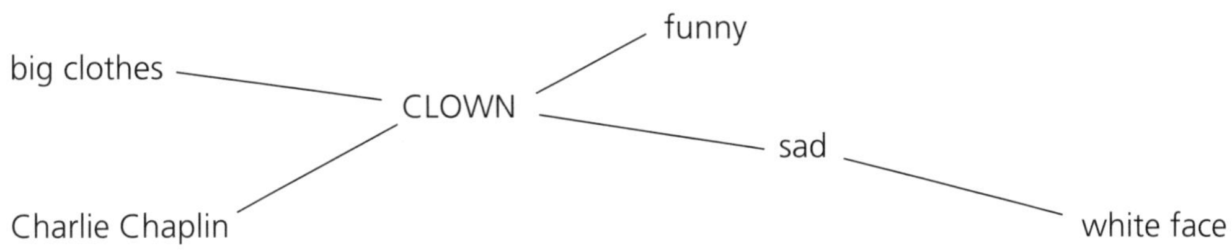

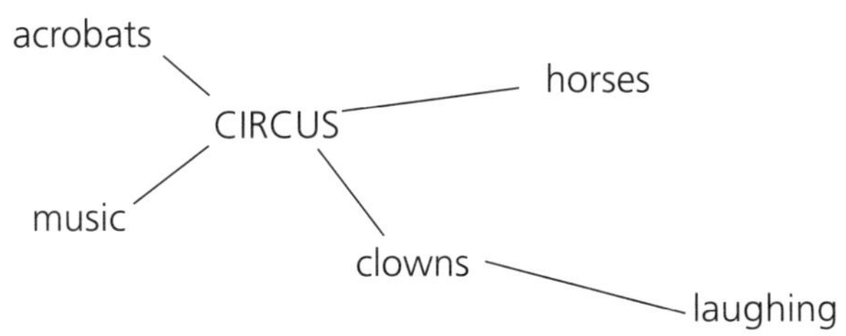

Compare your ideas.

2. The modern circus
Read the article on Page 20. Make a note of the differences between traditional and modern circuses. Add ideas of your own.

CIRCUSES	
TRADITIONAL	MODERN

Which type do you prefer? Write a paragraph to support your choice. Give your reasons.

3. Telling jokes
Do you know any good jokes? Write one of them here.
Exchange it with someone. Read your jokes. Do you both laugh?

Entertainment Worksheet 7

References: **All**

Focus:

Vocabulary Entertainment
Grammar Word order
Content Art, Design, L1, Music

Activities

1. What is entertainment?
There are lots of different types of entertainment, e.g. film, theatre. Write down as many as you can here.

Compare your ideas. Make a class list.

2. Each type of entertainment has different aspects, e.g. jobs, money, promotion, audiences, performers.

Look through this magazine and categorise the articles into type of entertainment (e.g. music, dance) and 'aspect'. Some of them may contain several examples.

ENTERTAINMENT: Analysis	ARTICLE	TYPE(S) OF ENTERTAINMENT	ASPECT(S)

3. Planning
Is there a good balance? How would you change it?
Plan a new magazine about Entertainment. Note your ideas here.

ENTERTAINMENT: New edition	ARTICLE	TYPE(S) OF ENTERTAINMENT	ASPECT(S)

References: **All**

Focus:
Vocabulary Entertainment
Grammar Present simple for descriptions
Content Art, Design, Geography, History, L1

Activities

1. Choose the entertainer
Look through *Entertainment* and choose one of the entertainers who interest you.

2. Promo time
You are going to design a website, an ad or a poster to attract people to an event where this entertainer will appear. You can work in pairs or in groups.

First of all, discuss and agree the important features of the event.
Make notes here.

DATE ______________________________

PLACE(S) ______________________________

TYPE OF EVENT ______________________________

MAIN FOCUS OF THE EVENT ______________________________

ROLE OF THE ENTERTAINER ______________________________

NAME OF THE EVENT ______________________________

MAIN SELLING POINT(S) ______________________________

OTHER ______________________________

Then decide:
What factual information to include.
What kind of picture best expresses the character of this event and the entertainer.
A title or slogan to attract people.

3. Organise an exhibition of the results. The class can vote on the most effective design.

Entertainment Test Worksheet

Name: ____________________

Total Points (1 per question) ____________

1. Look through Entertainment. Identify these articles. Write the page number and the title.

a. Read about a group from Liverpool.
   Page ________ Title ____________________
b. Meet a new group.
   Page ________ Title ____________________
c. Some musicians live near a famous river.
   Page ________ Title ____________________
d. Look at a funny little man.
   Page ________ Title ____________________
e. Do you like vegetable soup?
   Page ________ Title ____________________
f. Try a different kind of recipe.
   Page ________ Title ____________________
g. Find a new use for classical music.
   Page ________ Title ____________________
h. Life in a big tent.
   Page ________ Title ____________________
i. A crowd of spectators, some musicians – and lots of other things too.
   Page ________ Title ____________________
j. Here are two musicians with double lives.
   Page ________ Title ____________________

2. Are these statements true or false? Check them with the articles and circle T or F.

a.	Page 3.	It's easy tom organise a festival.	T F
b.	Page 4.	Festivals have lots of different kinds of entertainment.	T F
c.	Page 5.	Musicians only want to play their music.	T F
d.	Page 6.	Cabbage leaves squeak.	T F
e.	Page 8.	The Beatles were a great American group.	T F
f.	Page 11.	Che Guevara was born in Cuba.	T F
g.	Page 15.	Many serious musicians play commercial music.	T F
h.	Page 16.	Franz Ferdinand is a new group from Austria.	T F

3. What is the English word for these things?

a. A person who takes part in entertainment. ____________
b. This person watches entertainment. ____________
c. This machine makes voices and sounds louder. ____________
d. A person who writes poems. ____________
e. An enthusiastic supporter for a group. ____________
f. This person plays drums in a group. ____________
g. Special music for a film or TV programme. ____________
h. A public performance of music. ____________
i. The person who controls the sound in a recording. ____________

Topics

Teacher's Notes: **CONSUMERS** Intermediate

Ideas for use

This magazine explores different aspects of the modern consumer society. It does this from the starting point of the everyday lives and surroundings of the students themselves. They are encouraged to think about the nature of modern society in relation to themselves and to other people.

Crosscurricular links: History; Geography; L1 Language and Literature; other languages; Science and Technology; Music; Art.

Don't forget! You can find comprehensive ideas for different types of activity to use with all the titles in the Topics series on pages 113-117 of this Teacher's Book. Remember to identify the Consumer Spy activities for each article.

Cover and Contents

Encourage the students to browse through *Consumers* and look at the range of articles, illustrations and design styles.

Discussion: What do the photos suggest? Are they a good depiction of *Consumers*? What other images could be used? You may want to explore these linked words. Refer to a monolingual dictionary to check some of their uses.

- Consumer(s) *[noun]* People who buy and use things.
- Consumer *[adjective]* (always used with a noun) Relating something to consumers, e.g. consumer society.
- Consume *[verb]* To use a supply of something.
- Consumerism *[noun]* The activity or practice of buying and using things.

Page 1 – Letter

This letter contains a series of statements about the consumer world. They will serve as a general 'warm-up' for the topic and help to show what really interests each person.

Ask the students if they can suggest answers to the questions in the first paragraph: 'Who are the consumers?' 'What do they consume?' 'Are there better ways of having a happy life in our consumer society?'

What do the students think of when they see or hear the word 'consumer'? Build up a mind map on the board with their suggestions. E.g.:

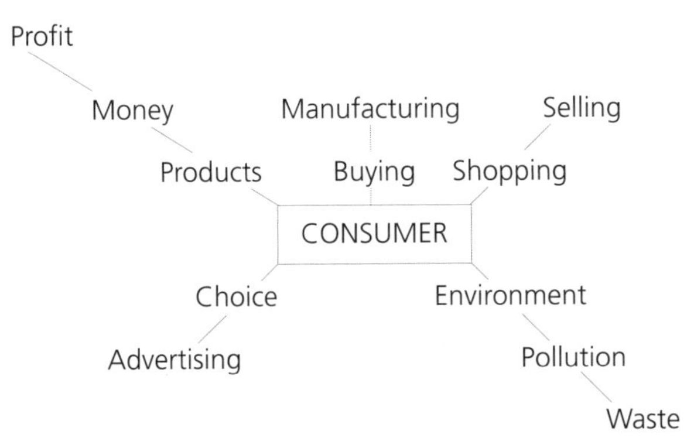

Make sure that the students understand (and can identify) the Consumer Spy icon.

Discussion. Which titles are easy to understand (e.g. *The state of our planet*) and which are more difficult (e.g. *UNICEF works!*)?

Speculation/Groupwork. The students can choose one title and write down what they think the article will be about. They can discuss their ideas within the group, or with other groups. They can then scan the article to check.

Discussion: What kind of articles would the students include in a new magazine about consumers and the consumer society?

Page 2 – Check it out

See page 118 for different activities to use with this reference page.

Page 3 – Let's go shopping!

Have the students look at the photos and identify the different types of shopping experience. How many types of shopping places can the students name (e.g. store, boutique, supermarket, street market…)? What are their favourite places to shop for various things (e.g. clothes, computer equipment, music, …)? Do they agree? Which are the most important factors: price, location, choice? Or others?

Writing. Ask the students to choose their favourite shopping place or store. Get them to write a paragraph about it for a local Tourist Guidebook. Before they begin, discuss what features they should mention in their description. Write these on the board. e.g.:

Name
Location / phone number / website
Opening hours
Speciality
One positive thing about it
One negative thing

Worksheet 1
Vocabulary – Shops, shopping, Buying, Selling
Grammar – Giving reasons, Word formation
Content – L1

Pages 4 and 5 – Fashion: What's new?

Identify the key words in the photos:

mini *pointed* *flares* *pony* *cut*

Can the students guess the meanings/make up definitions for these words (e.g. a pony is a small horse with a long tail) or apply them to other things (pointed ears)?

Ask the students to look at the pairs of pictures on Page 4. One shows modern fashion, the other a similar style from the past. Can they guess the dates of the older items?

Miniskirt - 1960s;
Pointed shoes – 18th century;
Flares – 1970s;
Ponytail – 18th century;
Cut cloth – 16th century.

Worksheet 2
Vocabulary – Describing clothes
Grammar – Collocation, Present Continuous
Content – Art, Design, L1

Discussion. The students can use the fashion pictures to discuss their likes and dislikes in clothes. Ask them to bring similar photos to class to discuss as examples of good and bad fashion. Ask them to discover what the article says about Ads, Rubbish, Recycling, Charities.

Ads – They encourage an appetite for change.
Rubbish – People often throw away their old clothes.
Recycling – You can make paper out of old clothes.
Charities – They can use the money from selling old clothes to help people.

The students can also choose one of these words and follow the page references to another article linked to it.

Ads – Page 6;
Rubbish – Pages 12/13;
Recycling and Charities – Pages 10/11.

They can present the extra information they discover there to the rest of the class (e.g. poster, spoken summary) and add their own ideas.

Pages 6 and 7 – Ad-speak

If necessary, explain that the term 'ad-speak' refers to the language of advertising. In the same way, 'child speak' is the language of children, 'teen-speak' the special language of teenagers, 'computer-speak' is the language of IT enthusiasts, and so on.

Warmup. Before they read the article, get the students to bring examples of ads to the class. Discuss the different styles and types of approach in these. Are they aggressive, persuasive, etc.? How does each ad use words, design, colours and images to send its message? What consumer group(s) is it addressing? Is the ad effective? (Links: L1 Language, Art)

The article identifies seven different types of ads and approaches. Have the students find these words and discuss what they mean. e.g.:

intriguing – you don't know exactly what it means
persuasive – it persuades you to do something
challenging
image-conscious
scientific
social-conscience
shock

Pairwork. The students choose one of these types. One student reads the description, the other asks questions about it (without reading the text). Can they add more ideas of their own? Do the ads the students have brought fit into these seven groups, or would they suggest others?

Possible extra project. Encourage the students to use the information in this article to analyse the language and design of ads in their own environment. Ask them to bring examples of ads from magazines and decide whether these are effective or ineffective. Encourage them to identify the target groups the ads are aimed at and to analyse the explicit and implicit messages.

Game. Ask the students to think of an object, and then to make up an advertising slogan for it without mentioning the object. e.g.: 'Time is precious!' (a watch or clock). The rest of the class try to guess the object in a 20 Questions game. They can only ask 'Yes/No' questions.

Worksheet 3
Vocabulary – Advertising
Grammar – Stating opinions and giving reasons
Content – Art, Design, L1

Pages 8 and 9 – Innovation, innovation, innovation!

Identify the two subject areas
a. Watching soaps on a mobile phone.
b. Renting a car or bike very cheaply.

Before they read the article, ask the students to guess what new ideas there could be for each of these.

Half the class reads about one of the ideas, and the other half reads about the other. They then form pairs (one from each half) and tell each other about the innovative idea. Their partner questions them about its cost, practicality, usefulness, etc.

Discussion: The students suggest innovative ideas for other products. These can be serious or crazy.

Page 10 – Charity shops

Ask the students what a charity shop is. *[It is run by a charity, and sells things which people have donated. In this way, it raises money for the charity.]* Do these shops exist in your area? Can they name any local charities? What do these do? (This is a preparation for the Consumer Spy activity.)

Have them look at the three photos: can they guess what each of these charities specialises in?

British Heart Foundation: heart disease
Cancer Research UK: cancer
PDSA: People's Dispensary for Sick Animals. This van collects things from people's houses

Encourage them to also identify any details in the photos that are different from those in their own environment.

Discussion. The question near the bottom: 'How much money goes to the people who need it?' What kind of expenses do charities have? Is it right that they keep some money for these expenses? How can we check on this?

Page 11 – The travels of a blouse

The article will have more effect if the students can follow the journey. Consult an atlas and draw a rough diagram on the board to show these places.

UK: Leicester (town); Southampton (port).
Ocean: Atlantic; Mediterranean; Indian Ocean; Suez Canal.
Mozambique: Beira (port); Tete (capital).
Zambezi River.
Zambia: Chipata (city).

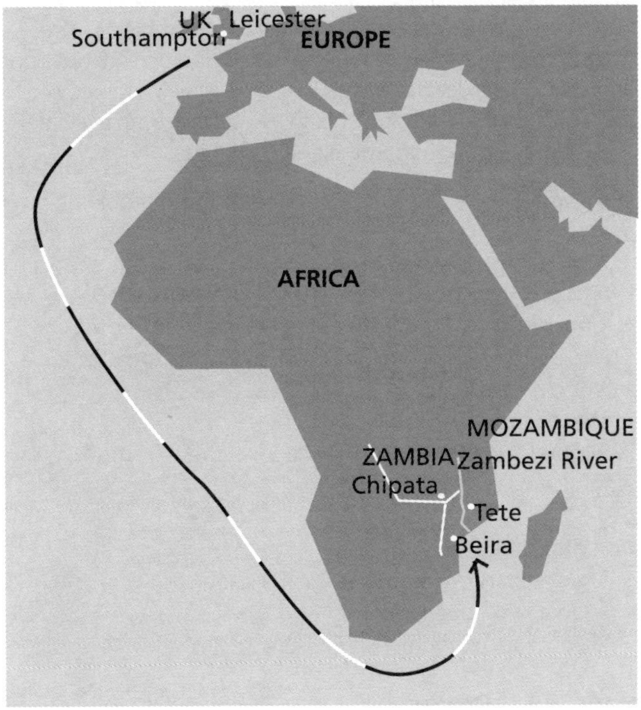

You can use this article for a jigsaw reading activity (see Page 9). Three groups of students can write questions about 'their' text, which another group answers (reading for information).

Quiz. Ask the students to answer these questions based on the text. Read the questions aloud to them and see who can find the answer first.

'How far did the blouse travel?' (16,000 kilometres)
'Where did its journey begin?' (In South-east England)
'Where did the journey end?' (In Zambia, in Africa)
'How did it travel?' (By lorry, ship, and another lorry)
'How much money did the blouse cost in Zambia?' (US$3)

Worksheet 4
Vocabulary – Journeys
Grammar – Past simple
Content – Geography, L1

Pages 12 and 13 – UNICEF works!

Check if the students recognise the name UNICEF. You can use the five questions on Page 12 to elicit information from the class, or they can read the questions and answers in pairs. Is this information new? Do they know anything else about UNICEF?

Speculation. Have the students look at the photo of the girl. Who is she? What nationality? What's her name? What's her problem?

Next ask them to look at the other photo. Can they identify any of the garbage? What is the boy doing? (Finding plates that are not broken and that can be sold.)

Text. Ask the students to find out what happened in these stages in the project.

Stage 1: UNICEF identified the problem. (e.g. A lot of unemployed people live on rubbish dumps. They also work there – they sell the rubbish.)
Stage 2: They helped the adults. (e.g. They helped them to form an association and to sell the rubbish direct.)
Stage 3: They helped the young people. (e.g. They helped them to make a youth centre, and they gave money to the families if the kids went to school.)
Stage 4: They solved some problems in the schools. (e.g. They had projects to help the students to integrate and to help the teachers too.)

Discussion. Is 'learning from experience' a good approach? Which groups of people are involved? Encourage the students to visit the UNICEF website, www.unicef.org and find out about other projects. They can report on these to the class.

Page 14 – Phones can do anything!

Find out what the students know about phones before they read the article. (e.g. When were they invented? Where? What were the first ones like? How were they different from modern ones? etc.) If most of the students use phones a lot, ask them to do a class survey on things like:

phones at home (Who has one?)
people with mobile phones (Who has one?)
public phones (Where are they? How much do they cost?)
types of phones (How many types are there?)
main uses of phones (student/family/friends)
useful numbers (emergency, information)
cost of phoning, etc.

Can any students find out and explain how phones work? (Link: Science)

Worksheet 5
Vocabulary – Telephone language
Grammar – General
Content – L1

Page 15 – The state of our planet

This article is an introduction to the Environmental Project described on Pages 16 and 17. Use the three numbered photos to focus on (1) traffic, (2) garbage/rubbish, (3) air pollution. Find out what the students know about these problems. What can be done to solve them?

Ask the students to look at the blue box above the Word File and find the 3 'R' words (Reduce/Reuse/Recycle) that the article suggests can help us with these environmental problems. Have them check the meanings of the words in a dictionary.

Pages 16 and 17 – An environmental project

Note: This project first appeared on a BBC educational website (www.bbc.co.uk/cbbc). The site also contains accounts of actual projects done in UK schools. Type 'environment projects' in the search box.

On these pages, there are four 'Missions' which the students have to complete in order to discover the final 'R' word: Respect. The places for these are ringed in the top screen and listed below it:

1. House 2. Room 3. School 4. Beach

Each Mission is presented as a quiz or puzzle. The students can solve these in pairs or individually.

Mission 1 (Reduce-House). The students choose the best ways to reduce the use of energy.

Mission 2 (Reuse-Room). They decide the best way to reuse some personal possessions.

Mission 3 (Recycle- School). Here they decide which objects can be recycled [R] and which ones should be thrown away [TA].

Mission 4 (Beach). First they choose the picture with the best clothes to wear [B] when cleaning a beach.

Then they decide which articles are safe to pick up to recycle [S] and which are dangerous [D].

Discussion. Understanding safety and danger, and choosing appropriate clothes, leads us to the 4th 'R' word: Respect (the environment). This is the answer to the question at the end of the article. Use the students' ideas as a basis for discussion about ways of solving these general problems. This prepares them for the Consumer Spy activity.

Writing. The students can make up similar quizzes.

Pages 18 and 19 – Consumer hot topics: obesity 🎧

Note: If obesity is a personal problem for any of the students, be careful how you discuss it.

You can treat this article as one long one, or two separate but linked ones. (*Food intake versus energy output* presents some facts on Page 18, and *Getting rid of the calories* suggests some solutions on Page 19.)

Use it for jigsaw reading and fact-finding activities.

Ask the students to look at the three factual tables in the article. Do any of the statistics surprise them? Can they suggest any other examples for each table?

Discussion 1. Which item would they choose to eat less of or give up?

Discussion 2. Favourite tips for fighting weight (serious and funny).

Pages 20 and 21 – Healthy living 🎧

Note: Again, you can treat these two pages as one long article on aspects of Healthy Living, or as two separate but linked ones: *Modern life: facts and figures* (Page 20), and *Problem solving* (Page 21).

Which of these - exercise/diet/emotional health - is the most serious problem? Ask the students to read what the article says about each one. Do they agree?

Discussion 1. Have their ideas changed after reading this? What is the most important idea in it?

Discussion 2. What do they think of the 'healthy diet' shown in the diagram? They can draw diagrams of their own diets (actual and/or ideal).

Are there other important 'Healthy living' problems? (e.g. Page 21 suggests ways of fighting eating disorders, depression and stress.) It is ideal for a jigsaw reading activity in three groups. Encourage the students to ask questions, to evaluate these ideas and to suggest their own solutions.

Writing. A similar list of tips for one of these problem areas.

Page 22 – Consumers quiz: Do you know?

1. Chocolate facts: The students can make up similar Chocolate quiz questions, or choose another topic, e.g. ice cream.

2. Water industry

3. Money word puzzle: They can use these as models for writing similar quizzes and puzzles.

✏ **Worksheet 6**

Vocabulary – Computers, Globalisation
Grammar – General
Content – Geography, IT, Science

Page 23 – Projects

Ask the students to read all the projects carefully. They must decide which ones are interesting for them. Which is the most/least interesting project for the class?

The projects can be done in groups, pairs or by students working alone. Some projects may fit in with those done in other school subjects, e.g. History or Science. The important thing is that each person chooses a topic that really interests them.

Encourage them to also review and present the things they have done in the various Consumer Spy activities and to present them as a class exhibition.

Page 24 – Chatrooms 🎧

Teens chat. The students can make up similar dialogues about one of their favourite possessions. They can also read this aloud, conveying the feelings through intonation.

Fun chat. What other money proverbs do they know in English or in L1?

Use the proverbs for a 'Find Your Partner' activity. Divide each saying into two parts and write each phrase on a piece of paper (eight phrases). e.g.:

Money doesn't...
...grow on trees.
Money makes...
...the world go round.

All that glitters...
...is not gold.
Love of money...
...is the root of all evil.

Give one piece of paper to each student. They go round the class to find a partner whos has the beginning or ending of their phrase. Then, together, they invent a new beginning or ending for 'their' proverb. Ask the pairs to read out their sentences to the class.

Can you believe it? The quotation from Wordsworth may link with similar thoughts from romantic poets in your country.

Worksheet 7
Vocabulary – Advertising
Grammar – Persuasion
Content – Art, Design, L1

Worksheet 8
Vocabulary – Arguing and justifying
Grammar – Giving reasons and justifying opinions
Content – L1

Title review. The students can do a review of the whole magazine to inform another class.They can do this on the magazine as a whole, or on specific articles. Have them discuss and design their own criteria, or draw this chart on the board as a model for them to copy or adapt.

CRITERIA	ARTICLE	STARS	COMMENTS
Interest			
Information			
Design			
Photos			
Checkout Spot			
Other			

Test Worksheet
The aim of the test is to encourage the students to look back through the magazine in order to check facts, notice details, and find specific information to answer the questions. It is not designed as a memory test!

Extra teacher's resources

These publications and websites are worth consulting for further information.

CBBC: www.bbc.co.uk/cbbc
FAIRTRADE: www.fairtrade.org
WWF: www.wwf.org
UNICEF: www.unicef.org
MARKETING: www.trendsetters.org

Consumers Worksheet 1

References: **Check it out** - Page 2
Let's go shopping! - Page 3

Focus:

Vocabulary	Shops, Shopping, Buying, Selling
Grammar	Giving reasons, Word formation
Content	L1

Activities

1. Different shops

Identify these different types of shopping places in the article.

a. It's usually outdoors, often in a street or square.
b. There are a lot of different shops in one place, usually indoors.
c. This shop sells a lot of different varieties of food – and sometimes clothes, CDs and other things, too.
d. A place to buy special clothes.

2. Who sells this?

What do these people sell? Use the items from the box. Add any ideas of your own.

cheese	coffee	cosmetics	fish	fruit	meat
magazines	medicines	newspapers	sugar	tea	vegetables

a. butcher
b. grocer
c. greengrocer
d. fishmonger
e. chemist
f. newsagent

3. Making decisions

Think of two things you have bought in the last month.
What made you choose them? E.g.price, fashion, usefulness, a friend.
Use the frame below. Describe each object and give the reason(s) why you bought it.
Finally, say whether you think you made a good or bad choice.

I bought this/these ____________________ . It's /They're ____________________ .
I chose it/them because ____ .
I think I made a good/bad choice because ____________________________
____

OBJECT A:

OBJECT B:

PHOTOCOPIABLE

Consumers Worksheet 2

References: **Fashion: What's New?** – Pages 4 and 5

Focus:

Vocabulary Describing clothes
Grammar Collocation, Present continuous
Content Art, Design, L1

Activities

1. Clothes vocabulary-check

Look at the photos on Pages 4 and 5. Identify these clothes and write their colour(s) next to them.

a. a denim miniskirt
b. striped flared trousers
c. baggy shorts
d. cut jeans
e. a long scarf
f. a hooded dress
g. a patterned jacket
h. modern high-heeled shoes

2. Notice the adjectives used to describe the clothes. Check the meanings in your dictionary.

baggy	cut	denim	hooded
long	modern	patterned	striped

What other clothes could each adjective describe? Write your suggestions here.

e.g. a striped sweater

a. ______________________________.
b. ______________________________.
c. ______________________________.
d. ______________________________.
e. ______________________________.
f. ______________________________.
g. ______________________________.
h. ______________________________.

3. Describing clothes

Write a short description of somebody's clothes here. Use suitable adjectives for each item.
Begin ' X is wearing __________ '

Now exchange Worksheets with a partner. Read the description and draw the clothes.
Check if the drawings are correct.

Consumers Worksheet 3

References: **Ad-speak** – Pages 6 and 7

Focus:

Vocabulary Advertising
Grammar Stating opinions and giving reasons
Content Art, Design, L1

Activities

1. Word-check

There are seven types of 'ad-speak' in the article.

challenging	image-conscious	intriguing
persuasive	scientific	shocking
	social conscience	

Read these definitions and match them with the types.

a. You don't know exactly what it means and so want to find out more.
b. These ads are designed to frighten you.
c. It tries to convince you through a lot of ' factual' information.
d. It uses reason and commonsense to convince you to do something.
e. It makes you feel that you need to have this object to be fashionable.
f. It makes you feel sympathetic – and so you give money.
g. It tells you that you have to do or buy this to be successful.

2. Ads and products

Each type is often used to advertise different types of products. Check the texts and the pictures. What products are often associated with each type of ad-speak?

Type	Typical products
Intriguing	
Persuasive	
Challenging	
Image-conscious	
Scientific	
Social-conscience	
Shocking	

Which type is designed to stop you from doing something? ______________

3. Analysing ads

Find an example of a good ad in a magazine.
What type is it? What is it advertising? How does it use words and/or visual impact to send its message?
What is the message? Which group of people (market) is it aimed at?
Why do you think it is effective?

4. Groupwork discussion

Bring your ad to class. Work in a group.
Look at the ads and read each others analyses. Do you agree with the opinions? Why (not)?

References: **The travels of a blouse** – Page 11

Focus:
Vocabulary Journeys
Grammar Past simple
Content Geography, L1

Activities

1. The journey

Find these places in an atlas. Then mark them on the map below.

England: Leicester (city); Southampton (port).
Atlantic Ocean; Mediterranean Sea; Indian Ocean; Suez Canal; Zambezi River.
Mozambique: Beira (port); Tete (capital).
Zambia: Chipata (city).

2. The people

Who did what in the story? Match the people and the events.

Dana Simons (x2)	Khalid	Mary	Priscilla Msimuko
a charity, Scope	a recycling company	a police guard	

a. ______________ decided to put her blouse in a recycling bank.
b. The bank belonged to ____________________________________
c. ______________ paid the charity for the things in the recycling bank.
They put the blouse into a package with other clothes. The package was put into a container. This travelled by ship to Mozambique.
d. The container went north by lorry to Zambia. It was valuable, so it had ______________
e. When it arrived in Chipata, a trader, ______________, bought the container.
f. His staff opened it and took out the package. A market trader, __________, bought it.
She opened the package and put the blouse on her stall.
g. A teacher, __________________, bought the blouse.
h. Back in England, _________________ felt happy to hear what had happened.

Consumers Worksheet 5

References: **Phones can do anything!** – Page 14

Focus:
Vocabulary Telephone language
Grammar General
Content L1

Activities

1. Phones Word-check
Six of these words and phrases are in the article. Three of them are not.
Match them with their definitions.

automatic connection	connect (verb)	dial (verb)	emergency numbers	long-distance call
mobile (adj.)	operator	phone card	ring tone	voicemail

a. A person who works for a telephone company and helps people with calls.
b. To press the buttons on a phone to call a person.
c. A plastic card to pay for phone calls.
d. Two phones are connected by machine or computer.
e. An electronic system to record spoken messages.
f. To make it possible for two phones to 'speak' to each other.
g. The sound which a phone makes when someone calls you.
h. An object that you can carry with you.
i. A call to a person in a distant place.
j. The numbers for the police or accidents.

2. What do people say?
Match the situations with the utterances on the right.

SITUATIONS

You call a friend in a big office. The person who answers:
a. Asks you to wait.
b. Tells you that you dialled incorrectly.
c. Suggests that you phone again later.
d. Says your friend is not there.
e. Explains that your friend is talking on the phone.

You want to know this information:
f. The number that indicates a city or part of a city.
g If you can leave a message for the person you want to speak to.

You hear this recorded message.
h. You can leave a message for your friend.
i. These are some different options.

UTTERANCES

'Sorry, you have the wrong number.'
'Hang on a minute, please.'
'That number's engaged.'
'What's the area code?'
'I'm sorry there's no reply.'
'Please speak after the tone.'
'Press 1 to hear the message again, press 2 to keep the message and press 3 to delete it.
'Can I leave a message?'
'Please call back later.'

3. Phone conversation
Choose one of the situations above, or one of your own. Write a short telephone dialogue for it.

Work with a partner. Act out your dialogues. Don't forget the sound effects!

References: **All**

Focus:
Vocabulary Computers, Globalisation
Grammar General
Content Geography, IT, Science

Activities

1. Computer word-check

Label the parts of this laptop computer with the words in the box.

battery	CD/DVD drive	graphics card
hard disc drive	memory card	micro-processor
power adaptor	power cord	removable memory stick

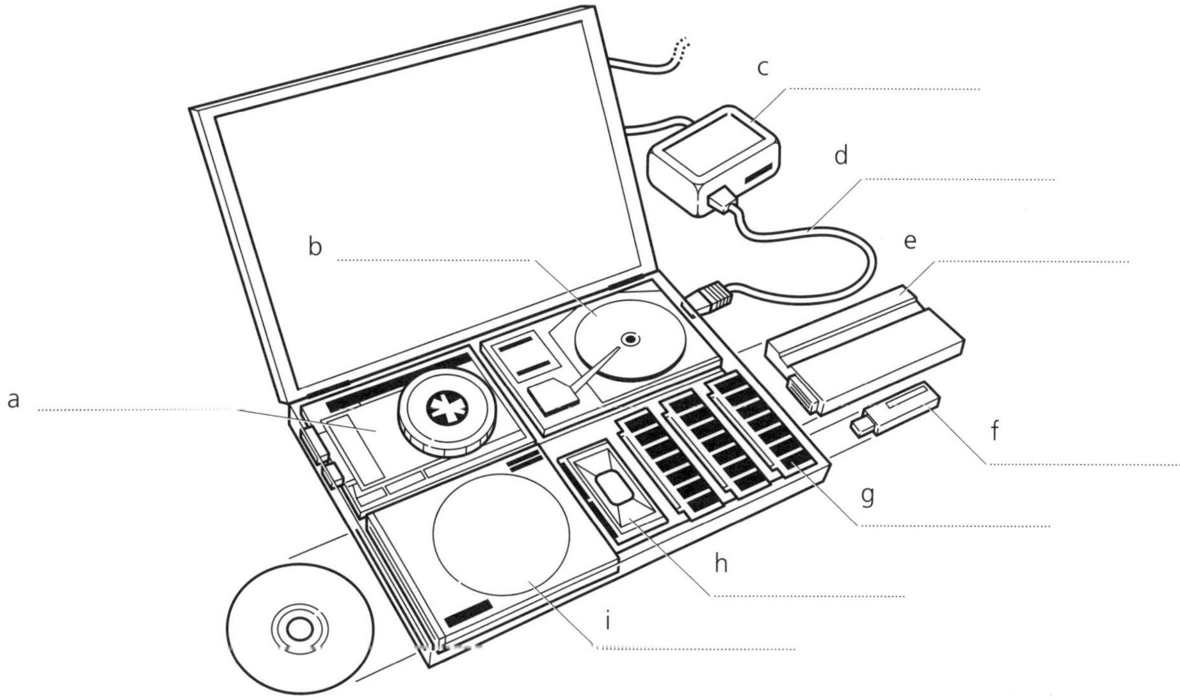

2. Consumer world!

The parts of this laptop come from a lot of different countries.
Unjumble the names of the countries to read about this product of globalisation.

a. It was designed in the ________________ and ________________. TINUED TESATS/WANITA
b. The battery comes from ________________. ECOMIX
c. The CD/DVD drive is from the ________________. SPINEPILIPH
d. The graphics card was made in ________________ NICHA
e. The hard disc drive is from ________________ PRESOGAIN
f. The memory is from ________________. GRENAMY
g. The micro-processor is from ________________. COATS CRIA
h. The power adaptor was made in ________________, but the power cord is from ________________. DITHNALA/NAIDA
i. The removable memory stick is from ________________. RASELI
j. The whole laptop was assembled in ________________. ASILAMAY

Consumers Worksheet 7

References:	**All**	
Focus:	**Vocabulary**	Advertising
	Grammar	Persuasion
	Content	Art, Design, L1

Activities

1. Consumer items

Look through Consumers and find the different kinds of 'consumer items' in it. Some of these are experiences (e.g. shopping, renting a car). Others are products (e.g. mobile phones, clothes). Make a list of them here.

PRODUCTS	EXPERIENCES

2. Advertising

Work in pairs or small groups.
Choose a product or an experience. You are going to design a website or poster to promote it.

Discuss and agree the important features of the item, e.g.
- the specific product or experience.
- its description.
- the important features that are 'new' or 'different'.

Make a note of these here.

3. Making decisions

Then decide:
- what are the key 'selling points';
- what factual information to include;
- what kind of picture best expresses the character of this item;
- a title or 'motto' to attract people.

Make a note of your decisions here.

4. Presentation and discussion

Organise an exhibition of the different projects. Vote on the most effective design.
Decide what makes it effective, e.g. visual impact, choice of words, unusual information.

References:	**All**	
Focus:	**Vocabulary**	Arguing and justifying
	Grammar	Giving reasons and justifying opinions
	Content	L1

Activities

1. Agreeing and disagreeing.
Read these quotations about the consumer world from some of the articles.
Decide if you agree or disagree with each one. Write your reasons underneath.

> 'People get bored quickly, so they want something new every few months.'
> Modern Life is Fast. Page 5

Agree: Disagree:
Reason: ______________________________

____

____

____

> 'It's not always easy to make things change. You have to go step by step. It's not enough to give money. You can solve one part of a problem, but then another part of it appears!'
> UNICEF works! Page 12.

Agree: Disagree:
Reason: ______________________________

____

____

____

> 'The government hopes that tourism will attract tourists to a really poor part of the country. All the money from this tourism will go to the communities in the area,'
> Can you believe it? Page 24.

Agree: Disagree:
Reason: ______________________________

____

____

____

2. Write your own statement about the consumer world here. Is it a good thing? What are the problems? Then exchange Worksheets with a partner and decide if you agree with each other's opinions.

> THE CONSUMER WORLD

Partner's Name: ____________________ Agree: __________ Disagree: __________
Reason: ______________________________

____

____

____

Consumers Test Worksheet

Name: ______________________

Total Points (1 per question) ______________

1. Look through *Consumers*. Find these articles. Write the page number and the title.

a. There are some photos of charity shops.
Page ________ Title ______________________

b. You can see an old telephone.
Page ________ Title ______________________

c. This article is about new and old fashions.
Page ________ Title ______________________

d. An international organisation that solves problems.
Page ________ Title ______________________

e. They're trying to sell you something!
Page ________ Title ______________________

f. In search of four 'R' words.
Page ________ Title ______________________

g. From Britain to Zambia… a long journey.
Page ________ Title ______________________

h. Balance food and energy.
Page ________ Title ______________________

i. Small car, big message!
Page ________ Title ______________________

j. Register for a special soap opera on your mobile phone.
Page ________ Title ______________________

2. Are these statements true or false? Check the article and circle T or F.

a. ☐ Page 3. A shopping mall has something for everybody. T F
b. ☐ Page 4. Mini-skirts are new. T F
c. ☐ Page 6. There are lots of different types of ads. T F
d. ☐ Page 7. Some ads want to stop us from doing something. T F
e. ☐ Page 9. Hire-cars can help to sell other products. T F
f. ☐ Page 10. Students don't like to work in charity shops. T F
g. ☐ Page 12. UNICEF only works with children. T F
h. ☐ Page 17. We should pick up all the rubbish on a beach. T F
i. ☐ Page 19. Drink 2 colas – you need to jog for an hour! T F
j. ☐ Page 21. Eating disorders can affect anyone. T F

3. What is the English word for these things?

a. The food we eat every day. ______________
b. A person who works for no money. ______________
c. An organisation that helps people. ______________
d. When the traffic cannot move. ______________
e. The British English word for 'garbage'. ______________
f. A person who steals things. ______________
g. A very new way to do something. ______________
h. To look at the shops without spending money. ______________
i. The money people get from their jobs. ______________
j. Very modern and fashionable. ______________

Teacher's Notes: **TRAVEL & TOURISM** Intermediate

Ideas for use
This title explores different aspects of the travel world. It does this from the point of view of people who travel for pleasure as well as that of people who work in tourism. Through this, the students are asked to think critically about the topic in relation to themselves and other people.

Crosscurricular links: Geography; History; L1 Language and Literature; other languages; Science and Technology.

Don't forget! Look carefully for the T&T Spy mini-projects with each article. You will find more general ideas to use with all the titles in the *Topics* series on pages 127-131 of this Teacher's Book.

Cover and Contents
Encourage the students to browse through *Travel & Tourism* and to look at the range of articles, illustrations and design styles.

Discussion. What do the big and small photos on the cover suggest? Are these a good depiction of the topic? Ask the students to suggest other possible images for the cover.

Use the large picture to speculate in groups about the people in it. Who are they? Where are they exactly? What are they looking at? The groups then compare their ideas and justify their decisions.

You can also use the two photos to discuss various aspects of travel, e.g. ecotourism, tourist attractions, working in the tourism industry, people's reasons for travelling.

Writing. The students can make up a story about the people in the large photo, or write an entry in a travel diary or blog for them.

Page 1 – Letter 🎧
The letter contains a series of questions about travel. It makes links between the topic and such areas as the environment and jobs. It asks if there is any difference between travel and tourism.

The letter also mentions that there is another type of virtual travel, which involves 'visiting' places on the Internet, reading books about them, looking at photos, or seeing a film.

Discussion. Ask the students if they agree with these viewpoints and if there are other aspects of the topic that they would include if they were writing a similar letter or magazine editorial.

Writing. Following the discussion, the students can plan and write their own letter or editorial in pairs or groups.

Discussion. Which titles are easy to understand (e.g. Souvenirs? Which are more difficult (e.g. L-Travel)? Encourage the students to guess what the articles are about and to flick through the pages to check this.

Page 2 – Check it out
See page 132 for different activities to use with this reference page.

Page 3 – Travel? Why? 🎧
Warm up. Ask the students how many different types of travel they have experienced personally. This may be ordinary travel (to school) or more exotic types.

Build up a summary of the class travel experiences on the board. Then ask them to think if the reasons for each example, e.g. to come to school, to visit my grandparents, to go on holiday. Then ask them to decide whether each travel experience was positive, negative or neutral. What made it so? Discuss good and bad travel experiences.

Note: These ideas can also be discussed first of all in groups and then reported to the whole class. Finally, ask the students to read the article and find out if any of the individual views expressed there match their own experiences. They can also speculate about the people, looking carefully at their photo and what they say and noticing their initials and where they live.

Writing 1. Ask the students to choose one of these people and to plan an interview with him or her. They can write their questions as an e-mail, or to be used face to face.

Writing 2. The students choose a person and write a profile of him/her.

Writing 3. The students write their own 'speech bubble' answering the questions 'Travel? Why' from their own point of view, using the opinions in the article as a model.

✎ **Worksheet 1**
Vocabulary – Describing people and places
Grammar – Present simple
Content – Geography, L1

Page 4 – A place to sleep
Find out if any students have ever stayed in a youth hostel. If so, ask them to describe the experience. If not, ask them to say what they think hostels are like.

Discussion. The students should read the article, look at the photos and decide which hostel they would most like to stay in. What are their reasons? What information would they want to find out before going there? They can discuss their choices and the questions in groups.

✎ **Worksheet 2**
Vocabulary – Describing places.
Grammar – Asking and answering about factual information
Content – Geography, History

Page 5 – Hostels: An inside view

This article is an interview with the manager of a hostel in Brazil, which is part of the International Hostels group.

Before they read it, ask the students to look at her photo and think of questions to ask her about her job. Write their suggestions on the board (or let them compile these in groups).

The students then read the article, and check whether the interviewer asks the same questions as theirs. Which things remain unanswered?

Writing. The students write an email to Beatriz with their unanswered questions.

Page 6 and 7 – The bicycle story

Note: The full name, bicycle is often shortened to bike or cycle. This can be extended to compounds, e.g. motorbike, motorcycle.

The article is in two parts: **The birth of bikes** (Page 6) and **Bikes today** (Page 7). Decide whether to read these separately or together.

Warm up. Check what the students know and think about bikes. How many different kinds can they think of? Who rides a bike? Do they do this for pleasure, for exercise, or just to get from place to place? Who has the oldest/newest/most interesting/fastest/strangest bike in the class?

Ask the students to read about the safety bike. Is the quotation at the bottom still true today? Do bikes still offer freedom to people? If so, what kind of people, and how?

Read these questions aloud. Ask the students to find the information in the article.

- What was the name of one of the first bikes in the 1880s?
- Where were the pedals on these bikes?
- What were the tyres made of?
- How many months did people have to work to pay for one of them?
- What was the name of the new type of bikes in the1890s?
- What size were the two wheels?
- What clothes did women wear on these bikes?

Writing. Divide the class into two groups ('velocipedes' and 'safety bikes'). Each group writes three quiz questions about their own type of bike. They exchange questions and find the answers about the other type.

✎ **Worksheet 3**

Vocabulary – Types of bicycles
Grammar – *Wh-* questions, Factual information
Content – History

Ask the students to read about the four different types of bike. Which one would they most like to ride? Why?

Groupwork. The article connects the bikes with six different things:
adventure, ecology, fashion, freedom, fun, speed.

Ask them work in groups and to put these in order of importance for them. Then ask them to add other positive and negative aspects of riding a bike. The groups compare their ideas.

Pages 8 and 9 – Two famous journeys

This article is also in two parts: **Odysseus** (Page 8) and **Marco Polo** (Page 9). As both parts are quite long, it is probably better to read them separately.

Warm up. Ask the students about any famous travellers and their journeys that they know of. These can be real, e.g. a famous explorer, or fictional, like Bilbo Baggins in *The Lord of the Rings*. What makes these journeys famous? The people, the places, the risks, the methods of transport or the events?

Odysseus. Check what the students know about Odysseus. *(Links with Art, History and L1.)* Encourage them to exchange their information. Before they read the article, ask them to look at the map of the Mediterranean and identify where Athens and Troy (probably) were. Then ask them if they know anything about these people:

Circe
Cyclops
the Lotus Eaters
the Sirens.

They then read Paragraph 4 to check their ideas.

Marco Polo. Brainstorm what these two places, Venice and China, mean to the students. Build up two mind-maps on the board with their suggestions.

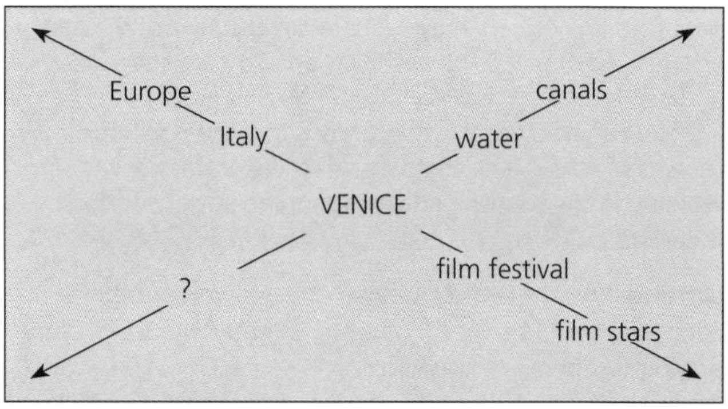

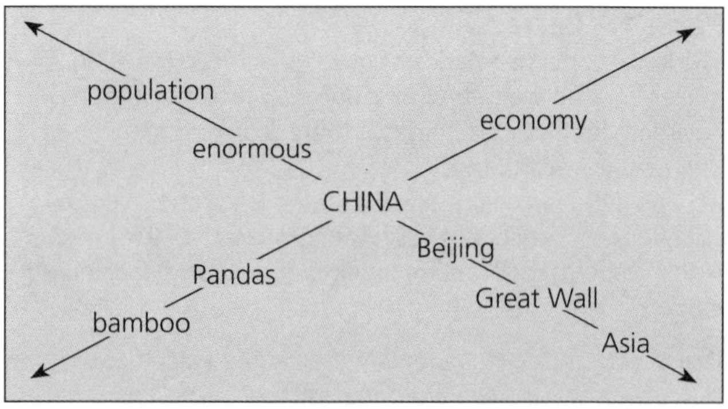

Then ask the students to read the article and find three things that amazed Marco Polo in China (paper money, coal, postal service).

Writing. Divide the class into two groups. One group writes a quiz about Odysseus and the other writes one about Marco Polo. Agree the number of questions they should write. Check the quizzes and then let them try them out on the other group.

Worksheet 4.
Vocabulary – Places
Grammar – Past simple for narrative
Content – Geograhy, History, L1

Page 10 – E-travel

Warm up. Ask the students what the title makes them think of (e-commerce, e-mail, e-bay, etc.) In those cases, the 'e' stands for 'electronic'. Here it is used because each of the three types of travel described begin with 'e': exploration, emigration, ecotourism.Have them speculate what might be in each of these sections.

Discussion. This can be useful preparation for the T&T Spy activity.

Exploration. What famous explorers do they know about? What did they do? What places do people still explore? Are there any places they would like to explore themselves? Why?

Emigration. Have any of their families been emigrants from another country? Do they know any other people who have emigrated? If so, what was the reason – e.g. economics, politics, religion? If so, do they still have any links with those places (culture, language)?

Ecotourism. What do they know about this? Have any of them experienced it? Are there any ecotourism projects in their area, e.g. hotels, trips, sightseeing?

Page 11 – L-travel

Ask for guesses as to what the 'L' refers to here (Learning). They may be able to guess this by looking at the three section headings (Exchange visits, Class trips, Research trips).

Warm up. Ask the students what people can learn through travel before they read the introductory paragraph. Do people agree with this? Check if any of them have been on 'learning travel' of any kind. What did they do? Where did they go? Did they learn anything new?

Exchange visits. Before going on an exchange visit, what information would they want to have about the place and/or profile? Where would they choose to go? Why?

Class trips. What trips have the class made? Were these linked to a specific subject. e.g. Geography, Art, Sports?Were they asked to find out information or do projects? Were the trips a success?

Research trips. Have any people been on 'field trips' to make a subject like History or Geography come alive? If so, what did they do? If not, what practical experience would they like to get in this way, like the students in the two photos?

Discussion. What learning trips would they like to go on? Are these better with the whole class, in smaller groups, or as individuals? They may like to plan an ideal trip or a programme of educational visits.

Pages 12 and 13 – What's it really like?

This two-page article contrasts the typical descriptions of places that are found in guidebooks with the 'inside view' of people who live in them or know them well. It focuses on three favourite tourist destinations: Mysore in India, Venice in Italy and Machu Picchu in Peru. Each place is described first of all through a typical guidebook description and a photo. Then the 'other voice' comments on this, with more photos (for Mysore and Venice).

Warm up. Ask the students if they have ever visited a place that was different from their expectations – either better or worse. If they live in a tourist area, what expectations do tourists have before they arrive? Are they surprised by the reality? What kind of things are the most surprising?

Discussion. Choose one of the places and ask the students to notice and discuss the differences between the two viewpoints, and to decide which gives the more accurate picture of it. They can then decide which kind of information they would prefer to have before they visit a place.

Writing. Ask them to write a similar pair of contrasting descriptions for their town or region, or any other place they know well.

Worksheet 5
Vocabulary – Personal opinions
Grammar – Comparing opinions with
on the other hand, but, however
Content – Geography, History, L1

Page 14 – Tourist info

Discussion. Check that they recognize the Information sign. What kind of information do tourists normally need when they visit a place? Where can they get this information? Write the suggestions on the board, e.g. maps, timetables, photos, guidebooks, personal anecdotes, etc. Group these into; factual information (e.g. maps) subjective information (e.g. guidebooks); promotional material (e.g. some brochures).

If possible, ask them to visit their local tourist office, or a travel agency, and to collect examples of travel literature. They should check and assess it for accuracy and for 'selling power'. This can act as preparation for the T&T Spy activity.

Page 15 – A career in tourism

This article presents factual information about some of the different careers that are possible in the travel and tourism industry.

Warm up. Write these five headings on the board:
Airlines
Hotels
Restaurants and cafés
Tourist offices
Travel companies

Ask the students to suggest jobs to put under each heading. E.g.

Restaurants and cafés			
Waiter Cook	Washer up	Accountant	etc.

Some jobs may fit into several different categories. Discuss which sectors and jobs are most attractive for them. Then ask them to consider the two questions at the beginning of the article: 'What are you good at?' and 'What do you like to do?'.

Discussion. Ask them to read the article and find out what advice is given about the three stages of each job:
Starting out
Getting on
Future career opportunities.
They can then decide if they agree with this and add other advice of their own.

Roleplay. In pairs, they act out a job interview for one of these jobs. They should choose the job together; the Interviewer then prepares a list of relevant questions and the Interviewee decides about his/her qualifications and qualities, as well as some questions to ask about the job.

Page 16 – Living with tourism 🎧

Warm up. This article presents a number of positive and negative opinions about living in a tourist place or area. These are grouped under three headings:
Crowds
Jobs
Shops and prices
Before they read the article, ask the students to predict what positive and negative opinions might be expressed under each heading. You can write their ideas on the board, or they can do this in groups and then compare their suggestions.

Discussion. They then read the article and compare the opinions voiced there with their own. Encourage them to add more ideas.

Page 17 – Souvenirs

This article discusses souvenirs from various viewpoints:
Their effect on the environment.
Their contribution to the local economy.
Their general aesthetic value.
It contains a mixture of objective and subjective opinions.

Warm up. Ask the students about any souvenirs they have ever bought . Were they worth the money? Why did they buy them? Were they made locally? Did they keep them?

Discussion.
Introduction and first paragraph. Ask them to read these and to answer the question: 'Are they worth it?'.
Helping the local economy. After reading this section, the students should suggest any souvenirs that help their local economy in some way, e.g. jobs, money, opportunities. Can they suggest any new ideas, e.g. Encouraging local artists.

Don't touch! There is more information about endangered species on the Oxfam and WWF websites (see Page 2). This can be used as a websearch project to give them practice in finding, analysing and selecting relevant information.

Further discussion. Has the article changed their opinions about souvenirs in any way? If so, how? What suggestions would the make to the local Tourist Board?

Pages 18 and 19 – Youth hostels

This factual article is linked to those on pages 4 and 5. It can be used as a basis for reading and checking information. Before they read the article, the students are given the questions to answer themselves. They then read the answers and check them with their own ideas.

Writing. The article can serve as a basis for writing (and answering) a quiz about youth hostels. e.g.
Do you have to bring your own towels?
Name three types of buildings that are used as hostels.
Who has priority when a hostel is full?

Pages 20 and 21 – A travel story 🎧

This two-page article describes a different type of travel – animal migration.

Warm up. Find out what the students know about the topic before they read the article. Which animals and birds migrate? What kinds of journeys do they make? How long are these? What dangers do they face? Do many of them survive?

Pre-reading. Ask the students to look at the photos and identify the animals: cheetah, hyena, lion, wildebeest and the group (herd).
Draw a diagram of the places in East Africa on the board, or use an atlas. Mark the distance (2000 miles) and identify these places:
- the Serengeti plains
- Lake Victoria
- the Mara River
- the Masai Mara Plains

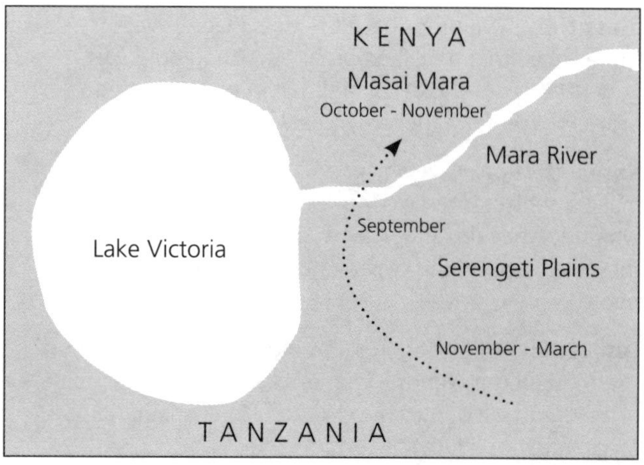

Write the names of the two main 'characters' of the story on the board: Kimbea (a female wildebeest) and Du-May (her calf). Ask the students to identify with one of these while they read the story and to find out what happens to them over the seven-month journey.

Writing. Write an alternative happy ending for the story.

Worksheet 6

Vocabulary –Wild animals
Grammar– Past simple for narrative
Content – Geography, Science, L1

Page 22 – Travel and Tourism Quiz: Do you know?

Writing: Tourist Office. Ask the students to bring in postcards of different places. They can then work in pairs or groups to make up similar quiz questions based on these.

Page 23 – Projects

Ask the students to read all the projects carefully in order to decide which ones are interesting for them. Find out which are the most/least interesting for this class and if any of them just interest one person.

These projects can be done in groups, pairs or individually. Some of them may link with those done in other subjects, e,g. History or Science.

Encourage the students to also review and present the things they have been doing in the various T&T Spy mini-projects. If appropriate, these can form a class end-of-term exhibition.

Pages 24 – Chatrooms

Teens chat. The students can read this chat exchange aloud in pairs, conveying the feelings through intonation.

Writing. They make up similar chat exchanges about their favourite school subjects.

Can you believe it? Discussion. Do they know of similar tourist ideas or places that exploit the memory of famous dead people? What do they think about this? What are the pros and cons?

Worksheet 7

Vocabulary – Personal opinions
Grammar – Stating opinions, Giving reasons
Content – Geography, History, Languages

Worksheet 8

Vocabulary – Visual styles, Content and impact
Grammar – Personalisation, Making personal judgements.
Content – Art, Design

Title review. The students can do a review to help inform other people. This can be of the whole magazine, or of specific articles. They can agree their own criteria, or you can put this framework on the board for them to copy and adapt.

Criteria	Article	Stars	Comments
Interest			
Information			
Design			
Photos			
T&T Spy			
Other			

Test Worksheet

The aim of the test is to encourage the students to look back through the articles in order to check facts, notice details and find specific information to answer the questions.

Extra teacher's resources

These books and websites are worth looking at for further information.

Books

Marco Polo *The Travels of Marco Polo*. Revised English translation published by Liveright, New York and London 2003.

Odysseus Homer's *The Odyssey*. Revised English translation published by Penguin Books 2003.

Che Guevara *The Motorcycle Diaries*. English translation published by Fourth Estate, London and New York 2003.

Websites.

HOSTELS: www.hihostels.com
UNESCO: www.unesco.org
Africa story: www.bbc.co.uk/radio4/science
OXFAM and WWF: www.oxfam.org.uk and www.wwf.org
Educational projects: www.hwdt.org

Travel & Tourism Worksheet 1

References: **Travel? Why?** – Page 3

Focus:
Vocabulary Describing people and places
Grammar Present simple
Content Geography, L1

Activities

1. Reasons for travelling

Read what the eight people in the article say about their reasons for travelling. Then identify the people here and write their initials on the right.

This person...

- wants to be healthy and likes to feel free. ____
- is curious about new places. ____
- is interested in wild animals. ____
- has to travel to the city every week for work. ____
- goes to school by bus. ____
- likes to meet new people and have new experiences. ____
- has to move house every few years. ____
- travels to find sun and warm weather. ____

2. Describing people

Read what the people say. Look at their photos. What are they like?
Suggest two adjectives to describe each person.

a. I.W ____________ ____________
b. K.T. ____________ ____________
c. W.L.G. ____________ ____________
d. J.A.A. ____________ ____________
e. L.L. ____________ ____________
f. B.J. ____________ ____________
g. T.Y. ____________ ____________
h. M.S. ____________ ____________

Compare your decisions with a partner. How many differences are there?

3. Design an ad for the destinations below. Think of the kind of people you want to attract. Emphasise their characteristics. Make up a good slogan for each place.

a. A safari. ____________
b. A warm, sunny island with lots of beaches. ____________
c. A tent in the mountains. ____________
d. A round-the-world airline trip. ____________
e. A big city. ____________
f. A small village in the country. ____________
g. An adventure trip in the jungle. ____________
h. A working holiday on a farm. ____________

References: **A place to sleep** – Page 4

Focus:

Vocabulary Describing places
Grammar Asking and answering about factual information
Content Geography, History

Activities

1. Cities and countries

Look at these cities and add the countries.

COUNTRY

a. Buenos Aires ______________________

b. Chicago ______________________

c. Fes ______________________

d. Stockholm ______________________

e. Sydney ______________________

f. Tokyo ______________________

g. Scotland ______________________

Then check your facts with the article. Correct anything that was wrong.

2. Collecting factual information

Choose one of these places. Find out about it. e.g. architecture, climate, population, scenery, sites. Write factual notes about your place here.

____

____

____

____

3. Using factual information: Let's go together!

Don't tell anyone else about your choice. Move around the class to find other people with the same one.
You can only ask 'Yes/No' questions, e.g. 'Is it on the coast?' 'Is it a modern city?'.
Use your information to answer other people.
From the size of the groups, decide which is the most and least popular destination in your class.

Travel & Tourism Worksheet 3

References: **The Bicycle Story** – Pages 6 and 7

Focus:
Vocabulary Types of bicycles
Grammar *Wh*-questions, Factual information
Content History

Activities

1. Identify the bike

safety bike	messenger bike	mountain bike
unicycle	velocipede	yellow bike

Without looking at the article, write the name of the bicycle after each description.

a. A bike with one wheel. ________
b. A bike with a big front wheel. ________
c. A bike for busy people in the city. ________
d. A very light bike. ________
e A historically important bike for women. ________
f. An ecologically-friendly bike. ________

Read the article and check your answers.

2. Read the descriptions on page 6 quickly to answer these questions

Velocipedes

a. When were they popular? ________
b. How many wheels did they have? ________
c. Why were they difficult to ride? ________
d. Why were they uncomfortable? ________

Safety bikes

e. Why were they more comfortable? ________
f. Why were they useful for working people? ________
g. Why were they important for women? ________
h. Who wore 'bloomers' ________

3. Read the descriptions on Page 7. Write a similar question about each of these bikes.

Mountain bikes
a. ________
Messenger bikes
b. ________
Yellow bikes
c. ________
Unicycles
d. ________
Exchange worksheets with a partner. Answer each other's questions.

4. Choose one of the six types of bikes in the article

Notice what it is associated with (fashion, speed, etc.). Consider its strong and weak points. Then make up an advertising slogan to convince people to use it.

____

____

You can display your slogans round the class and vote on the best one in each category.

References: **Two famous journeys** – Pages 8 and 9

Focus:
Vocabulary Places
Grammar Past simple for narrative
Content Geography, History, L1

Activities

1. Complete these sentences with the names of the people from the story about Odysseus

Argos	Circe	Cyclops
Lotus Eaters	Penelope	Sirens

a. ___________ was a monster with one eye.
b. The ___________ were women with very beautiful voices.
c. ___________ turned the sailors into pigs.
d. The ___________ never did any work.
e. ___________ recognised his master – and died.
f. ___________ waited for many years for her husband to return.

2. Find the words or phrases in both sections with these meanings

ODYSSEUS
a. A very long and complicated journey.
b. The place where dead people went, according to the Ancient Greeks.
c. A person who goes on journeys.
d. A piece of land with sea all round it.
e. The vocal sound a dog makes (verb)

MARCO POLO
f. A person who asks people to pay their taxes to him.
g. Money that is very light to carry.
h. People who attack ships to get money or objects.
i. One person tells a story and the other person writes it down.

3. Finding places

The place where...
a. Odysseus' journey home began.
b. his family were waiting.
c. Marco Polo was born.
d. the Great Khan was the ruler
e. Marco was put in prison.

4. Comparing journeys

Compare Odysseus' journey home with March Polo's journey to an exciting place.
Use the information in the article to complete this table.

	ODYSSEUS	MARCO POLO
Where the journey began.	____________	____________
Where he went to (one way).	____________	____________
Method(s) of transport.	____________	____________
Length of the journey	____________	____________
A problem during it.	____________	____________
The problem after it.	____________	____________
Your opinion.	____________	____________

Travel & Tourism Worksheet 5

References: **Living with Tourism** – Page 16

Focus:
Vocabulary Personal oppinions
Grammar Comparing opinions with *on the other hand, but, however*
Content Geography, History, L1

Activities

1. Different opinions

The article quotes different opinions about the effects of tourism on shops and prices, jobs and crowds. Make a note of the positive and negative points here.

SHOPS AND PRICES
Positive:

Negative:

JOBS
Positive:

Negative:

CROWDS
Positive:

Negative:

2. Now use your notes to write a sentence about each of these things, contrasting the positive and negative opinions, points. e.g.

JOBS: *'There are lots of extra jobs, but they're not all interesting!'*

Use connectors like:

but	however	on the other hand

SHOPS AND PRICES:

JOBS:

CROWDS:

3. Think of a place you know that is popular with tourists.

What are their positive and negative effects on it?
Write a paragraph describing the place and the effects of tourism on it.

Exchange descriptions with a partner. Would you like to visit these places? Why (not)?

References: **A Travel Story** – Pages 20 and 21

Focus:
Vocabulary Wild animals
Grammar Past simple for narrative
Content Geography, Science, L1

Activities

cheetah	crocodile	hyena	leopard	lions	monkeys
small birds	vultures	wild dogs	wildebeest	zebras	

1. What part do these animals play in the story?

a. Two of these animals are the main characters. ____________

b. These animals often travel with them. ____________

c. Du-may's birth is delayed because of this animal. ____________

d. These big birds watch the new animals. ____________

e. This animal follows Du-may in the Serengeti Park. ____________

f. These animals make a lot of noise and warn Du-may of danger. ____________

g. This animal attacks Kimbea in the river. ____________

h. These animals hide in the long grass on the plains. ____________

i. This animal is sleeping in a tree. ____________

j. Movement alarms these animals. ____________

k. These animals kill Du-may. ____________

2. Summarising the events

Complete this summary, using the Past simple.

November
A group of zebras and wildebeest, ________ (begin) to travel north in search of food and water. One of them ________ (be) pregnant.

February
The female ________ (delay) the birth of her calf because there ________ (be) hyenas nearby.

March
The calf ________ (escape) from a cheetah because some monkeys ________ (make) a lot of noise and ________ (frighten) her.

June
The animals ________ (move) through the forests towards the Mara River.

September
A crocodile ________ (try) to eat Kimbea but she ________ (escape). She ________ (go) back to find her calf.

October
Kimbea ____________ (escape) from a big fire. A leopard ________ (hear) Du-may's calls and ________ (begin) to move towards him, but some small birds ________ (warn) him and he ________ (run) away.

November
The animals ________ (begin) to return south. They ________ (cross) the river again. Some wild dogs ________ (see) that Du-may was ill. When he ________ (fall) over, they ________ (attack) him and ______ (tear) him apart. Then the vultures ________ (come) down.

Reread the whole summary. Check with the article if anything important has been left out. If so, add it.

Travel & Tourism Worksheet 7

References: **All**

Focus:
Vocabulary Personal opinions
Grammar Stating opinions, Giving Reasons
Content Geography, History, Languages

Activities

1. Agreeing and disagreeing.
Read these three quotations about travel from some of the articles.
Decide if you agree or disagree with each one. Write your reasons underneath.

'TRAVEL ADVICE: First of all, plan where, when and how to go. Collect a lot of information about the place. Plan when your trip will be, how much it will cost each day. Find out how to travel around the country, what the food is like and about the season – will it be winter or spring?'
Beatriz Borges, Page 5.

Agree: __________ Disagree: __________

Reason: ______________________________

'EMIGRATION: The more we can learn about other people, the more we understand why they do things in a different way. That's interesting – and it also make us think more about our own cultures, as well.'
E-Travel, Page 10.

Agree: __________ Disagree: __________

Reason: ______________________________

'RESEARCH TRIPS: Doing practical research is much more interesting than learning a lot of facts.
L-travel, Page 11.

Agree: __________ Disagree: __________

Reason: ______________________________

2. Write your own statement about travel here. Is it a good thing? What are the problems? Then exchange Worksheets with a partner and decide if you agree with each other's opinions.

References: **All**

Focus:

Vocabulary Visual styles, Content and impact
Grammar Personalisation, Making personal judgements
Content Art, Design

Activities

1. Identifying visual styles

Look through the magazine and identify the different styles of illustration in it. Write the article and page number references against each one.

VISUAL STYLE	ARTICLE	PAGE
Cartoon	______	______
Computer graphic	______	______
Diagram	______	______
Drawing	______	______
Photo	______	______
Other	______	______

2. Design priorities: personal criteria

How do you choose a good illustration for an article? Put these qualities in order of importance (1 = high). Add your own ideas.

colourful	eye-catching	modern
mysterious	reflects the article	strange

QUALITIES

1. ______	5. ______
2. ______	6. ______
3. ______	7. ______
4. ______	8. ______

3. Applying personal criteria

Now choose one article. Read (or reread) it. Then use your criteria to evaluate the overall design. Give each item a score out of ten.

PAGE	ARTICLE
CRITERIA	SCORE

4. Making suggestions

Write an e-mail to the editor about the illustration and design. Say what works well for you. Then give suggestions for improvements. Begin like this:

To: Magazine Editor From: ______

Date: ______ Topic: ______

Travel & Tourism Test Worksheet

Name: ______________________________

Total Points (1 per question) ______________

1. Look through *Travel & Tourism*. Identify these articles. Write the page number and the title.

a. An ancient adventure in the Mediterranean Sea.

Page ________ Title ______________________________

b. Different faces, different voices, different opinions.

Page ________ Title ______________________________

c. A lot of hostels to choose from.

Page ________ Title ______________________________

d. One big wheel from the past and one smaller wheel from the present.

Page ________ Title ______________________________

e. Don't believe everything in the guidebooks!

Page ________ Title ______________________________

f. Is tourism for you?

Page ________ Title ______________________________

g. Not all journeys have a happy end.

Page ________ Title ______________________________

h. Learning can be fun.

Page ________ Title ______________________________

i. Tourism – not all good or bad!

Page ________ Title ______________________________

2. Are these statements true or false? Check them with the articles and circle T or F.

a. Page 3. Everybody likes to travel. T F
b. Page 6. Bikes helped women to be independent. T F
c. Page 8. Odysseus gave his name to a type of journey. T F
d. Page 9. Everybody believed Marco Polo's stories. T F
e. Page 10. Space travel is safe now. T F
f. Page 12. India is a good place for cows and bulls. T F
g. Page 13. Governments do not always agree with UNESCO. T F
h. Page 14. There's an international sign for 'information'. T F
i. Page 17. Some tourists buy animals as souvenirs. T F

3. What is the English word for these things?

a. A small hotel. ______________
b. A hotel for young people. ______________
c. A bike with one wheel. ______________
d A lot of traffic in one place – nothing can move. ______________
e. To travel by plane. ______________
f. A traveller who discovers new places. ______________
g. A person who goes to live in a new country. ______________
h. A kind of tourism that doesn't harm the environment. ______________
i. A book with information and advice about a country, region or city ______________

ANSWER KEY

Topics

PEOPLE

People Worksheet 1
Check it out – Page 2
Activities
1 MOTHER
FATHER
GRANDMOTHER
GRANDFATHER
2 Mother / Father
Mum / Dad
Mummy / Daddy

Grandmother / Grandfather
Grannie / Grandad
Grandma / Grandpa

3

C	M	K	D	G	C	O	U	S	I	N
P	A	O	F	R	Y	C	J	O	Y	A
N	U	T	B	A	H	Q	I	R	B	Z
V	P	Z	U	N	C	L	E	G	Q	E
G	R	A	N	D	M	O	T	H	E	R
S	H	U	I	F	O	S	R	W	J	L
I	J	N	E	A	T	D	L	P	K	A
S	H	T	I	T	H	G	W	F	C	B
T	F	A	T	H	E	R	S	E	V	D
E	X	K	W	E	R	X	U	T	L	F
R	N	G	B	R	O	T	H	E	R	M

4 Student's own answers

People Worksheet 2
Personal identity – Page 3
Activities
1 Student's own answers
2 Student's own answers
3 Student's own answers
4 Student's own answers

People Worksheet 3
My life: past, present and future – Page 4
1 Student's own answers
2 Student's own answers
3 Student's own answers
4 Student's own answers

People Worksheet 4
I have a voice! – Pages 6 and 7
1

B	J	R	P	R	U	S	S	I	A	Y
C	A	M	B	O	D	I	A	O	F	E
G	S	O	A	G	T	E	Z	U	W	M
U	E	L	Y	R	F	R	A	N	C	E
I	D	D	S	N	U	R	P	B	E	N
N	Q	O	K	O	Q	A	G	O	J	B
E	L	V	I	T	A	L	Y	L	M	H
A	N	A	H	C	B	E	H	I	A	U
L	E	S	O	T	H	O	T	V	X	T
X	G	E	R	M	A	N	Y	I	D	A
M	I	V	I	F	C	E	L	A	K	N

Britain
2 Guinea, Lesotho, Sierra Leone
Bolivia
Bhutan, Cambodia, Yemen
Britain, France, Germany, Italy, Moldova, Russia
G8 countries – Britain, France, Germany, Italy, Russia
Europe
3 Student's own answers

People Worksheet 5
Statues – Pages 8 and 9
1 a Easter Island b Brazil
c a beach d New York
e a cold place f a garden
2 a True b False c False d False
e True f False g True h True
Student's own answers
3 a stone b marble c terracotta
d metal e wood f plastic
g fibreglass h mud

People Worksheet 6
Happy Birthday! – Page 12
1 Age in Britain:
a 13 b 15 c 16 d 16
e 18 f 17 g 17 h 18
Age in student's country: Student's own answers
2 Student's own answers
3 Student's own answers

People Worksheet 7
All
1 a page 1 or 2 b page 11
c page 2 d page 16
e page 5 f page 7
g page 3 h page 9
i page 13 j page 3
k page 15 l page 16
2 Student's own answers
3 Student's own answers

People Worksheet 8
All
1 Student's own answers
2 Student's own answers
3 Student's own answers

People Test Worksheet
1 a 8, Statues b 4, My life: Past, present and future c 12, Happy Birthday!
d 6, I have a voice! e 10, People and Clothes f 3, Personal Identity
g 9, Statues h 9, Statues
i 13, A song to a special person
j 16, Topics chatrooms
2 a True b True c False d True
e True f True g False h True
i True j False
3 a personality b blog
c brave d grandmother
e uniform f nameday
g mum h fave
i beach j personality

PLACES

Places Worksheet 1
Check it out – Page 2
1 ROOM
My dream place — Page 3
TUNNEL
Connecting Places: Tunnels — Pages 10 & 11
NEST
Animal Places — Page 12
CANAL
Connecting Places: Bridges — Pages 8 & 9
HOLE
Connecting Places: Tunnels — Pages 10 & 11
BRIDGE
Connecting Places: Bridges — Pages 8 & 9
HOTEL
Places to live, work and play — Pages 6 & 7
OPERA HOUSE
Places to live, work and play — Pages 6 & 7
2 Student's own answers
3 Student's own answers

Places Worksheet 2
My dream place – Page 3
1 Girl - room, window, colour, walls, notice, friends
Boy – room, website, colour, shape, size, password
2 a black
b walls, ceiling, floor
c silver
d they're really big
e things can be hidden in them
f modern, cool, big, tidy
g the dream room
3 Student's own answers

Places Worksheet 3
Doors going out and coming in – Pages 4 and 5
1 Unable to answer until table has been completed
2 Suggested answers:
a bank b hotel/shop
c revolving d exam room/doctors
e plane
3 Student's own answers

Places Worksheet 4
Places to live, work and play – Pages 6 and 7
1 Suggested answers:
LIVING: house, caravan, doorway, hotel, yurt
WORKING: art gallery, opera house, house, parliament building, hotel
PLAY: art gallery, house, caravan, opera house, hotel, yurt
2 Student's own answers

Places Worksheet 5
Connecting places: bridges – Pages 8 and 9
1 CITY: Sydney, Rio de Janeiro, Prague, London, Gateshead, Millau, Florence, Venice
BRIDGE: Sydney Harbour, Rio-Niteroi, Charles, Tower, Millennium, Millau, 'Old Bridge' 'Bridge of Sighs'
2 BRIDGE: Old Bridge-Florence, Tower Bridge-London, Millennium Bridge-Gateshead, Charles Bridge-Prague
BRIDGE: 'Bridge of Sighs', Sydney Harbour, Rio-Niteroi, Millau
3 Student's own answers

Places Worksheet 6
A strange place – Page 13
1 a submarine b yellow
c blue d green e friends
f more friends g the band
h aboard
2 Student's own answers
3 Student's own answer

Places Worksheet 7
All
1 Student's own answers
2 Student's own answers

Places Worksheet 8
All
1 Student's own answers
2 Student's own answers
3 Student's own answers

Places Test Worksheet
1 a 4, Doors: going out and coming in
b 12, Animal places
c 13, Strange places: a song
d 10, Connecting places: tunnels
e 8, Connecting places: bridges
f 3, My dream place
g 3, My dream place
h 7, Places to live, work and play
2 a True b False c True
d False e False f False
g True h True i True
3 a password b entrance
c homeless d pedestrian
e cyclist f tomb
g nest h outside

ANIMALS

Animals Worksheet 1
Check it out – Page 2

1

Animal	Colour(s)	Page
BUTTERFLY	green & black	6, 4
CUCKOO	grey & yellow	5
DONKEY	brown	7
EAGLE	black & white	3
FROG	red	6
HORSE	brown	16
OSTRICH	grey & white	3, 14
RABBIT	grey	10
SNAKE	green	4, 2
TIGER	yellow, black & white	14, 2
WOLF	grey	5, 10, 11
ZEBRA	black & white	4

2 Suggested answers:
a wolf b elephant c eagle
d cat e giraffe f rabbit
g bull h tiger
3 Student's own answer

Animals Worksheet 2
Feet Talk! – Page 3
1 Insert word box with the six words encircled, as per worksheet page 43
2 ostrich, eagle, duck, woodpecker
3 a ducks & swans, skin
b The eagle, long, sharp claws
c woodpeckers, because they have two toes at the front and back of their feet to help them clim
d ostrich, very flexible
4 1 cat 2 dog 3 cow
4 elephant 5 sheep 6 horse
5 Student's own answers

Animals Worksheet 3
Families – Page 5
1 a Cat b dog c horse
d cow e sheep f duck
g swan/goose h chicken/chick/goose
2 a COW b HEN c SWAN
d DUCK e HORSE f GOOSE
g CAT h SHEEP i DOG
Student's own pictures
3 a kid b kid

Animals Worksheet 4
Birth, life and death – Page 6
1 BUTTERFLY, CATERPILLAR, CHRYSALIS, FROG, TADPOLE
Student's own pictures
2 a frog b She c tadpoles d tadpoles, frogs e caterpillar f caterpillar, chrysalis g chrysalis, butterfly
3 Student's own answers

Animals Worksheet 5
WWF – Pages 8 and 9
1 Student's own answers
2 a International
b In about 100 countries
c Nature
d A panda
e It's the international motto
3 Student's own answers
4 Student's own answers

Animals Worksheet 6
1 - 3 Student's own answers

Animals Worksheet 7
Check it out – Page 2
1 - 6 Student's own answers

Animals Worksheet 8
All
1 – 4 Student's own answers

Animals Test Worksheet
1 a 7, A Working Life
b 5, Families
c 6, Birth, life and death
d 12, Animals attract tourists!
e 3, Feet talk!
f 4, It's a dangerous world!
g 10, Pet's corner
h 4, It's a dangerous world!
i 8, WWF Across the world
2 a True b False c True
d False e False f False
g True h False i True
3 a footprint b reptiles c zebra
d signet e tadpole f buddy
g bull h ark i frogs

SPORTS

Sports Worksheet 1
Check it out – Page 2

1

C	E	L	E	B	R	A	T	E
O	Q	O	W	N	Z	V	R	K
M	E	S	U	P	P	O	R	T
P	R	E	A	Q	T	U	L	C
E	E	Y	H	I	T	W	I	N
T	R	A	I	N	G	J	P	E
E	W	T	S	C	O	R	E	E
P	R	A	C	T	I	S	E	R

Horizontal words – 5
Vertical words – 2
a SCORE b SUPPORT
c WIN d LOSE
e CELEBRATE

2 FOOTBALL:
a stadium b referee
c goals d forward, midfielder
TENNIS:
a tennis court b umpire
c points d racket

3 a athlete b competitor
c spectator d fan
e commentator f coach
g team h club

Sports Worksheet 2
Sport: To do or to watch? – Page 3

1 a Way of Life b TV Addict
c Health d Travel
e Excitement f New Skills

2 a where b why c why
d why e how f what

3 Student's own answers

Sports Worksheet 3
Marathon and Marathons – Pages 6 and 7

1 DATES:
First marathon took place
New marathon took place
New York marathon
NUMBERS:
Runners in new marathon
Runners to finish New York marathon
Sumatran rhino in the world
Soldiers in Athenian army
Soldiers in Persian army
Runners in New York marathons now
DISTANCES:
The new marathon
A hot marathon
Distance run by Pheidippide

2 Student's own answers

3 a A 93-year-old marathon runner
b A famous Ancient Greek runner
c A famous Greek postal worker

4 Student's own answers

Sports Worksheet 4
A – Z of Sport – Pages 8 and 9

1 Student's own answers

2 a diving b long jump
c figure-skating d skateboarding
e windsurfing f table tennis
g judo h baseball
Student's own answers

3 – 4 Student's own answers

Sports Worksheet 5
Two sides of Sport – Page 12

1 – 3 Student's own answers

Sports Worksheet 6

1 Student's own answers

2 CRICKET: England, India, West Indies, Australia, New Zealand, Pakistan, Sri Lanka
POLO: China, Persia, India: England, US, Ireland, Australia, Argentina
JUDO: China, Japan: All over the world
Student's own answer

3 – 4 Student's own answers

Sports Worksheet 7
All

1 – 3 Student's own answers

Worksheet 8
All

1 – 3 Student's own answers

Sports Test Worksheet

1 a 11, The Beautiful Game
b 4, The Olympics Story
c 3, Sport: to do or to watch?
d Marathon and Marathons
e 6, Marathon and Marathons
f 10, The price of sport
g 8, The A-Z of Sport
h 7, Marathon and Marathons

2 a True b False c True
d False e True f True
g False h True i False

3 a sports fan b spectator
c stadium d paralympics
e holiday f train
g dive h sportswear
i cheer j champion

FESTIVALS

Festivals Worksheet 1
Check it out – Page 2

1 a band b bonfire
c mask d procession
e fireworks f anniversary
g lantern/candle h musician
i float

2 – 3 Student's own answers

Festivals Worksheet 2
Let's begin with the New Year – Page 3

1 New Year - 1st January
Student's own answer
January/February March/April
September March/April
Student's own answer

2 – 3 Student's own answers

Festivals Worksheet 3
Chinese and Scottish New Year – Pages 4 and 5

1 CHINESE NEW YEAR:
a 15 b 5 c clean their houses
d red envelopes/money e animals
f vegetarian g fireworks h animal
i lanterns j Asia
SCOTTISH NEW YEAR:
a longest b good c warmth
d food e happiness f old
g old year h 4 i wind
j 'Sorry. No party tonight! But come back next year…'

2 – 3 Student's own answers

Festivals Worksheet 4
Festival Food – Pages 6 and 7

1 CHRISTMAS: Italy, France, Eastern Europe
Fish, turkey, goose, mince pies, panettone
MARDI GRAS: Britain, France
Pancakes
BONFIRE NIGHT: Britain
Gingerbread, sausages
THANKSGIVING: USA, Turkey
sweet potatoes, pumpkin pie

2 Student's own answers

3 a put b whisk c add d beat
e leave f melt g pour h cook
i put j spread k keep l make
m eat
Student's own answers

Festivals Worksheet 5
Your Carnival, My Carnival, Whose Carnival? – Pages 8, 9 and 10

1 Student's own answers

2 CITY/CITIES/REGION:
Andes Rio, Salvador, Recife Quebec
Nice Venice New Orleans
London Notting Hill August
Student's own answers

3 Student's own answers

Festivals Worksheet 6
Life and Death – Pages 11 and 12
1 Suggested answers:
scary sweet
2 a Korea b United States
c Mexico d Mexico
3 – 4 Student's own answers

Festivals Worksheet 7
All
1 – 4 Student's own answers

Festivals Worksheet 8
All
1 – 5 Student's own answers

Festivals Test Worksheet
1 a 11, Life and Death
b 6, Festival Food
c 10, Carnival in August!
d 4, Chinese New Year
e 12, Family Festivals
f 8/9, Your Carnival, My Carnival, Whose Carnival?!
g 3, Let's begin with New Year
h 5, Scottish New Year
2 a False b True c True d False
e False f False g True h True
i False j True
3 a Hogmanay b Thanksgiving
c calypso d ancestors
e Mardi Gras f 4703
g lunar h mask
i lent

ENVIRONMENT

Environment Worksheet 1
Check it out – Page 2
1 Suggested answers:
a destroy b pollute
c researching d protect
e contaminate f lose
g consume h increasing
i decreasing j preserve
k save
2 a flood b fire c earthquake
d drought e tornado f famine
3 Student's own answers

Environment Worksheet 2
My environment – Page 3
1 a move quickly
b is full of fumes
c they get ill
d the doctors and hospitals are very busy
e they decide to build a big ring road
f to move quickly around the city
g the air becomes better
h there is more pollution outside the city
i affects the food supply
j use more chemicals on the crops
k can't find food
l disappear from the countryside
2 Student's own answers

Environment Worksheet 3
Using water – Pages 4 and 5
1 Suggested answers:
1. washing dishes/wasting fresh water
2. farmland/crops need irrigation
3. dam ?/transportation by water
4. vineyard/salt water levels rising
2 Student's own answers
3 a 19 litres
b waste water
c drinking, washing, cooking
d animals, irrigation, fish
e produce electricity
f agriculture
4 a because b so c because
d because e so

Environment Worksheet 4
The food chain – Page 6
1 Plants are producers: they produce energy. First some animals eat plants to get energy: they are first-level consumers. Then, some animals and birds eat other animals – alive or dead: they're second or third-level consumers. After that some organisms consume dead plants and animals. They are decomposers. Finally, this food returns to the earth. The cycle begins again.
2 Student's own answers
3 Student's own answers

Environment Worksheet 5
Making a difference – Pages 8 and 9
1 Suggested answers:
Hebridean, whales, dolphins, research, educational, cetaceans, observers, environmental.
Student's own answers
a The family of whales, dolphins and porpoises
b local people
c Introducing students to different kinds of cretaceans
2 RESEARCH:
a 24 b water is polluted by people using boats, which also kills the plankton the whales eat c visitors
d observation sheet e 8
f location, description, behaviour, number of whales etc, state of the sea/weather.
EDUCATIONAL PROJECTS:
a for research/as a floating classroom
b science, maths, computer studies, geography
c 9 metres, blowholes, plankton, pollution

Environment Worksheet 6
Natural Disasters – Page 13
1 Student's own answers
2 a What are they?
b Why do they happen?
c Where do they happen?
d How do they affect people?
e What can people do?
3 Student's own answers

Environment Worksheet 7
All
1 – 3 Student's own answers

Environment Worksheet 8
All
1 – 4 Student's own answers

Environment Test Worksheet
1 a 13, Natural Disasters
b 16, Topic Chatrooms
c 12, Energy: Where the wind blows
d 5, Identifying water problems
e 10/11, Feeding the world
f 9, HWDT – The Hebredian Whale and Dolphin Trust
g 3, My environment
h 4, Using Water
i 6, The food chain
2 a False b True c True d False
e False f False g True h True
i True j True

COMMUNICATION

Communication Worksheet 1

Hello – Page 3

1 Suggested answers:
a hello! b Nice to meet you! c Good morning! d Hi! e How are you?
2 a kissing b hugging c shaking hands d bowing e rubbing noses
3 Student's own answers

Communication Worksheet 2

Computer Chat – Pages 4 and 5

1 a chat rooms b e-mails
c search engines d blogs
e surfing f e-commerce
2 a e-commerce b surfing
c e-mail d search engines
e chat rooms f blogs
3 Suggested answers:
a Only give your address to friends
b Don't give personal information
c Update it every few days
4 Student's own answers

Communication Worksheet 3

Non-Verbal Communication – Pages 8 and 9

1 Suggested answers:
1 Black lorry pointing downhill on yellow board/This hill is very steep for lorries/road sign
2 Bicycle on wall/We repair bikes here/ wall picture
3 Red traffic light/Stop!/traffic lights
4 Red line through cigarette/No smoking!/public place
5 White arrow pointing left/One way: go left/street sign
6 Red hand on lights/Stop!/road sign
2 Suggested answers:
a Fire
b Stop, go to meeting place and await instructions, don't panic
c Stop/Get out of the way in a safe manner
d Signature tune
3 Student's own answers

Communication Worksheet 4

The Story of English – Pages 12 and 13

1 a Asian culture b Australian English
c Yiddish culture d Russian culture
e Chinese culture f Asian culture
g Native American h Australian English
i Native American j Native American
k American English
2 Student's own answers

Communication Worksheet 5

Inventions – Pages 14 and 15

1 Student's own answers
2 a The first phones were not mobile but now you can speak from anywhere using mobile phones.
b You could not see the other person with the first mobile phones, but now you can send pictures with a cameraphone.
c Cameraphones are easy to steal, so phone crime is rising in many countries.
3 Student's own answers
4 Student's own answers

Communication Worksheet 6

From A to Z: the alphabet story – Pages 20 and 21

1 Student's own answers
2 STEP 1: Byblos/1800BC/Combined an Egyptian symbol with each Canaanite sound
STEP 2: Greece/1000-900BC/Extra vowel symbols
STEP 3: Rome/600BC/Used some Greek letters
STEP 4: The Americas/India, South-east Asia, Australia/International communication
Student's own answers

Communication Worksheet 7

All

1 – 4 Student's own answers

Communication Worksheet 8

All

1 – 4 Student's own answers

Communication Test Worksheet

1 a 6, Safe Surfing
b 8, Non-Verbal Communication: Using the senses
c 20, From A – Z: the alphabet story
d 18, Don't forget the animals!
e 14, Inventions: Steps to better communication
f 17, Teen speak
g 10, Say it with flowers
h 3, Hello
i 11, Mixed messages
2 a True b False c True d False
e False f True g True h False
i False
3 a chat rooms b surfer
c holly d emigrant
e thou f cameraphone
g code h disguise
i ideogram

ENTERTAINMENT

Entertainment Worksheet 1

It's Festival Time! – Page 3

1 Suggested answers:
a **Insurance** is needed in case someone has an accident on site.
b **Tickets** cannot be too expensive for young people, but must be high enough to cover costs.
c They need to have enough **toilets** for several thousand people.
d The volume of **traffic** needs regulating, with enough space for cars to park.
e If there's bad **weather**, some facilities may need to be undercover.
2 TYPE OF MUSIC:
a jazz b reggae c country
d electric e folk f blues
g alternative
h Student's own answer
PEOPLE:
Student's own answers
3 Student's own answers

Entertainment Worksheet 2

Festivals – More than the music – Page 4

Behind the music – Page 5
1 a Gilberto Gil b Rui Veloso
c Beatles d Paul McCartney
2 a R b G c G d R e G
Student's own answers
3 Student's own answers

Entertainment Worksheet 3

What strange music! – Pages 6 and 7

1 a5, b7, c1, d6, e3, f4, g2
2 a7, b6, c1, d3, e4, f5, g2
3 Student's own answers

Entertainment Worksheet 4

Where do movies come from? – Pages 10 and 11

1 Student's own answers
2 Student's own answers
a Homer
b Trojan and Greek
c Prince of Troy ran away with Helen, Greek King of Sparta's wife
d Outside the City of Troy
e 10 years
f Odysseus
g A wooden horse
h It was burned by the Greeks
3 a He told the director about the diary/ journey
b He encouraged the director to make the film
c Walter Salles/Brazilian
4 Student's own answers

Entertainment Worksheet 5

Music opens doors: The Amazon Youth Cello Choir – Pages 12 and 13

1 Student's own answers
2 Suggested answers:
a on the delta, near the equator
b hot and wet/tropical
c wild animals are in the streets
d secondary school, Belem
e University of Missouri – Columbia
f teach cello
g 'It's like the human voice'
h they made good friends
i expensive, travelling long distances, bus and taxi, adult-sized cellos
j travelling, finding a place to practise, the heat
k they gave concerts
l Teatro da Paz in Belem
m Mark Rickards
n make a radio programme about them
o interviews, music
p two cellos
q concert organisers in the Netherlands
r money was donated to buy instruments
s Student's own answers

Entertainment Worksheet 6

The (modern) circus is coming – Page 20

1 – 3 Student's own answers

Entertainment Worksheet 7

All

1 – 3 Student's own answers

Entertainment Worksheet 8

All

1 – 3 Student's own answers

Entertainment Test Worksheet

1 a 8, The Beatles
b 16, Franz Ferdinand
c 12, The Amazon Youth Cello Choir
d 21, The Clowns' Story
e 6, The First Vienna Vegatable Orchestra
f 18, A recipe for making music
g 14, Music sells
h 20, The (modern) circus is coming
i 4, Festivals: more than the music
j 5, Behind the music.
2 a False b True c False
d True e False f False
g True h False
3 a performer b spectator
c amplifier d poet
e fan f drummer
g soundtrack h gig
i sound technician

CONSUMERS

Consumers Worksheet 1

Check it out – Page 2
Let's go shopping! – page 3

1 a market b shopping mall
c supermarket d boutique
2 a meat
b cheese, coffee, sugar, tea
c fruit, vegetables
d fish
e medicines, cosmetics
f magazines, newspapers
3 Student's own answers

Consumers Worksheet 2

Fashion: What's New? – Pages 4 and 5

1 a blue b grey/white c black
d blue e green f red/white
g orange/black
h white
2 – 3 Student's own answers

Consumers Worksheet 3

Ad-speak – Pages 6 and 7

1 a intriguing b shocking
c scientific d persuasive
e image-conscious f social conscience
g challenging
2 cigarettes trainers hot fashion consumer items: mobiles/backpacks/watches healthy foods and drinks/medicines/ health clubs charities aids/drugs/smoking/ alcohol

Consumers Worksheet 4

The travels of a blouse – Page 11

1 Student's own answers
2 a Dana Simons
b a charity, Scope
c A recycling company
d a police guard
e Khalid
f Mary
g Priscilla Msimuko
h Dana Simons

Consumers Worksheet 5

Phones can do anything! – Page 14

1 a operator
b dial (verb)
c phone card
d automatic connection
e voicemail
f connect (verb)
g ring tone
h mobile (adj.)
i long-distance call
2 a 'Hang on a minute, please.'
b 'Sorry, you have the wrong number.'
c 'Please call back later.'
d 'I'm sorry there's no reply.'
e 'That number's engaged.'
f 'What's the area code?'
g 'Can I leave a message?'
h 'Please speak after the tone.'
i 'Press 1 to hear the message again, press 2 to keep the message and press 3 to delete it.'
3 Student's own answers

Consumers Worksheet 6

All

1 Student's own answers
2 a United States/Taiwan b Mexico
c Phillipines d China
e Singapore f Germany
g Costa Rica h Thailand/ India
i Israel j Malaysia

Consumers Worksheet 7

All

1 – 4 Student's own answers

Consumers Worksheet 8

All

1 – 2 Student's own answers

Consumers Test Worksheet

1 a 10, Charity Shops
b 14, Phones can do anything
c 4, Fashion: What's New?
d 12, UNICEF Works!
e 6, Ad Speak
f 15, The state of our planet
g 11, The travels of a blouse
h 18, Consumer hot topics: Obesity
i 9, Innovation, Innovation, Innovation!
j 8, Innovation, Innovation, Innovation!
2 a True b False c True d True
e True f False g True h True
I False j True
3 a intake/diet b volunteer
c charity d traffic jam
e rubbish f thief
g innovative h window-shopping
i salary j up to date

TRAVEL & TOURISM

Travel & Tourism Worksheet 1

Travel? Why? – Page 3

1 MS, KT, IW, JAA, BJ, LL, TY, WLG
2 Student's own answers
3 Student's own answers

Travel & Tourism Worksheet 2

A place to sleep – Page 4

1 a Argentina b USA
c Morocco d Sweden
e Australia f Japan
g Scotland
2 Student's own answers
3 Student's own answers

Travel & Tourism Worksheet 3

The Bicycle Story – Pages 6 and 7

1 a unicycle b velocipede
c messenger d mountain
e safety f yellow
2 Suggested answers:
a 1880s
b 2
c pedals on wheels
d solid tyres
e air filled tyres
f getting to work/for pleasure
e they could ride in skirts
h women
3 Student's own answers
4 Student's own answers

Travel & Tourism Worksheet 4

Two famous journeys – Pages 8 and 9

1 a Cyclops b Sirens
c Circe d Lotus Eaters
e Argos f Penelope
2 Suggested answers:
a An odyssey/incredible adventure
b underworld
c traveller
d island
e bark
f tax collector
g paper money
h pirates
i dictate
3 a Island of the Lotus Eaters
b Ithaca c 13th Century
d China e Venice
4 Suggested answers:
ODYSSEUS:
Ithaca
Troy
Sail boat
10 years
Had to fight a Cyclops
Nobody recognised him
Student's own answer

MARCO POLO:
Venice
China
Sail boat, horse, on foot
21 years
He was ill for one year
Imprisoned
Student's own answer

Travel & Tourism Worksheet 5

Living with Tourism – Page 16

1 Suggested answers:
SHOPS:
Good bargains
Specialist shops disappearing

JOBS:
More jobs available during holidays/weekends
Strangers always around at family run businesses, like a B&B

CROWDS:
Funny information being given to tourists
Too many people walking around the streets
2 Student's own answers
3 Student's own answers

Travel & Tourism Worksheet 6

A Travel Story – Pages 20 and 21

1 a wildebeest b zebra c hyena
d vultures e cheetah f monkeys
g crocodile h lions i leopard
j small birds k wild dogs
2 began, became, delayed, were, escaped, made, frightened, moved, tried, escaped, went, escaped, heard, began, warned, ran, began, crossed, saw, fell, attacked, tore, came

Travel & Tourism Worksheet 7

All

1 – 2 Student's own answers

Travel & Tourism Worksheet 8

All

1 – 4 Student's own answers

Travel & Tourism Test Worksheet

1 a 8, Two Famous Journeys
b 3, Travel? Why?
c 18, Youth Hostels
d 6, The Bicycle Story
e 16, Living with Tourism
f 15, A career in Tourism
g 20, A Travel Story
h 11, L-Travel
i 16, Living with Tourism
2 a False b True c True
d False e False f True
g True h True i True
3 a Bed and Breakfast
b hostel
c unicycle
d traffic jam
e fly
f explorer
g emigrant
h eco-tourism
i guidebook

TAPESCRIPT

CD A

People

TRACK 1
▼ **Page 1 Welcome to People**
Come and meet some interesting people. Look at their photos, read their ideas and discuss their opinions.

You can do projects about people, too. There are suggestions for these with every article.

Share your ideas with the other people in your class. Do the project. Reading is just the first step!

Enjoy 'People' with us.

TRACK 2
▼ **Page 3 Personal identity**
Anna: Who are you?
Ben: Who am I? What a strange question! *Me*, of course!
Anna: It's not really strange. We all have different roles. For example, think about your family. You are a child, a grandchild, a brother, a sister... It depends on the relationship. To some people, you are young. To others, you are old.
Ben: Oh, I see. You mean... different people have different 'views' of us?
Anna: Yes. Your friends see one person. Your teacher sees another. They're not totally different. But which one is the real you?
Ben: That's a difficult question! Hey - what about famous people? It's true for them, too, isn't it? I mean, we see Madonna – but her kids see 'Mum'.
Anna: Exactly. Remember, we often see people as stereotypes. For example, teenagers are 'difficult'. Business people are 'busy'. Actors and music stars are 'glamorous'. Of course, this can be true – but not always!
Ben: Mm, I see what you mean. It's the same with nationalities, too, isn't it? Italians, Brazilians, British people. There are lots of stereotypes.
Anna: That's right! Most people have many personalities and roles. Talk to them. Find out about them.

TRACK 3
▼ **Page 13 A song to a special person.**
There are a lot of poems and songs about special people: parents, kids, boyfriends, girlfriends, best friends. Sometimes the words are *about the* person, but sometimes they are *to* him or her.

Here's a famous one. Do you know the writers of it? Or the music group? Why are some of the words in French?

Michelle, ma belle.
These are words that go together well,
My Michelle.

Michelle, ma belle.
Sont des mots qui vont tres bien ensemble,
Tres bien ensemble.

I love you, I love you, I love you.
That's all I want to say.
Until I find a way
I will say the only words I know that
You'll understand.

Michelle, ma belle.
These are words that go together well,
My Michelle.

I need you, I need you, I need you.
I need to make you see,
Oh, what you mean to me.
Until I do I'm hoping you will
Know what I mean.

I love you.

I want you, I want you, I want you.
I think you know by now
I'll get to you somehow.
Until I do I'm telling you so
You'll understand.

Michelle, ma belle.
Sont des mots qui vont tres bien ensemble,
Tres bien ensemble.

I will say the only words I know that
You'll understand, my Michelle.

TRACK 4
▼ **Chatrooms**
TEENS CHAT
Anna: Hi! Do you like this photo?
Ben: Mm....What is it?
Anna: They're statues! It's for our Statues Project. Or this one...
Ben: No, I like the first one.
Anna: Me too! They're statues and they're modern. They're different from the other ones.
Ben: Mm. But there's a problem...
Anna: Why?
Ben: Well, what are the statues?
Anna: Two giraffes, of course.
Ben: And what's the project?
Anna: Statues.
Ben: Yes. Statues of what?
Anna: Oh – people! So ...
Ben: Sorry! But it's a great photo.
Anna: Huh! Bye!

CAN YOU BELIEVE IT?
Look at Page 3 again. It's about our different roles and identities, isn't it?
Well, Shakespeare has the same idea!

> 'All the world's a stage
> And all the men and women merely players.
> They have their exits and their entrances,
> And one man in his time plays many parts .... '

As You like It Act 2. 1599

BYE FOR NOW!
That's the end of 'People'. Don't stop finding out about different people. See you soon!

Places

TRACK 5
▼ **Page 1 Hello! Welcome to Places**
It's full of exciting photos and articles about the topic. Some of the places in it are old and others are new. There are private places and public ones, too. All these places are interesting in different ways. Read the articles, look at the photos and find out more about all these places.

There are projects with every article, too. Share your information with the other people in your class. Do the projects. Reading is just the first step!

Enjoy exploring Places with us!

TRACK 6
▼ **Page 3 My dream place**
'I share a room with my sister. My dream is to have my own room.

I want a big room, with a big window. My favourite colour is blue. I want blue walls, like the sky. On the door outside, there's a big notice. It says: PRIVATE!. But my friends can come here for sleepovers, of course.'

'My dream place? Well, it's a special space. In fact, it's a website. So I guess it's a *virtual* place. I can go there any time. And, of course, I can change it, too! Size, shape, colours, the things in it... I can change them all. It's easy!

It's a really private place. My friends have a secret password to enter it, of course. And I can keep other people out. I just change the password!

I'm really in control. It's a great place.'

TRACK 7
▼ **Page 13 A strange place**
Here's part of a famous song about a very strange place to live in.
Do you know the song writer? Do you know the music group?
And why is 8th December 1980 an important date?

We all live in a yellow submarine
Yellow submarine, yellow submarine
We all live in a yellow submarine
Yellow submarine, yellow submarine

And our friends are all aboard
Many more of them live next door
And the band begins to play
We all live in a yellow submarine
Yellow submarine, yellow submarine
We all live in a yellow submarine
Yellow submarine, yellow submarine

As we live a life of ease
Everyone one of us has all we need
Sky of blue and sea of green
In our yellow submarine
We all live in a yellow submarine
Yellow submarine, yellow submarine
We all live in a yellow submarine
Yellow submarine, yellow submarine
We all live in a yellow submarine
Yellow submarine, yellow submarine
We all live in a yellow submarine
Yellow submarine, yellow submarine

TRACK 8
▼ **Chatrooms**
TEENS CHAT

Anna: Hello! There's a new History Quiz Game on the Internet.
Ben: No.... I don't like History!
Anna: But this is fun. It's about places.
Ben: Places? That's Geography, not History!
Anna: Well – think of a place. How about 'Rio de Janeiro'? Why does it have that name?
Ben: I don't know!
Anna: Easy! The explorer Amerigo Vespucci saw the place in January. A point to me.
Ben: On New Year's Day, I think..
Anna: OK – one point to you. In 1502. That's another point to me. Here's another one. 'Via 22 Marzo' in Italy – what's the story behind that date?
Ben: I don't know!
Anna: Try this one. Lots of towns in Italy have a 'Garibaldi' or ''Cavour' place – why?
Ben: OK, OK, I understand. History, Geography... just look at a map. And music. What about John Lennon airport in Liverpool?
Anna: You see! OK, let's begin.

CAN YOU BELIEVE IT?
This is Janus. He's an Ancient Roman god. People often put his face over their doors and gates. He looks in two opposite directions. He watches entrances and exits. So... he's also the god of change, and of the past and the future.

BYE FOR NOW!
That's the end of Places. But don't stop doing your projects. Find out about all the places around you. Discover the facts about the places you visit on holiday, too. It's your turn now. See you soon!

Animals

TRACK 9
▼ **Page 1 Welcome to Animals!**
There are a lot of animals in the world.
And there is a lot of information about animals, too. In books, on the Internet, in TV programmes. It's easy to find out interesting things about animals.

Become an animal expert. It's exciting!

TRACK 10
▼ **Page 3 Feet Talk!**
Look at your feet.
What can you do with them? You can run, jump, walk...
What about animals? They use their feet for different activities. And we can guess their activities from their feet.

Let's look at some birds first. Different birds have different feet. It depends where they live.

Woodpeckers
These birds climb up trees. They want to find insects to eat. And their feet help them to climb. They have two toes at the front and two toes at the back of each foot. Climbing is easy for them.

Ducks
Ducks and swans swim in the water. They have skin between three toes. They can push the water with their feet, so they can swim fast. They can also dive under the water.

Ostriches
These big birds can run fast. Their feet are very flexible, so they can run over the grass.

Eagles
These birds catch animals for food. They have big, strong feet. The claws are long and sharp. They can hold the animals with their claws.

Footprints
You can find animal footprints on the beach, or on wet ground. Or in the snow, of course.

TRACK 11
▼ **Page 4 It's a dangerous world!**
The animal world is full of danger. Some animals eat other animals. How can animals survive?

Where is it?
Some animals hide.
Stick insects live in grass or in trees. It is very difficult to see them, because they look like a part of the tree.

Zebras and giraffes are big animals, and they have special patterns and colours. It is often difficult to see them under the trees, or in the grass.

Wow! What's that?
Some animals dazzle their enemies.

The butterfly at the top of the page is a Peacock. When a bird comes near it, the butterfly moves its wings very quickly. Flash! The bird sees lots of bright colours: red! black! white! yellow ...! Flash! The bird is afraid and it flies away. The butterfly is safe!

Don't touch!
Some animals look fierce. For example, snakes. In fact, some snakes *are* very dangerous: they can spit their poison at their enemy!
And lizards look fierce, too But, in fact, they're not dangerous at all! Shh!

Conservation spot
Of course, animals are in danger from other things.

Global warming: It is difficult for some animals to find food.

Humans: They build lots of houses and roads. These cause lots of pollution!

Industrialisation: People cut down trees and destroy the environment.

TRACK 12
▼ **Page 12 Animals attract tourists!**
This is Hamish. He lives in Scotland. He's a Highland bull. He is ten years old. He attracts a lot of tourists.

Tourists stop and take photos of Hamish. They make comments:
'Look!', 'Isn't he sweet!', 'Have a sandwich, Hamish!'
(Hamish likes to eat grass, not sandwiches!)

There is a tourist shop next to Hamish's field. So the tourists go into the shop. They buy souvenirs. And, of course, they buy Hamish souvenirs. Hamish biscuits. Hamish chocolates. Hamish soap... The people in the shop get lots of money: pounds and dollars and euros.

What does Hamish get? Nothing!

Is it bad to use animals in this way? Or is it just fun?

TRACK 13
▼ **Page 13 An animal song**
The animals went in two by two, Hurrah, Hurrah,
The animals went in two by two, Hurrah, Hurrah,
The animals went in two by two,
The elephant and the kangaroo,
And they all went into the Ark, just to get out of the rain.

The animals went in three by three, Hurrah, Hurrah,
The animals went in three by three, Hurrah, Hurrah,
The animals went in three by three,
The butterfly and the bumble-bee,
And they all went into the Ark, just to get out of the rain.

The animals went in four by four ...
The fat hippopotamus stuck in the door ...

The animals went in five by five ...
They were so glad to be alive ...

The animals went in six by six ...
They threw out the monkey because of his tricks ...

The animals went in seven by seven ...
They thought that they were going to heaven ...

The animals went in eight by eight ...
Then Noah went to shut the gate ...

The animals went in nine by nine ...
Then Noah went to cut the line ...

The animals went in ten by ten, Hurrah, Hurrah,
The animals went in ten by ten, Hurrah, Hurrah,
The animals went in ten by ten,
If you want any more we can sing it again,
And they all went into the Ark, just to get out of the rain.

TRACK 14
▼ **Page 16 Chatrooms**
FUN CHAT
Hi, guys. Take a look at these cartoons. Know what? They're all animals!
A black sheep
A fat cat
A dark horse
A hot dog
A busy bee
A piggy bank

TRACK 15
TEENS CHAT
Sarah: Hi, there. Do you have any pets?
Lesley: No, I don't. I had goldfish. But they all died!. What about you?
Sarah: My pet's a cat... Mesty.
Lesley: How old is she?
Sarah: Oh....She's about 11 or 12.
Lesley: What colour is she?
Sarah: She's all sorts of colours. She's grey, with sort of black ... She's got white socks. And a white belly. She's a lot of different colours.
Lesley: A technicolour cat! What does she eat?
Sarah: She's quite a strange cat. She likes different things.
She sometimes also comes home with birds or mice...
Lesley: Oh, I don't like that!
Sarah: No, but she's a cat, so...
Lesley: Mmm.

CAN YOU BELIEVE IT?
People in Britain love animals. And the winters are often cold. So horses often wear coats!

BYE FOR NOW!
That's the end of 'Animals'. Of course, you can continue with your Animal Detective work. See you soon.

Sports

TRACK 16
▼ **Page 1 Welcome to Sports**
People play and watch sport all over the world. It's a good international link – a way to find friends in other countries. We explore the international face of sport here.

Become a sports expert. Good luck!

TRACK 17
▼ **Page 3 Sport: To do or to watch?**
Some people play a sport. Others prefer to watch it. What are their reasons?

Way of life
I live near the sea so swimming is part of my life! I meet my friends on the beach, and we have fun. There are exciting sports, like surfing, too.

Excitement
Soccer's my favourite sport. It's really exciting. It's good to play and it's good to watch. I always want my team to win. In fact, I identify with my team. When they win, I'm really happy. But when they lose, I'm in a bad mood all day!

Travel
Sports people travel a lot. Players go to other cities to compete. Sometimes they go to other countries. Today, spectators travel, too. There are matches and competitions everywhere. Some people take their holidays to watch sport: the World Cup, the Olympics. Sport is international!

Health
I play tennis. You feel great. You run and jump, and you're in the fresh air.
I always want to win!
I watch tennis on T.V., too. It's exciting. I love the Wimbledon championships. Every year, I have a favourite player. It's a good game for men *and* women.

New skills
It's exciting to learn a new skill. At first, you can't do something and then, one day, you can do it! Success is good for people. It makes them feel self-confident.

T.V. Addict
I love to watch sport – on T.V.! It's all there – skiing, hang gliding, horse jumping, and lots more. I can't see these things in my town, but I can watch them at home. I can dream and perhaps, one day........!

TRACK 18
▼ **Page 10 The price of sport.**
Sports fans buy soccer shirts for their favourite teams. They collect autographs from their favourite players, too. Trainers, sports caps and tracksuits are part of fashion today. People want the 'in' labels and designs. They also want cheap prices.

Sports clothes are big business too! When there's a big sport event, like the World Cup, or the Olympic Games, the big sportswear companies want to sell clothes with the 'magic' logo.

Where do these things come from? Who makes them? It's not always a happy story.

Workers in Asia make many of these things. Look at the labels. Many of them come from Indonesia, China, Cambodia and Thailand. And in some factories, people work long hours and receive low pay. Here is an example from a report in 2004. This report is from Oxfam, an international charity.

'I have many health problems: headaches, stomach flu, back pains... My target is 120 pairs of trousers in an hour. In the normal working day I make 960 pairs! We work from 8 am, ... and we work until 2 am or 3 am in the peak season.'

Some companies now have rules to protect their workers. And there's a new report from Oxfam, 'Play Fair at the Olympics'. It wants the IOC (International Olympics Committee) to help them.

TRACK 19
▼ **Page 12 The two sides of sport.**
POSITIVE
There are some positive reasons for doing sport on page 3. Here are some more positive ideas, serious and not-so-serious.

Social effects
Sport can help people in poor parts of the city. Doing sport can help them to fight against drugs and crime.

Lifeskills
There are winners and losers in sport. And there are winners and losers in life, too. So sport can prepare people for life. It can help us to overcome problems, and to help other people.

Fashion
Many sports clothes are great fashion. So doing sport can be a reason for looking good!

Fun
Sport gives lots of opportunities to have fun.

NEGATIVE
It's not all good news! Sport has its problems, too. Here are a few of them.

Training, training, training
Good athletes train every day. They often have no time for friends or fun. They forget about a 'normal' life. After years of this, some of them say 'No more!'. Many tennis stars begin when they are four or five years old, and stop before they are twenty.

Drugs
Athletes want to win. They eat special diets to be strong. Their bodies are very important for them. And sometimes they want to 'help' their bodies. Drugs can do this – but then the competition isn't fair. Sports people do tests of their blood and urine to detect drugs. Good players don't want to cheat.

Isolation
Sport is great if you like it. If all your friends are good at sport, and you are not, it's no fun. Sport at school can be horrible for some people.

Violence
It's natural to support a football team. It's normal to want your team to win. It's good to be excited, and to cheer a goal. And it's great to celebrate after the match.

But some fans make a lot of trouble. They fight other fans. They drink a lot of alcohol, and are violent. The police have to control them. It's not sport, it's war. And that's sad for the players, and sad for the other spectators.

TRACK 20
▼ **Page 16 Chatrooms**
TEENS CHAT
Sarah: Hi. Do you like sports?
Lesley: Well ... I go to the gym sometimes. What about you?
Sarah: Me too. And I'm into American football. I like to watch it.
But there isn't a team at school. They play ordinary football, of course.
Lesley: What other sports?
Sarah: Oh – swimming. Athletics. Golf ... But I'm not a sporty person!
Lesley: I'm not either. All my family loves to do sports, but not me.

CAN YOU BELIEVE IT?

What's this?	A tree.
Who's this man?	A competitor.
What's he doing?	He's throwing a tree!
Where?	In Scotland.
Why?	It's a popular competition.
What's its name?	'Tossing the caber.'
How tall is it?	Between 5 and 6 metres.
And what does it weigh?	About 70 kilos.
Wow!	

GOODBYE!
Well, that's the end of 'Sports'.
Of course, you can continue with your projects.
And playing and watching sports.
See you in the next Topics title.
Bye for now!

Festivals

TRACK 21
▼ **Page 1 Welcome to Festivals!**
Festivals are part of our lives. We have personal festivals, like birthdays. And we have big festivals, like Carnival and Christmas and New Year. Then there are national festivals, like Independence Day, and Republic Day. In some towns, there are special, local festivals to celebrate local events.
Now over to you!

TRACK 22
▼ **Page 3 Let's begin with the New Year**
Which New Year?
Every year has a first day: New Year's Day. Do you know when this is? Easy, isn't it? 1st January!

Well - yes and no! Some New Years are on different dates. This depends on the calendar. Let's look at some facts.

Dates
In the Western World, the New Year usually begins on 1st January. But there are exceptions. The Muslim New Year begins in March or April. So does the Indian New Year. But the Jewish New Year begins in September.

Then there's the Chinese New Year. This begins in January or February. The Chinese have a lunar calendar, so the beginning and end of every month depends on the moon. There are 12 months in their year, and every year has a different sign - and personality. There are 12 signs, so a sign comes back every 12 years. The Chinese calendar is very old: the western year 2005 is the Chinese year 4702 (the Year of the Rooster). And so 2006 is the Chinese year 4703 (the Year of the Dog). The Chinese New Year is a big holiday in many parts of Asia.

Celebrating
There's one important thing about New Year in every culture: it's a time to celebrate! We 'kill' the old year, and all its problems, and we welcome the New Year. It's a new beginning, a time of optimism.

Sometimes the New Year celebrations represent different traditions. For example, in Rio de Janeiro on 31st December, there are fireworks and concerts on the beach. And there is also the 'Iemanja' festival with fires and candles and little boats. Two different ways of saying 'goodbye' to the old year and of welcoming the future.

TRACK 23
▼ **Page 10 Carnival in August**
The Month: August
The Music: Calypso, soca, hip-hop, salsa...
The Instruments: Steel drums
The Food: Rice, chicken and peas, tropical fruit
The Place: London
London? Yes, London! London, England? That's right!

There is a famous carnival in London: Notting Hill Carnival. It's different from many carnivals. For one thing, it happens in August, not February or March. And London is in Europe, but the Notting Hill Carnival is West Indian! Why?

Well, Trinidad is an island in the West Indies. And back in 1833, the slaves in Trinidad became free. And every year they remember this at Carnival time. They celebrate with calypso music and dance.

What's the link between Trinidad and London? See the History Note.

Now more than two million people take part in this special carnival in the Notting Hill area of London. (Remember the *Notting Hill* movie, with Julia Roberts and Hugh Grant?)

There are steel bands, floats, processions, music, and West Indian food. Black and white people dance to calypso and soca in the streets of London!

TRACK 24
▼ **Page 12 Family Festivals**
New Year and Carnival are big, public festivals. But there are lots of smaller, 'private' ones, too. Some festivals are national, or belong to special groups of people. Some of them celebrate a national event, like Independence. Let's take a look at some of these. Which ones do you recognise?
Teacher's Day
Children's Day
Women's Day
World Environment Day
Mother's Day
Father's Day
Birthday
Name Day
Valentine's Day
Columbus Day
Here are some descriptions of these events. Which description goes with which festival?

1. A very personal festival: it commemorates your first day here!
   Birthday
2. Children give presents to their mums to say 'thank you'.
   Mother's Day
3. Another personal festival. In some cultures, it commemorates a saint.
   Name Day
4. Children are the focus of this October festival.
   Children's Day
5. 15th October is a good day for teachers!
   Teacher's Day
6. The festival for lovers. It is a saint's day on 14th. February in some countries.
   Valentine's Day
7. Dad deserves a big hug!
   Father's Day
8. Christopher Columbus wanted to go to Asia, but he sailed to the New World.
   Columbus Day
9. An international green festival on 5th June.
   World Environment Day
10. Women support women on this day in March.
    Women's Day

TRACK 25
▼ **Page 13 Festival raps, songs and rhymes**
Valentine's Day
Roses are red,
Lavender's blue,
Sugar is sweet
And so are you!
Be my Valentine.

Bonfire Night
Please remember
The fifth of November,
Gunpowder, treason and plot.
I see no reason
Why gunpowder, treason
Should ever be forgot!
Penny for the Guy! Penny for the Guy!

Christmas
Jingle bells, Jingle bells,
Jingle all the way,
Oh what fun it is to go
In a one-horse open sleigh!

Christmas/New Year
We wish you a Merry Christmas,
We wish you a Merry Christmas,
We wish you a Merry Christmas
And a Happy New Year!

Environment

TRACK 27
▼ **Page 1 Welcome to Environment**
It's a great opportunity to explore our world: the

- Financial guidelines. / Visit bank.
Debbie Whait - Barclays.

They eat a lot of different dead animals. Ugh! But, in fact, this cleans up the environment!

Decomposers
There are other important organisms in the food chain. Examples are fungi and bacteria. These consume dead plants and animals, and then this food returns to the earth.

Why are food chains important?
They remind us that, if we damage or destroy one
chain, this affects the next one. So if
amage plants, the producers, there is no
ne first-level consumers. This can affect
d-level consumers and the third level
s, too. The damage to plants can be from
uses (flood, drought or climate change),
man causes (pollution or destruction). The
be the same. Ultimately, there will be no
umans, either.

3 Natural disasters
nderstand a lot about the environment
don't understand everything! Every
are big and small disasters in different
e world. Some of these happen very
some of them are a big shock. How do
al disasters affect humans? Can we do
bout them?

s
they?
rms with strong winds. They start at
n travel a long distance. They have
mes in different places: 'hurricanes' in
Ocean, 'typhoons' in the Pacific Ocean,
clones' in the Indian Ocean and around

or whirlwinds, are similar, but begin over

ey happen?
vaporates from the warm sea. This
n the atmosphere. More and more hot,
s up. It becomes a strong wind.

they happen?
arm parts of oceans. Tornadoes are
parts of the U.S.A, Australia, and Japan.

ey affect people?
fect ships, blow down houses, cause
disrupt traffic.

people do?
n usually track hurricanes, but they
them.

they?
n rivers, lakes or the ocean rises above its
l and goes onto the land.

ey happen?
lot of rain, or very strong winds, floods
n.

they happen?
s in Bangladesh and India flood every
e expect it, so there is no panic. When
go down, there are lots of minerals in the
an grow good plants.

hey affect people?
floods are a surprise, many people can
ery year, people lose their houses and their

ods happen every year, some people are
them. But many people (and governments)
epare properly.

What can people do?
Dams can reduce floods – but some dams can cause them! There are often 'flood warnings' on the radio.

TRACK 31
▼ **Page 16 Chatrooms**
TEENS CHAT
Anna: Hi. How's life?
Ben: Fine. What're you doing today?
Anna: Nothing much. I'm doing a project for school – the environment. I'm tired! Hey, feel like doing a quiz?
Ben: A quiz? What's the topic?
Anna: Guess! The environment!
Ben: Mm. It's not my favourite topic, but...
Anna: Come on, there are lots of fun questions... It's not serious.
Ben: OK. Test me!
Anna: The cows are lying down. What's going to happen?
Ben: Easy. It's going to rain. Now it's my turn. It's evening. The sky's red...
Anna: Everyone knows that! It's going to be a good day tomorrow.
There are lots of red berries on the bushes and trees.
Ben: Ummm ... I don't know.
Anna: It's going to be a cold winter. How about this puzzle?
'A cloud was my mother and the wind is my father. My son is a cool river and my daughter is the fruit of the land. My bed is a rainbow, and the earth is my final resting place.'
Ben: Wow. Ummm ...

CAN YOU BELIEVE IT?
You need a lot of breath when you climb a hill.
This sign in India gives some good advice.
Your lungs are at work. please do not smoke.
What's this? It's a sign!
Where is it? In India.
What's its purpose? It's an environmental warning.
Who is it for? Tourists.
What's the message? Don't smoke!
Why? It's bad for your health - you can't breathe properly!
Note: it's also bad for the plants!

GOODBYE!
Well, that's the end of 'Environment'. We hope you'll continue with your Environmental Eye work. See you in the next Topics title. Bye for now!

CD B

Communication

TRACK 1
▼ **Page 1 Welcome to Communication.**
There are lots of ideas here – and they're all about communication. That's an important topic for all of us. The world needs good communicators.

We really hope you'll enjoy reading and using this Topics title.

TRACK 2
▼ **Page 3 HELLO!**
Greeting people in English is easy, isn't it?
'Hello' 'Hi!' 'How are you?' 'How're you doing?'
'Good morning. Good afternoon. Good evening.'
'Nice to meet you!'.

These words *look* easy, don't they? We say them when we're greeting someone. But what about the other things? Gestures. Behaviour. Do you touch the other person? Do you stand very near to them? It all depends ... on what? On age, on relationships, on culture, on the situation.
In fact, the way we greet other people gives them information about ourselves.

Kissing
In some cultures, only friends kiss. In others, it's polite to kiss strangers. O.K. – you just have to notice what other people do. But there are other things to notice, too. How many times? In some areas, one kiss is normal. In others, two. And in really friendly places – three kisses! Then, of course, there's the question of 'Where to begin?'. On the right, or on the left? Get that wrong, and your noses will bump! Kissing is a nice way to greet someone, but it's not so easy, after all.
NOTE: And in Paris – it's 4 times!

Hugging
This is like kissing – it's important to get it right! In some cultures, like Russia, close physical contact is important. In others, you only hug your best friends. In fact, in some cultures, people stand at quite a distance from each other. They don't touch. They certainly don't hug the other person!

Shaking hands
Adults do this with other adults. It's formal. But how formal? Well, that depends. In France, students often shake hands with older people, like their teacher.

Bowing
Bowing indicates social position. In many societies, it's only done in extreme situations. For example, if you meet royalty, or the president. But in Japan, Thailand and India, bowing is part of normal greeting. And it has its rules, too. Who bows first? How low do you bow? Do you do anything special with your hands, as in India?

Rubbing noses
Here's a greeting we associate with just two cultures - the Inuit and Maoris. Do they really greet each other this way? What are the rules?

Don't forget!
Good communication is often more than just choosing the right word. Gestures and behaviour send messages, too. These non-verbal signals can communicate a lot of extra things. You'd better learn this language!

TRACK 3
▼ **Page 12 The story of English**
What kind of English do you speak? American English? Or British English? Or a different variety?

Question: Why are there different types of English?
Answer: Because of History, Politics and Geography. Let's find out.

1. **From England to New England**
In 1620, this group of people sailed from England to North America. Their religion was very important for them, and they wanted to be free to live in their own way. They took the English Bible with them. They spoke English: 17th century English. This was the language of Shakespeare, and many of the words, and the pronunciation, were different from modern English.
'Whither goeth thou?' 'Where are you going?'

The eastern part of the continent became an English colony. The language here was English, but it began to change. The immigrants needed new words for the plants and animals there. They often used Native American words for these. American English was becoming different from the English in England.
moose wigwam tomahawk Potomac

2. **Independence!**
In 1776, after six years of war with England, the United States of America became independent. American English continued to develop. And the English-speaking area got bigger and bigger. The French sold Louisiana to the new United States. Spain gave up its colonies in the south. And as English-speaking people from the east coast went west, to look for gold, or to establish enormous cattle ranches, they took English with them. They invented new words for their lives there.

Another influence on American English, of course, was the language of the slaves: Afro-American English. In 1885, Mark Twain's *Huckleberry Finn* used this language in print.
'... Aunt Sally she's going to adopt me and sivilize me and I can't stand it.'

3. **Immigration, immigration, immigration**
During the 19th and 20th centuries, more and more people went to live in North America. They came from many different countries, and they went there for political, religious or economic reasons. They wanted to start new lives.

These new immigrants to North America brought their languages – Spanish, Italian, Chinese, Japanese, Russian, Yiddish – and they all contributed words and phrases to American English.
chutzpah! gulag 'I should worry!' gung-ho

TRACK 4
▼ **Page 13**
4. **English travels east**
Back in Britain, English was developing too. Politics and trade changed it. During the 18th and 19th centuries, the British Empire grew and grew. People described it as 'The Empire where the sun never sets'. The soldiers, administrators, traders who built this Empire took English with them. The language travelled to India, to Australia, to Asia, New Zealand and Africa. In many places, it became the language of government.

5. **Different Englishes**
Britain was a small, overcrowded country, and many people went out to find better lives overseas. They used local words for the new things they found there.

Different varieties of English began to develop: Indian English, Singapore English, Australian English. Which one is this?

> *Once a jolly swagman camped by a billabong*
> *Under the shade of a Coolibah tree ....*

6. **Movies or films?**
In the 20th century, because of the invention of the cinema, American English began to travel back again to Britain. It affected British English. Gradually, speakers of British English became accustomed to hearing American accents. They knew that 'sidewalk' and 'pavement' were the same thing. The two languages became closer in many ways.

British English has had other influences in the last few years. There is a big immigrant population from India and Pakistan. Asian music and Bollywood movies are very popular among young people – and Asian English is now a part of general British 'teen speak'.

'She looks so Angrez!'
'Don't be so badmash!'
'He's really jungli!'

7. **Still moving!**
Films have helped to take American English all over the world. But don't think this is the end of the story. People now speak English all over the world as a first, second, or foreign language. Non-native speakers of English use it as an international language of communication. And people often use English words when they are speaking other languages. French, Spanish, Italian and Portuguese speakers all recognise a 'mouse' – which doesn't eat cheese – or a 'bug' – which isn't an insect!

Listen carefully – there are many different forms of English. It's still developing. The language belongs to the world!

Question: Which type is correct?
Answer: All of them!
Question: So ... do you speak American English, or British English ... or international English?

TRACK 5
▼ **Page 17 Teens speak**
'Teenagers are.........!' Adults will probably finish this sentence in one way; teenagers in a different way. Why? Well, communication across generations is often difficult. This seems strange! After all, adults were teenagers themselves once. Perhaps they have short memories. Or perhaps it's because the world is changing so quickly. Being a teenager then, and being a teenager now is different!

It's often easier for a group of teenagers from different countries, with different native languages, to understand each other. Their language relates to their culture: teenage culture.
Here's part of a Teenager English Phrasebook.
All the words and phrases come from a teenager magazine. Which ones are new for you? Does this language follow any patterns? Over to you!

Describing things
fab, fave, funky, glam, gorge, hottest, mega-cool, nifty, quirky, sassy, yummy

Things (Stuff)
bling, clobber, freebie, gear, moby, pressies, sunnies, trackies

People
bloke, bro, celeb, freak, mates, old fogey, sis

The things people do or are
blinging, clothes-swap, cringe, get hitched, get the goss, in a strop, in the buff, to be savvy

TRACK 6
▼ **Page 24 Chatrooms**
TEENS CHAT
Ian: Hi. D'you know any good jokes?
Kirsty: I know some silly ones. What has 4 legs and only 1 head?
Ian: Mmm - a bed! Try this. What would you do if you found an elephant in your bed?
Kirsty: Sleep somewhere else! What's the longest word in the English language?
Ian: No idea!
Kirsty: 'Smiled'.
Ian: Why'?
Kirsty: There's a mile between the first and last letters!
Ian: OK! Look at this photo. Can you guess the proverb?
Kirsty: Mmm ... people whispering secrets – I know: Walls have ears!
Don't talk too much – you never know who's listening! Good advice.

CAN YOU BELIEVE IT?
A friend was on holiday.
Where?
In Brazil, in the Amazon, four hours away from the nearest city. She visited an Indian village.
What did she see?
This notice for visitors. PROPINAS. TIPS HERE.
English is an international language!

GOODBYE!
We're at the end of 'Communication'. We hope you'll continue to find ways to be a good communicator. See you in the next Topics title.
Till then...

Entertainment

TRACK 7
▼ **Hello! Welcome to Entertainment**
Entertainment means having fun. Enjoying yourself. Being happy. This depends on age, and personal tastes. What entertainment do older people like? Or kids? And how about the differences between you and your friends? To what extent does entertainment depend on fashion? Maybe on advertising, too?

We really hope you'll enjoy using 'Entertainment'.

TRACK 8
▼ **Page 3 It's Festival Time!**
Woodstock! Glastonbury! Rock in the Park! Rock in Rio!

In parts of the world, summer means 'festival time'. It's an opportunity to hear famous bands and singers 'live' - to be part of a big event, with several thousand other people. Also to dress up (or down), to dance, to do crazy things.

Some music festivals are only for one day. Others go on for several days. They are usually out of doors. They often have 'tent cities' where people can sleep. There are places to buy food and drink. They become a 'special world' for those few days.

For the organisers, there are huge practical problems, of course. What about the traffic? Are there enough places for cars? Will there be too much noise? Will the police cooperate? And what about insurance for accidents? Are there enough toilets and showers for several thousand people? What is the best price for the tickets? They mustn't be too expensive for young people, but they must cover the festival costs. And – especially in some countries - will it rain?

The biggest festivals often contain many different types of music. Jazz, reggae, country, electric, folk, blues, alternative – you can find all your favourite music styles on the programme. Other events are very specialised. Perhaps they only have one kind of classical music, or one style of folk music. Some festivals also include talks, or theatre, or clowns, or events like bungee-jumping.

TRACK 9
▼ **Page 6 What strange music!**
The First Vienna Vegetable Orchestra.
Organic music... this is the latest thing in some European cities. It's experimental. It makes something out of nothing. It encourages people to think. And it sounds (and tastes) good! Are you puzzled? Here are a few facts.

Who's in the orchestra?
In 1998, a small group of artists got together to work on a new project. They wanted to experiment with musical sounds. They decided to use vegetables as musical instruments.

How many people are in the group?
At present, there are eight or nine musicians, one sound technician – and a cook. You see, at the end of the concert, the cook makes soup out of the vegetables. And the audience can taste it!

TRACK 10
▼ **Page 12 Music opens doors: The Amazon Youth Cello Choir**
The Amazon. What do you immediately think of?
Brazil. The rainforest... and... umm...
Yes. And cellos?
Cellos? No...
And an orchestra – playing music by Villa Lobos, and Bach, and more modern composers?
No, of course not!
Well, you're going to have a surprise.

The place
The state of Pará is in the far north of Brazil. The huge River Amazon runs through it. Its capital city, Belém, is on the delta, near the equator. It has a hot, wet, tropical climate – and, of course, the Brazilian rainforest is famous all over the world.

Brazil is a huge country, and the north is a long way from the big cities of São Paulo and Rio de Janeiro. A lot of people in the south do not know much about it. As one teenager from the group said, 'They think there are wild animals in the streets here!'.

A hundred years ago, Belém was a rich city, because it exported rubber from the Amazon area all over the world. Students from other parts of the state still come to study here. However, not all of them have the opportunity to have a good education. In fact, it's a surprising place to find a cello orchestra, especially one with an international reputation!

The people
Aureo DeFreitas was born in the state of Pará, and went to secondary school in Belém. There, he had a very good music teacher – and began to study the cello. He continued his music studies in the U.S., at the University of Missouri-Columbia.

When he returned to Brazil, he began to teach the cello in Belém. He welcomed a lot of students to his classes and he persuaded the music school to lend them cellos to play on. He began to experiment with new methods to teach large classes. More and more students decided to join the group. Their ages were from 10 to 18.

The students were very enthusiastic about the instrument. 'It's like the human voice', one of them said. At one time, 85 of them were learning it. Playing together in the orchestra, they made good friends. They could discuss their problems – school, family, money, boyfriends, girlfriends – everything.

The problems
It wasn't easy for them, however. Cellos are big instruments – and expensive. They are difficult to carry around. Not many families could afford to buy one. As well as their normal school work, the students had to practise a lot. And many of them had to travel for long distances on buses.

Some of the players were quite young – and small. Normally, young players play smaller-sized instruments. But all *their* cellos were full-sized – made for adults. The kids had to carry their instruments on the bus. They usually had to stand at the back, as the cellos were too big to fit into a seat. They were afraid their instruments might hit something, and break. As well as this, some of the players live in dangerous parts of the city. One of the parents is a taxi-driver – and he's a great help!

But they were determined to succeed. The Amazon Youth Cello Choir was born.

TRACK 11
▼ **Page 14 Music Sells!**
Ever seen this guy?
He's George Frederick Handel. He was a German, though he went to live in England. He was born in 1685 and died in 1759. Over 300 years ago.
He composed a lot of music: 'The Messiah' (remember the 'Halleluiah' chorus?'), 'The Water Music'…

What's that got to do with us, today?
Wait! I'm sure you know what these are!
Sure – they're jeans
But they're not 300 years old… They're *modern*!
Well, that's the link.

The new Levi's campaign
Levi's jeans launched a new advertising campaign in Europe. Like most ads, these used music. And what did the advertising agency choose? Handel's 'Sarabande in D Minor'.

Handel wrote this piece for a single harpsichord. Levi's rearranged it for a full orchestra. It's very dramatic – just like the ad. In it, two people do amazing things. They crash through walls, run up trees, and then jump into a huge night sky. Wearing Levi's, of course!

Levi's have used classical or old pieces of music for their ads in the past. And these pieces often become hits. They are recorded in an exciting way, and so they seem modern. They introduce teens to classical music AND they sell things. Handel may soon be 'Top of the Pops' all over Europe!

TRACK 12
▼ **Page 16 The story of a group – Franz Ferdinand**
Who are they?
A band from Glasgow, in Scotland.
Are they new?
Quite new. They got together in 2001.
So why are they important?
Well, people think they're going to have a big future. They're very popular in the U.S. We thought you might like to be some of the first people to know about them!
O.K. Tell us something about them…

There are four of them:

The drummer:	Paul Thomson. He worked at Glasgow School of Art.
The bass player:	Bob Hardy. He was a student there.
The singer:	Alexander (Alex) Kapranos. He was studying English at university, but he had lots of friends at the art school.
The guitarist:	Nick McCarthy. He used to live in Germany, but he moved to Glasgow.

What kind of music did they decide to play?
They felt that post-rock music was too serious. They wanted to make good music for dancing. Their first gig was at a fashion show at Glasgow Art School. Some female art students asked them to provide music for it.

Here is part of a track from the album 'Franz Ferdinand'.
'You see her
You can't touch her
You hear her
You can't hold her
You want her
You can't have her
You want to
But she won't let you…'

TRACK 13
▼ **Page 24 Chatrooms**
TEENS CHAT
Emma: Hi! Have you heard about the latest MP3 player?
Ian: No … so what's new?
Emma: It's denim!
Ian: What? Denim? Like jeans!
Emma: Yeah. It's really cool!
Ian: But… what's it like?
Emma: There's a pocket – it's covered in denim. And you can attach it your clothes.
Ian: So … The player's inside this pocket? Sounds funny … How do you switch it on and off?
Emma: There are buttons. They're covered with denim too … It's really cool.
Ian: Sounds funny to me … Are you joking?
Emma: No, I read about it. It was the big thing at some Media Festival. Oh, and you can put it in the washing machine, too!
Ian: Now you must be joking … That's crazy!

CAN YOU BELIEVE IT?
People have festivals for all sorts of things. In some places, bread is really important. They even have special days to celebrate it. People dress up, they play music, have competitions – and they make, and eat, lots of bread! Can you guess which country this festival is in?

GOODBYE
That's the end of 'Entertainment'. We hope you've enjoyed it. See you in the next one.

Consumers

TRACK 14

▼ **Page 1 Welcome to Consumers!**

We have lots of articles about different aspects of our modern world. Who are the consumers? What do they consume? Are there better ways of having a happy life in our consumer societies?

We really hope that you enjoy exploring these ideas.

TRACK 15

▼ **Page 3 Let's go shopping!**

Different people like to shop in different places. It all depends on you.

Something special for that special date? Go to your favourite specialist fashion shop. Great clothes, great ideas… but they can be expensive.

Money a problem? Want a bargain, something really cheap? Then maybe a street-market is best for you.

A lot of variety? No time to visit lots of different places? Just go down to the supermarket.

Perhaps you just want a chance to look at the newest fashions. Why not go window-shopping? This is the cheapest way to shop!

But if you want *all* of these - ideas, variety, space, and special shops - then the shopping mall is the place for you. And, of course, it's also a place to hang out with your friends, to chat, and to make plans. Did you know that some of the newest malls in the U.S. and Canada now have special lounges for teenagers? There's a lot of life in a mall!

TRACK 16

▼ **Page 6 Ad speak**

Advertising is all around us. It's on T.V., in magazines, in newspapers, on websites. It's difficult to escape it. Ads tell us about the product, right? Yes – but they do this in lots of different ways. They use images, words, sounds and word association.

Let's do a bit of ad analysis. We can find out what kind of message the advertisers are using. Are they trying to manipulate us? Or are they just giving us information?

For a start, ads can be intriguing, persuasive, challenging…

Intriguing ads

These often use beautiful – or strange – photos. They are designed to catch our attention, and to be memorable. The most extreme ads of this type do not even give the name of the object! They want to make us stop and look at them in a subtle way. This type of ad is often used for cigarettes. Cigarette advertising is controlled in many countries, so advertisers try to find 'soft' ways to sell their product.

Persuasive ads

This type often uses 'gentle' messages. They 'suggest' something. It's like having your best friend whispering in your ear and smiling at you. 'Why don't you…?' 'Have you ever considered…?'.

Challenging ads

'Be one of the group!' 'All the coolest kids use this product!' 'Why be different?' These ads often use aggressive language and images. They generally promote 'hot fashion' items – things that will go out of fashion very quickly!

▼ **Page 7**

Image, image, image…

'Here's the coolest… wildest… hippest… funkiest… object!'

'The image-conscious person cannot do without it!'

This style is ideal for fashion and consumer objects (mobiles, backpacks, watches, and so on). It's the most common form of advertising for many products. But don't forget all those other types of message. Be clever: don't let the advertisers fool you!

Scientific ads

These ads often contain a lot of text. There's a 'scientific' explanation to support the product. Often there are letters from 'real people' who have benefited from the product. Sometimes these ads use diagrams and statistics to give them an image of truth. You can find these ads for products like healthy food and drinks, medicine – and even health clubs.

Social conscience ads

Some advertising is designed to shock us. Sometimes the advertisers want to make us feel sorry for people who are less fortunate than us. They use images like starving kids, or people sleeping in the street. These remind us of the negative side of the consumer world. The photos are often in black and white. They appeal to our hearts and our consciences. Their message is 'Give money'. Charities use this type of advertising very effectively.

Shock! Horror!

These ads are not selling anything. They want to stop you from doing something. Think of problems like AIDS, smoking, drugs, alcohol. They use shocking visual images, strong colours and often statistics to shock us.

TRACK 17

▼ **Page 18 Consumer hot topics: Obesity**

Food intake versus energy output

Isn't it strange? A large percentage of the world's population can't get enough to eat. But in 'advanced' societies, there's a different health problem. Obesity. And this problem is spreading to lots of different countries. Why is this happening? What does it mean? Let's look at some of the facts. Modern life is fast. Everyone is rushing. Right? So there's not much time for meals. And 'fast food' is easy to find (if you have the cash). Fast food is fashionable. Millions of dollars are spent on ads to promote fast food and snacks.

The message?

Fast food is modern! It's cool! It's fun!

The facts?

Most fast food contains a lot of calories. And if the consumers don't take a lot of exercise, those calories produce fat.

Exercise?

If you live in a big city, and travel by car or bus, you probably don't take much daily exercise. This is worse if you sit at your computer, or watch videos, in your spare time.

It takes a lot of regular exercise to balance the effects of this kind of food. Let's look at four popular fast food products. How many calories do they contain?

Cola (500ml bottle)	= 210
Burger and chips	= 699
Banana milk shake	= 396
Chocolate bar (large)	= 445

TRACK 18

▼ **Page 19 Getting rid of the calories**

Here's what you have to do to 'negate' the effects of that food, and burn up those extra calories.

Cola:	More than 30 minutes' jogging.
Burger and chips:	Play football for more than 1 hour + jog for 43 minutes.
Milk shake:	One hour's cycling.
Chocolate bar:	Play football for more than one hour.

Surprised? Are there enough hours in the day to do these activities? Or is it easier to cut the calories?

Activity chart

Let's look at this problem in a different way. You have 60 minutes to take some exercise. What is the best activity to do? How many calories do different activities burn up in 60 minutes?

Aerobic dancing	390
Cycling	372
Dancing	270
Jogging	390
Playing football	420
Playing tennis	432
Running uphill	582
Walking	210

So… the choice is yours!

TRACK 19

▼ **PAGE 21 Problem solving**

Take a look at these tips. What do you think of them?

Eating disorders

If you, or one of your friends, has an eating disorder, here are some things to remember.

* People with eating disorders often use food as a way of showing that they are unhappy.
* Being thin doesn't mean they have an eating disorder. There are other signs to look for.
* If you're worried about a friend, try to encourage them to get help.
* Never change your own eating patterns to fit in with theirs.
* If someone has an eating disorder, the first step to recovery is to admit it.
  This takes courage.
* Eating disorders can affect everyone.

Depression

Here are a few ways to feel happier.

* Do something you enjoy: watch a film you love, or listen to your favourite music.
* Get physical! Doing exercise usually makes you feel good about yourself.
* Share your problem. Discussing it with a friend often helps.
* Remember that sad feelings will go away. Nothing lasts forever.
* Don't hesitate to talk to sympathetic teachers and parents.
* See a health professional. Remember that they will respect your privacy.

Stress

Sometimes, life seems full of problems.

* It's normal to be nervous before exams!
* Headaches, stomach pains, sleeping problems and no interest in food can all be signs of stress. Be alert!
* Write a list of the things that make you feel stressed. Think of a solution for each one.
* Make an action plan, and discuss this with a friend.
* Eating properly can reduce stress. Every day, try to eat five portions of fruit and vegetables and to drink eight glasses of water.
* Laughing is a great way to reduce stress! People say that 100 laughs are as good as 15 minutes on your bike!

TRACK 20
▼ **Page 24 Chatrooms**
TEENS CHAT
Emma: Hi! Guess what...
Kirsty: What?
Emma: I lost my phone last week...
Kirsty: Again!
Emma: I know, I know.
Kirsty: So - d'you have a new one?
Emma: Sure. It's really nice.
Kirsty: What's it like?
Emma: Small... silver... takes pix... great memory.
Kirsty: OK, OK...
Emma: Look...
Kirsty: Wow! Cool! Did it cost a bomb?
Emma: It's my birthday present
Kirsty: No comment!

FUN CHAT
Money, Proverbs and Sayings
Money doesn't grow on trees.
Money makes the world go round.
All that glitters is not gold.
Love of money is the root of all evil!

CAN YOU BELIEVE IT?
William Wordsworth is one of the most famous English poets. He criticised many things in his 'modern' society. He thought that things connected with nature were better.

'The world is too much with us: late and soon,
Getting and spending, we lay waste our powers:
Little we see in nature that is ours.'

He wrote this in 1806. Two hundred years ago, people used a lot of energy to make and to consume things. In fact, Britain was already a consumer society! How about your country?

GOODBYE!
We're at the end of 'Consumers'.
We hope that you'll continue with the Consumer Spy ideas. Be an intelligent consumer! See you in the next Topics title. Till then...

Travel and Tourism

TRACK 21
▼ **Page 1 Hello! Welcome to Travel and Tourism.**
In it, we visit some exotic places – and we also ask a lot of questions. Why do people travel? What 'sells' a place to us? What do we do there? What kind of souvenirs do we want to buy? Where can we stay?

Let's start this journey together.

TRACK 22
▼ **Page 3 Travel? Why?**
I want to work with animals when I'm older. So I like to go to different places and observe them. That's what I do every holiday. I go to the beach, or the mountains – and I look at the animals and the birds. Sometimes I take photos, too. I belong to a few Animal Observation Forums on the Internet, too. So I have friends all over the world.

(K.T.)
Curiosity! I want to see different places. I like to read about them, and then go to see what they're really like. I've had a few surprises... And it makes me appreciate the good things at home, too.

(W.L.S.)
Why do I travel? The climate! Here in Northern Europe, the winter's really long. It's so good to see the sun, and to forget about rain. Sometimes I go with my family - sometimes with my friends. We do different things, of course – but it's nice to have a big change like this. I feel great when I get back.

(J.A.A.)
I travel because I have to! I don't like to travel – but there are no good jobs in my town. So I go to the capital every week. And I hate big cities!
(M.S.)
Is cycling a kind of travel? Well, you're moving. So I guess it is. Anyway, I cycle to keep healthy. I love to go into the country with my friends, of course. But even cycling in the city is fun – if there's not too much traffic. You feel free. You can go anywhere. And it's great exercise, too.

(T.Y.)
My parents move every few years. It's because of their work. So we have to go too. New school, new friends, new house. It's hard, but it makes you independent. Trouble is, you don't want to get too friendly with anyone – it makes moving harder. I guess when I'm older, I'll never move again!

(B.J.)
Travel? I never travel! Well, I go to school, of course. On the bus. But we don't have a car. We live in a small town, so I walk a lot. Oh, I went on a plane once, with my grandparents. It was strange. But I'd like to fly again. It was kind of exciting, arriving at a new place so quickly.

(L.L.)
I just love it! I like to see new places, have new experiences, meet new people.

TRACK 23
▼ **Page 12 What's it *really* like?**
Guidebooks present one view of a place. They are often full of facts – dates, names, distances. If there are pictures, the place usually looks wonderful. The descriptions use words like 'beautiful', 'exciting', 'exotic'.
However, very often, the people who live there have another view. No place is perfect – it's a mixture of positive and negative things. They also know personal things about the place – the sights, sounds – even the smells! - that make it special for them. Visitors also have their individual memories – the kind of things they tell their friends when they get home. A bit of personal advice is always a good idea. Let's look at the guidebook view of a few places – and some more personal comments.

MYSORE, India
'This charming city is a favourite with tourists. It enjoys a good climate, and has preserved its heritage. The city is famous for its silk, and for sandalwood and incense. Until Independence, Mysore was a princely state. The maharajah's palace is now a major tourist attraction.'

'Yes, that's true – the palace *is* amazing. But the things I remember best were the cows in the street! They're sacred, so they can go anywhere. The traffic just goes round them. Oh, and on a hill outside the city there's a gigantic statue – the Nandi Bull. It's nearly two metres high, and was carved out of rock. People leave gifts of food for him – and touch him for good luck.'

TRACK 24
▼ **Page 13 VENICE, Italy**
'Perhaps no other city in the world has inspired the superlatives heaped upon Venezia by writers and travellers through the centuries. It is built on 117 small islands and has about 150 canals and 409 bridges.You can drive your car to Venezia and park it, but there is nowhere to drive once you arrive.'

'When you read this, it's difficult to imagine how this affects everyday life. You have to walk everywhere (or take a boat). A distance of one or two kilometres is no longer a few minutes in a car. You have to think carefully before carrying anything heavy.

It means that everything in the city has to move by boat. The food comes from the mainland and the other islands to the market by water. Fire, police, hospital workers, builders – they all have to move around by boat. So the Grand Canal (and the small ones) are full of all sorts of working boats.

Of course, there are gondolas, too. Local people use them to cross the Grand Canal quickly. And tourists pay a lot of money to see the city from the water. But the real daily life is based on all those other working boats – and your feet!'

MACHU PICCHU, Peru
'The ancient Inca city is on a plateau on a high mountain. It is in quite a good state of preservation because the Spanish conquistadores never found it in the 16th century! It was deserted, and stayed hidden in the jungle for centuries. In 1911, an American archaeologist found it by chance.'

'Sounds good, doesn't it? And it is a fantastic place. The problem is that there are too many tourists – 400,000 in one year. Think of the environmental damage from so many people! The Government wants to attract more tourists, but UNESCO wants to reduce the number. What's the answer?'

TRACK 25
▼ **Page 16 Living with Tourism**
People who live in a tourist spot often have mixed feelings. There are 'plus point' and 'minus points' about it! We talked to a few people who live in these places. Here are some of their comments.

Shops and prices
'Tourists have more money than us. Music events, eating places – even ice cream... They all cost more here because of the tourists.'

'There are lots of good places to buy cheap sweaters! That's what the tourists come for, and you can get really good bargains.'

'All the small specialised shops are disappearing. The rents are too expensive. And in the winter, out of the tourist season, lots of places close. The town is dead!'

Jobs
'Tourism really helps with jobs. There are lots of possibilities for weekend and holiday jobs – working in cafés and restaurants, or in some of the shops. It's quite easy to earn some extra money now.'

'I'm thinking of tourism as a career. I like meeting people, and I'm quite good at languages. I think you can find really interesting jobs. I mean, I'd like to be a tour guide for a bit, and visit other places.
Or perhaps I'll train to be a hotel manager. There are lots of possibilities.'

'My Mum runs a 'bed and breakfast' place. It's awful – there are always strangers in the house. You can't make a mess or a noise. And I have to help clean the rooms at the weekends, or in the holidays. I even have to get up early and help to make the breakfasts! All my friends are still in bed… O.K., I earn a bit of money, but I'd prefer to choose what to do. I want to help Mum, of course – but it's my life, too!'

Crowds
'You can't walk along the street at busy times. There are crowds of people walking really slowly. They stop and look at things – and they always move in groups. It makes me mad.'

'You're walking along, and suddenly you see a person with an umbrella, and a crowd of people behind. It's a tour guide and some tourists. They all move together. They're just like sheep!'

'It's funny to hear some of the information that the guides give. You hear lots of wrong facts. Dates, names – they often get them wrong. Most tourists never notice. But sometimes one person in the group has a guidebook. They check up – and that's funny, too.'

'A lot of tourists seem to think the city is a beach! They wander around in silly clothes. Or sunbathe.'

TRACK 26
▼ **Page 20 A Travel Story**
In Africa, a lot of animals move around every year in search of food. They make long, difficult and dangerous journeys. Often the end of the story isn't a happy one. Here's an account of one animal, a wildebeest. A group of scientists tracked her progress, and made a radio documentary about her.

The journey: From the Serengeti Plains in East Africa to the Masai Mara - over 2,000 miles!
The animal: A four-year-old wildebeest, Kimbea (her name means 'Run' in Swahili).
The dangers: Other animals - lions, hyenas, cheetahs.
Natural dangers: deep rivers, forest fires, no food or water.

NOVEMBER: Over a million animals in the Serengeti Plain begin to move in search of food and water. Wildebeest and zebras often travel together. One of these is a female wildebeest. She is pregnant. The animals move slowly north for several months.

FEBRUARY: Kimbea is ready to give birth. Her contractions begin. However, just then she sees a hyena. It's looking for a meal. She controls her contractions and delays the birth until it is safe. Then a male calf, Du-may, is born. She takes it to join the other new animals. All around, hyenas and vultures watch and wait.

MARCH: The animals are still in the Serengeti. There is grass to eat, but there is danger, too. A cheetah sees the young calf. She begins to follow it. However, some monkeys see this, and make a loud noise. The cheetah goes away – this time.

JUNE: The animals move west, towards Lake Victoria. There are thick forests here – and more dangers. The animals will have to cross the wide Mara River.

TRACK 27
▼ **Page 21**
SEPTEMBER: There has been a lot of rain, so the river is very wide, and the water is moving fast. It's easy to be swept away by the current. There is another danger too: crocodiles.They know the places where the animals usually cross the river, and lie in wait. Kimbea goes down the bank and begins to cross the river. Suddenly, a crocodile grabs one of her legs. They struggle in the water, but finally she pulls herself free, and goes up the bank. Then she notices that Du-may isn't with her. She goes back through the dangerous waters, red with blood, and finds him. Then they have to cross the river again.

OCTOBER: The animals arrive in the Masai Mara plains. There is good grass, and water – but a lot of lions are waiting to attack them. Fire is another danger. The dry grass burns easily. One day, Kimbea is caught in a ring of fire. She panics – but finally finds a way out. Where is Du-may? She calls for him, but at first there is no answer. Then she hears a calf calling for its mother. It's him!

Kimbea is not the only animal to hear Du-may's calls. A leopard is sleeping in a tree, and the sound wakes it up. It comes down and moves towards the calf. The movement disturbs some small birds. They make a noise, and Du-may runs away. He's safe!

NOVEMBER: It's time to begin the return journey. The animals are moving back south to the Serengeti Plains again. The grass there is now tall and green. They have to cross the Mara River again, but this time they find a place where the water is shallow. There are no crocodiles – it's much easier.

Du-may is now ten months old. He doesn't always stay near his mother now. But there's something wrong with him – he walks in a strange way, and he moves away from the other young animals.

Du-may is sick – and the wild dogs that always follow the animals notice this. They move closer. Du-may falls over. He has an infection that affects the brain. The dogs get closer and closer – and then attack him. It's the end for him. They tear him apart. Then the vultures come down.

Kimbea does not see this. She is eating the grass, getting her strength back. Soon, she and the other animals will begin their long journey all over again. And again. And again… it's a journey to survive.

TRACK 28
▼ **Page 24 Chatrooms**
TEENS CHAT
Kirsty: Hi! What're you doing today?
Ian: Studying...
Kirsty: Studying? Today?! It's a holiday.
Ian: Yes, but we've just started this really interesting subject – Tourism. It's cool. In fact, I think I want to work in the travel industry.
Kirsty: What do you do in Tourism?
Ian: Lots of projects on tourism in different countries. Where people go - beaches, cities, eco-tourism. And what they want to do. We did a project on tourism here, too. I've never thought about this place like that.
Kirsty, Stop, stop. OK, I can see you'll have a great future in tourism. Just tell me when you have time to talk about something different!

CAN YOU BELIEVE IT?
Hey! Did you see the *Motorcycle Diaries* film? Well, travel companies are now selling Motorcycle Diary tours! Look at these suggestions. We found them in a travel brochure.

'Join a 3-week tour from Buenos Aires to Lima. Optional extra: a 3-day river tour on the Peruvian Amazon. With trips into the rain-forest and a visit to the San Pablo leper colony.'
'An 18-night tour to Cuba, visiting all the key revolutionary places.'

'Even Bolivia – where Che was killed – now has a Che Guevara tourism route. The government hopes it will attract tourists to a really poor part of the country. All the money from this tourism will go to the communities in the area.On the building where he was killed, the tourists can read a notice: 'Through this door one man walked out to eternity.'

Tourism? Exploitation of a film? A cynical way to get money? What do *you* think?

GOODBYE!
Well, that's the end of 'Travel and Tourism'.
We hope you've enjoyed it. Perhaps you can even find a job in it in the future. There are lots of possibilities – for travellers and tourists!
See you in the next Topics title. Bye!

TRACK 28
Copyright information.